British civilian internees in Germany

MANCHESTER
1824

Manchester University Press

British civilian internees in Germany

The Ruhleben camp, 1914–18

Matthew Stibbe

Manchester University Press

Manchester and New York

distributed exclusively in the USA by Palgrave

Published by Manchester University Press
Oxford Road, Manchester M13 9NR, UK
and Room 400, 175 Fifth Avenue, New York, NY 10010, USA
www.manchesteruniversitypress.co.uk

Distributed in the United States exclusively by
Palgrave Macmillan, 175 Fifth Avenue,
New York, NY 10010, USA

Distributed in Canada exclusively by
UBC Press, University of British Columbia, 2029 West Mall,
Vancouver, BC, Canada V6T 1Z2

British Library Cataloguing-in-Publication Data is available

Library of Congress Cataloging-in-Publication Data is available

ISBN 978 0 7190 7085 3 paperback

First published by Manchester University Press in hardback 2008

This paperback edition first published 2014

The publisher has no responsibility for the persistence or accuracy of URLs for any external or third-party internet websites referred to in this book, and does not guarantee that any content on such websites is, or will remain, accurate or appropriate.

Printed by Lightning Source

To my grandfather

Edward Victor Stibbe (1890–1966)

Contents

Figures

Figures 2, 3, 5, 8, 9, 10, 11, 12, 14, 15, 16, 17 and 18 are reproduced with the permission of the Brotherton Library, University of Leeds. Figure 13 is reproduced with the permission of Chris Paton. Figures 1, 4, 6 and 7 are from the author's private collection.

Tables

Acknowledgements

Over the past few years I have been contacted by a number of people who have been willing to share with me their knowledge of Ruhleben and its impact on their own family history. In particular I owe an enormous debt to Norman Stockall for allowing me to cite from his father's unpublished account of his time in the camp. Frank Stockall, like my grandfather, Edward Stibbe, was in Chemnitz when the war broke out, and his memoir has had a meaning to me over and beyond its undoubted value as a historical source. Thanks also to Elizabeth Beasley and Mary Firth for sending me material relating to their relatives' experiences, and to Louise Argent, Hazel Basford, and Joy Lumsden for their correspondence and the interest they have shown in this project. Anyone reading this book who has a family or local connection with Ruhleben should definitely look at Chris Paton's excellent website at http://ruhleben.tripod.com.

Several scholars have read all or parts of this book in manuscript form and have offered their friendly advice and constructive comments. Many thanks in particular to Rebecca Gill, Adrian Gregory, Christoph Jahr, Heather Jones, Kevin McDermott and Benjamin Ziemann. Jenny MacLeod and Pierre Purseigle, co-founders of the International Society for First World War Studies and co-organisers of its first conference at Lyon in September 2001, have done much to encourage contact between historians across national boundaries and have greatly enriched my own understanding of the period. I am also indebted to Professor John Horne at Trinity College, Dublin, for his support and interest, and to Alison Welsby and Emma Brennan at Manchester University Press for their enthusiasm in taking the book on and seeing it through to the end.

At Sheffield Hallam University I would like to thank all my colleagues in History and English, who between them have provided a conducive and stimulating environment in which to teach, write and carry out research. Special mention should also be made of the librarians at the Collegiate and

Adsetts Learning Centres who have met my numerous requests for inter-library loans with great speed and efficiency.

The staff of the eighteen archives and museums I have visited in the course of my research on Ruhleben are too many to mention individually by name, but I hope that collectively they will accept my expression of gratitude. The research trips themselves were funded by the British Academy, which provided a much-needed travel grant in 2003, and by the Humanities Research Centre at Sheffield Hallam University.

Finally, as always, my love and thanks go to Sam and Nicholas who have provided much fun and laughter, holidays, walks in the park, football, and many other distractions on the way.

I dedicate this book to the memory of my grandfather, Edward V. Stibbe, Leicester hosiery and knitwear machinery salesman and Ruhleben internee, 1914–18, who died in 1966, three years before I was born.

Matthew Stibbe
Chorlton-cum-Hardy, Manchester

Abbreviations

AA	Auswärtiges Amt (German Foreign Office)
ACICR	Archive du Comité International de la Croix-Rouge, Geneva
AEG	Allgemeine Elektrizitäts-Gesellschaft, Berlin (general electric company)
BA Berlin	Bundesarchiv, Berlin-Lichterfelde
BNV	Bund Neues Vaterland
EZA	Evangelisches Zentralarchiv Berlin
FEC (FEWVRC)	Friends Emergency Committee (Friends Emergency War Victims Relief Committee), Society of Friends Library, London
FO	Foreign Office (British)
GCL	Grimsby Central Library
GLA Karlsruhe	Generallandesarchiv Karlsruhe
HLL-EC	Ettinghausen Collection, Harvard Law Library, Cambridge, Massachusetts
HStA Stuttgart	Hauptstaatsarchiv Stuttgart
ICRC	International Committee of the Red Cross
IISG	Internationaal Instituut voor Sociale Geschiedenis, Amsterdam
IRC	*In Ruhleben Camp*
IWM	Imperial War Museum, London, Department of Documents
LA Berlin	Landesarchiv Berlin
NA	National Archives, Kew, London (formerly the Public Record Office)
NCOs	non-commissioned officers
NHStA Hanover	Niedersächsisches Hauptstaatsarchiv Hanover
POW	prisoner of war

RCM	*Ruhleben Camp Magazine*
RXD	Ruhleben Express Delivery
SPD	German Social Democratic Party (founded 1875)
StA Hamburg	Staatsarchiv Hamburg
USPD	Independent German Social Democratic Party (founded 1917)
VAT	value added tax
WUA	Das Werk des Untersuchungsausschusses der Verfassunggebenden Deutschen Nationalversammlung und des Deutschen Reichstags, 1919–1928 (proceedings of the Reichstag's committee of inquiry into the causes of the war and of Germany's defeat)
YMCA	Young Men's Christian Association

Introduction

On 17 October 1914 an important meeting took place in Berlin between representatives of the Prussian Ministry of War, the Foreign Office and Reich Office of Interior, the federal states and the deputy general staff and deputy admiralty. Part of the discussion centred on future policy towards British subjects living in Germany, following reports of the systematic abuse of German civilians in British hands and allegations of spying and sabotage by enemy agents working inside Germany at Britain's behest. Most of the participants supported an earlier proposal made by the deputy general staff to begin an immediate internment of all British males of military age. The Foreign Office representative nonetheless raised a series of legal–political objections (to be discussed in Chapter 1) and also cast doubt on the accuracy of some of the press reports concerning the treatment of Germans in Britain. The meeting therefore ended without agreement, and instead the matter was referred to the German general headquarters at Charleville.

On one issue, however, the deputy general staff was adamant. If internment was to be introduced, its spokesman declared, 'then the prisoners should not be accommodated in or near Berlin, because otherwise we will be faced with a constant stream of visits by representatives of foreign powers'. It was therefore recommended that the Prussian Ministry of War, which was responsible for the administration of prison camps, begin looking for alternative sites away from the Reich capital.[1] Too much international publicity was considered a bad thing, especially given the recent success of allied accusations of German atrocities against civilians in Belgium.[2] It was also recognised that overcrowding in a German internment camp was likely to be at least as bad as the overcrowding in Newbury and other British camps now roundly condemned in the German press.[3]

Roughly three weeks later, on 6 November 1914, the deputy general staff's wishes were met when the vast majority of British males in Germany were interned under an order issued from Charleville and carried out by the police and military authorities at home. However, contrary to its warnings, the site chosen for this venture was the Ruhleben *Trabrennbahn*, a racecourse complete with cinder track situated just 2 miles to the west of Berlin, between the industrial district of Spandau and the densely populated borough of Charlottenburg. Between November 1914 and November 1918 some 5,500 Britons were imprisoned here, with a population ranging from 4,273 in February 1915 to around 2,300 at the time of the armistice.[4] The site was easily reached thanks to its position adjacent to the main railway line linking Berlin and Spandau with Hamburg, and instantly recognisable courtesy of its high-profile status in the German and British press. As if to confirm the deputy general staff's fears, it became the most regularly visited, most widely publicised and most frequently written-about prison camp in the whole of the German empire, dwarfing references to all other camps, at least in the English-speaking world. This was in spite of the fact that the word 'Ruhleben', translated literally into English, means 'quiet life'.

Ruhleben, in fact, was not only a prison camp; over the four years of its existence it was or became an 'imagined community' with its own unique cultural institutions and forms of self-representation.[5] Its inmates were an extremely diverse group, and included people from all social classes and all corners of the British empire. There were fishermen from Hull and Grimsby, black sailors from West Africa and the West Indies, Jewish tailors and music hall artists from the east end of London, professional football players and golfers, jockeys from the royal racecourse at Hoppegarten, and a host of criminals, conmen and drifters who happened to be in Berlin or Hamburg when the war broke out. Around one-fifth of the inmates were openly pro-German in outlook (*deutschgesinnt*) and many others had German wives and children and were thus deemed to be *deutschfreundlich* (friendly towards Germany without necessarily supporting the German war effort). Bi-lingualism and attachment to German culture were extremely common, even among the pro-British prisoners. There were also Afrikaans, Arabic, French, Hebrew, Italian, Russian, Spanish, Welsh and Yiddish, speakers, and classes were available in all of these languages. The captains' committee was led by Joseph Powell, a self-made businessman and cinema owner from Leeds, and his deputy, L. G. Beaumont, who was released early in March 1916. Other famous inmates included Sir John Balfour (the nephew of the Conservative statesman Arthur Balfour); Sir Timothy Eden (the elder brother of the future Prime Minister Anthony Eden); Carl Fuchs (a celebrated cellist who played for the Hallé orchestra in Manchester); Sir Ernest MacMillan (conductor, pianist and composer); Israel Cohen (journalist and Zionist spokesman); George Merritt (actor on stage and screen who starred in

1960s British TV classics like *The Avengers* and *The Prisoner*); Nico Jungmann (artist and designer); Robert Smyllie (a Scots-born journalist who went on to become editor of the *Irish Times* from 1934 to 1954); Cecil Duncan Jones (a writer who had just published his first novel); Freddie Pentland and Steve Bloomer (professional football players turned coaches); and Wallace Ellison (businessman, serial escaper, MI5 officer, government advisor and Liberal party agent to Winston Churchill MP in his Dundee constituency between 1919 and 1922).

Ruhleben attracted international attention for other reasons, too. Philatelists, for instance, were much taken with the Ruhleben express delivery service, an internal mailing system with its own special stamps which rapidly became (and still are) collectors' items.[6] Others were interested in the shops in the camp which sold arts and crafts made by the prisoners themselves, and the workshops used for teaching bookbinding, engraving, watch mending and other trades.[7] The high-brow *Strand Magazine* in 1916 praised the dedicated journalism that went into the *Ruhleben Camp Magazine*, noting that its staff had 'every reason to be proud of their production', particularly for its varied illustrations and content.[8] According to Peter Liddle and S. P. MacKenzie, the Ruhleben camp school also pioneered the development of professional and university education through correspondence courses, a practice adopted by British military prisoners of war only in the Second World War (and later redeveloped by the Open University in the 1960s and 1970s).[9] Among its teachers were the future Nobel-prize winning physicist James Chadwick, the Italian scholar and art critic Matthew Prichard and the Oxford historian John Masterman, later to become master of Worcester College and head of MI5's counter-intelligence unit in Britain during the Second World War.

Finally, Ruhleben often featured in the propaganda war conducted between the British and German governments and thus became an 'imagined community' from without as well as from within. For instance, the British government published selected extracts from its correspondence with the US embassy in Berlin concerning conditions at Ruhleben, and the German military commissioned regular feature-length reports which appeared in popular newspapers like the *Berliner Illustrierte Zeitung* and *Die Woche*. From 1916 questions were raised at frequent intervals in both Houses of Parliament about the physical and mental health of the internees, and about the slow pace of exchange negotiations. The Ruhleben prisoners also campaigned on their own behalf, through publications while in captivity and after release and through connections with prominent sympathisers at home. In the UK their cause was championed by an unlikely coalition of interested parties, ranging from Quakers and pacifist MPs to the rabidly nationalist Northcliffe press.

In Germany, the SPD/USPD Reichstag deputies Wolfgang Heine, Eduard Bernstein and Oskar Cohn openly criticised their government's internment policies, particularly those directed towards British subjects; later in the war they were joined by a number of liberal bourgeois politicians, including Ernst Müller-Meiningen and Matthias Erzberger. After 1916 leading German bankers, diplomats, academics and businessmen also donated funds to help the Ruhleben prisoners and their families, including (to name but a few) Hans Delbrück, Bernhard Dernburg, Albert Einstein, Prince Karl von Lichnowsky, Walther Rathenau, Hugo Simon, Oskar Tietz and Max Warburg.[10] Internment was indeed rarely out of the public eye, and often acted as a barometer for public attitudes towards the war more generally.

The aim of this book is to tell the story of Ruhleben both as a prison camp and as an 'imagined' or symbolic community. Particular emphasis will be placed on exploring how the experience of internment was mediated by differences in class, race, nationality and level of education. Many of the Ruhlebenites kept diaries during the war, or found alternative means of preserving and recording their experiences, for instance through art, poetry, music and photography. Others wrote memoirs after 1918, sometimes for publication and sometimes for private use. These accounts make for fascinating reading in their own right. They are also of much relevance to current debates about who history is written for, and why some events become part of 'collective remembrance' whilst others are quietly forgotten or buried under intervening 'layers of memory'.[11]

Before continuing with this theme, however, it might be useful to consider what the Ruhleben prisoners shared in common with the hundreds of thousands of other civilian and military detainees across Europe and the rest of the world between 1914 and 1918. For here we can fit the story of Ruhleben into the bigger framework of historical writing on the experience of captivity in all countries during the First World War, and the politics of remembering and forgetting after 1918.

Civilian internment and the First World War

Between 1914 and 1918 at least 300,000 enemy civilians were deported and/or interned in western and central Europe, a further 300,000 in the Russian empire and probably around 50,000 to 100,000 in the rest of the world.[12] This represented a difference in scale, if not in substance, when compared to previous conflicts. True, the Spanish war in Cuba (1896–97), the British campaign against the Boer insurgents in South Africa (1899–1902) and the Balkan wars (1912–13) had all seen the mass detention and/or deportation of non-combatants in localised contexts. There had also been a deliberate act of genocide committed by German imperial troops against the Herero and Nama peoples in German South West Africa in the years 1904–8.[13] However, it was only in 1914 that the internment of enemy civilians became a truly global phenomenon, undertaken by all belligerent states in all continents.[14] Compulsory military service in most European countries and a growing propensity to adopt the territorialist French 'nation-in-arms' model of citizenship as a key element in state-building partly explain this development. So, too, do the advances in railway and steamship travel and the unprecedented growth in the movement of people as well as goods and capital which characterised the period of intensified global economic integration from the late nineteenth century onwards.[15] A final factor was the technical ability of occupying armies to deport large numbers of enemy civilians for punitive reasons or as a source of cheap labour, a practice carried out by both Russia and the Central Powers with unprecedented levels of brutality, and even by Britain and France in colonial settings.[16]

In spite of this, astonishingly little has been written about the treatment of 'enemy aliens' and civilian internees during the First World War. Since the 1980s, only one major English-language work has devoted so much as a chapter to this group of detainees, Richard B. Speed III's *Prisoners, Diplomats and the Great War* (1990).[17] The French historians Annette Becker and Tristan Robert, and the British scholar Helen McPhail have also written extensively about the deportation and internment of French civilians in Germany as part of their attempt to 'rediscover' the hidden suffering of occupied populations behind enemy lines.[18] Nonetheless, their work remains something of an exception in European historiography, which still likes to present a 'sanitised' version of the Great War. Few people today, for instance, remember that France had its own 'concentration camps' in the 1914–18 period.[19] In Germany, too, interest in civilian prisoners of war (POWs) has been minimal, with the exception of two excellent essays by Christoph Jahr published in 1999 and 2006, one on Ruhleben and one on southern Bavaria, and an impressive masters dissertation completed by Sebastian Tripp at the University of Marburg in 2005.[20] Rainer Pöppinghege also includes civilian internees in his comparative study of prison camp journals.[21] Otherwise, in the few instances where scholars have turned their attention to First World War captivity, the focus has been on combatant prisoners of war alone, as illustrated by the contributions of Odon Abbal, Gerald H. Davies, Niall Ferguson, Uta Hinz, Giovanna Procacci, Alon Rachamimov and others.[22]

Admittedly the phenomenon of civilian internment was granted a two-page entry in the mammoth, 1,001-page *Enzyklopädie Erster Weltkrieg*, edited by Gerhard Hirschfeld, Gerd Krumeich and Irina Renz (2003), but here the state of knowledge could be dealt with only in summary form.[23] Meanwhile, the somewhat over-ambitious survey of twentieth-century camps by the Belgian/French scholars Joël Kotek and Pierre Rigoulot, which first appeared in 2000, surprisingly devotes nearly the whole of its short chapter on the First World War to France and Britain, with only half a page on the much more extensive internment camps in Germany and German-occupied territory, and nothing at all on Russia, Romania, Bulgaria and Austria-Hungary.[24] This cursory treatment of an important subject undermines rather than strengthens their case for seeing the violence of the 1914–18 conflict as a kind of precursor for the totalitarian regimes that followed.

Apart from these examples, specialist works on civilian prisoners and internees have either taken a top down approach, looking at the interaction between the state, public opinion and internment, or have tended to focus exclusively on the experience and behaviour of the detainees themselves.[25] Captors, neutral observers and prisoners' families are usually kept well in the background. Even studies which have attempted to broaden the scope of inquiry to include some of the above factors are contained within certain methodological or national boundaries which can sometimes act to obscure the wider picture. Indeed, since the 1980s it is possible to identify three different forms of academic writing on civilian internment.

Firstly, some scholars have approached the subject from the point of view of anti-alienism and anti-immigrant sentiment within the captor nations. In this sense the harsh treatment of 'enemy aliens' between 1914 and 1918 is often depicted as an irrational act, born of wartime hysteria and the nationalist hatreds this gave rise to, and not as a considered or deliberate response by governments to the onset of war. Official and unofficial racism is also said to have played a part. The argument is presented roughly as follows: in the eighteenth and nineteenth centuries great trading cities like Hamburg, London, Marseilles, New York and St Petersburg attracted immigrants from throughout the world, as did large industrial towns like Manchester, Lille and Breslau. The state, anxious to promote the development of free markets and trade routes, protected the rights of these alien subjects and enacted legislation setting out standard procedures for naturalisation. Those who were naturalised could expect to enjoy legal equality along with the other members of that state; those who remained non-naturalised at least enjoyed the right of semi-permanent residency and the expectation that they be protected against arbitrary arrest or interference by the state in their private lives. In this way the protection of foreigners was seen as complementary to the rule of law and the protection of private property.

From the late nineteenth century, however, anti-immigrant sentiment and the entry of the masses into politics caused national or state parliaments in Britain, France, Germany, Russia and the USA to place restrictions on the entry of aliens.[26] The outbreak of war in 1914 accelerated this process, leading to the suspension of civil law or the introduction of emergency legislation against 'enemy aliens' and other foreigners, with the result that 'long-standing [global] networks were destroyed' and long-standing immigrant communities were subject to abuses of state power.[27] Panikos Panayi, in his book on the history of racism in Britain, gives two examples of this: the wholesale internment of German and Austrian men in the aftermath of the Lusitania riots of May 1915, and the Nationality and Status of Aliens Act, passed by parliament in 1918, which gave the home secretary the right to revoke the naturalisation certificates of immigrants and order their deportation in certain circumstances. In Panayi's view, the driving force behind these and other racist actions lay with an 'intolerant' press and public opinion which targeted not only Germans, but also other minorities, including Irish and black immigrants, Belgian refugees and Russian Jews.[28]

The problem with this approach, however, is that while it highlights important links between globalisation, popular attitudes towards immigrants and official state-sanctioned internment policies, it also shuts out other important questions about the development of 'war cultures' and 'mentalities' at different stages in the respective war efforts. In particular, it underplays the real divisions that appeared in combatant societies as the war progressed. As we shall see later, critics of internment emerged in both Britain and Germany, as well as in neutral countries, and included those who came into regular contact with prisoners, such as Red Cross officials, private philanthropists and representatives of the churches. In addition, newspaper articles, photographs and even direct sightings of British (or French or German or Russian) prisoners in transit or behind barbed wire brought the war home to 'ordinary' civilians and provoked contradictory responses which are hard to quantify. While some professed hatred for the enemy, others were moved by feelings of sympathy, or reminded of relatives held in prison camps abroad. In short, there was never any clear-cut popular consensus in favour of internment, a fact which both the German and British governments privately acknowledged, even if this did not lead to significant changes in their policy, at least until 1916–17.

The second type of writing on internment focuses not on 'enemy aliens' resident within the captor nation, but rather on enemy subjects deported from occupied territories, who made up a separate and, in the case of Germany, Austria-Hungary and Russia, numerically much larger body of civilian internees. Tristan Robert, for instance, in his study of the fate of French civilians from the Picardy region, has shown that after the battle of the Marne, when German hopes of a quick victory were dashed, the German military moved beyond temporary hostage-taking among prominent citizens (a policy already evident in 1870–71) towards a more systematic deportation of whole communities – men, women, children, young and old, able-bodied and infirm – with the simple aim of terrorising, subduing and even 'criminalising' an occupied population. Worse still, these actions were not only covered up, but actually instigated by the German high command, giving rise to a new dynamic between ordinary soldiers and wartime violence. Occupied civilians and deportees in turn became part of the French war effort and war culture (*culture de guerre*), helping to recast it as a gigantic 'struggle for civilisation' against a barbaric foreign invader:

> The conditions of incarceration experienced by these deportees sheds light on a different war to that experienced by combatants in the trenches … These civilians, held indiscriminately in military camps, felt the need to create a new kind of 'front' inside Germany, in order to fight in their own way for the motherland.[29]

This theory has been developed by Stéphane Audoin-Rouzeau and Annette Becker, who have adapted it to their broader concepts of 'violence', 'crusade' and 'mourning' as a means of exploring the eschatological framework in which the war was experienced by soldiers and civilians.[30] In their view the treatment of displaced populations and POWs after 1914 was something fundamentally new in the history of warfare: 'exile, loss of liberty, labour and hunger in the blockaded nations which could not feed them … aggravated by the duration of internment and by the acts of reprisal' undertaken against them by the states which held them captive.[31] Furthermore, the use of forced labour and the compulsory wearing of coloured armbands by civilian prisoners in parts of occupied France, although 'still relatively unsophisticated', nonetheless represented 'a step in the organisation of a concentration camp system'.[32] In occupied territory in particular moral qualms were 'overcome … and total war gained ascendancy'.[33]

However, the chief criticism here is that although there were numerous camps for civilians in Germany and elsewhere, they were by no means all modelled on the lines suggested by Audoin-Rouzeau and Becker. Instead, internees' experiences were a 'patchwork of tales' (to borrow a phrase used by Bernice Archer[34]) and depended on a variety of factors, not least the precise attitude of their captors towards them. For instance, classification of prisoners by coloured armed bands was rare, and space for the development of individual creativity and alternatives to the dominant war culture were much more varied than the model provided by Audoin-Rouzeau and Becker allows for. The internment camps in Germany and elsewhere were not all instruments of total war designed to punish individuals and communities through exile or forced labour. Nor were they sites for the development of a uniform war culture uniting soldiers and civilians in a 'crusade' or 'struggle for "civilisation"'. In fact, neither the belligerent governments nor the prisoners themselves were hegemonic when it came to determining the regimes, structures and cultures within the camps.[35] Away from occupied territory there were greater checks on the use of violence and reprisals, and civilians as well as combatant prisoners were at least partly protected by the domestic military laws of the country which held them captive and by their captors' fear of retaliation or retribution. They in turn were held back from violently resisting their captors by the same laws rather than by fear or lack of arms alone.

In other words, there was never any consistency or ideological certainty about the purpose of internment, and certainly no movement towards genocide, as under the Nazis. Even the physical lay-out of the camps was different. Whereas Wolfgang Sofsky has shown that the geography of the 'modern' Nazi concentration camp system was based on an 'ideal plan … [where] even the architecture signified repression and violence',[36] First World War camps were often make-shift prisons set up in old fortresses, castles, military barracks, schools or racecourses. Overcrowding was pretty much universal, individual acts of brutality were not uncommon, and some of the camps were mismanaged by senior officers to the point of causing extreme suffering and even death among the prisoners, but in no sense were they 'prototypes' for the type of terror camps that emerged in the 1930s and 1940s.[37] Mortality rates differed from camp to camp and country to country, but until 1918 rarely exceeded 5% of the captive population. For most of the war they were much lower than this.[38]

In short, Audoin-Rouzeau and Becker's concepts of 'violence' (numbness), 'crusade' (anger) and 'mourning' (grief) are too rigid and fail to do justice to the multiplicity, variability and range of civilian captives' experiences between 1914 and 1918. Even so, they deserve credit for highlighting some of the more horrific sides of internment, especially in contexts where no outside monitoring of conditions took place. That the German atrocities against French and Belgian civilians in 1914, the scorched earth policy adopted by the Russians during the retreat on the eastern front in late spring 1915, the massacre and deportation of Serbs during the two Austro-

Hungarian invasions of 1914–15 and 1915–16, the Turkish genocide against the Armenians in 1915–16, and the increased use of deportations and forced labour on the home front in Germany after 1916 all, in their different ways, left an unresolved legacy of terrible, incomprehensible violence, and lowered inhibitions towards the deliberate targeting of civilian populations during the remainder of the war and in subsequent conflicts, is indisputable. However, it is equally important not to ignore countervailing trends, and to point to instances where considerations of state interest, or the simple force of circumstances or individual personalities, did act effectively to prevent serious abuses of human rights and of the rules and conventions of war.[39] This is a theme I shall also address throughout this book.

The third category of writing about civilian internment attempts to place it in the context of changes in international law and human rights legislation, including efforts to investigate, monitor and prosecute alleged 'war crimes' during the increasingly violent conflicts of the twentieth century.[40] This is the most fruitful approach, and has been applied successfully in comparative studies of combatant prisoners of war.[41] As these studies show, from the late nineteenth century belligerent nations were increasingly anxious to avoid censure from neutral states, and, more importantly, to protect the interests of their own servicemen in enemy hands. For this reason they were willing, in most cases, to adopt mutually binding agreements to alleviate the condition of military POWs, including the provision of accurate lists of who was being held and where (the so-called *Gegenseitigkeitsprinzip*). However, special difficulties arose in connection with civilians caught up in war owing to the lack of clear, internationally accepted guidelines on their status. Thus civilian POWs were not included in the Geneva convention of 1864 (revised 1906) or the Hague convention of 1899 (revised 1907), which dealt only with the treatment of wounded and captured soldiers. Likewise alien subjects and refugees, including women and children, had no formal protection in international law with the exception of a few vague references in articles 42–56 of the 1907 Hague convention on the laws and customs of land warfare (Hague IV) to the rights of populations living in occupied territories. Apart from this, countries at war were directed to the preamble to Hague IV, known as the 'Martens clause', which simply stated that:

> In cases not included in the regulations adopted by them, the inhabitants and belligerents remain under the protection and the rule of the principles of the law of nations, as they result from the usages established among civilized peoples, from the laws of humanity, and the dictates of public conscience.[42]

Until 1914 it was expected – not least by organisations like the International Committee of the Red Cross (ICRC) – that belligerent governments would restrict internment to enemy combatants only. At worst enemy civilians might be retained by the hostile power for a month or two before proper exchanges could be arranged. However, once hostilities began the Central Powers and the Allies not only interned male enemy nationals of military age, but also seized and deported hundreds and thousands of civilians (including women and children) for purely punitive reasons or – in the case of Russia – as part of an extensive programme of expropriation and expulsion of minority groups. Germany, Austria-Hungary and Russia also considered that they had a right to take reprisals against prisoners and enemy civilians in occupied territory in retaliation for alleged acts of resistance or on grounds of 'military necessity'. This caused a humanitarian crisis on a large scale, prompting a rethink on the part of the ICRC and other human rights groups. Eventually a special section of the ICRC's *Agence Internationale des prisonniers de guerre* was set up in Geneva to deal specifically with civilian detainees, and links were formed with other interested parties, including the national red cross societies of Denmark and Sweden. Much good work was done, especially in terms of forwarding food parcels and clothing to those that needed it most, and in facilitating contact between prisoners and their families back home. Even so, the ICRC ultimately failed in its campaign to secure the release of all non-combatants from internment and outlaw the use of reprisals, but not for want of trying. Part of the problem, indeed, is that some internees were actually subjects of the states imprisoning them, this being the case with up to 300,000 civilians of various nationalities deported from the western districts of Tsarist Russia between 1914 and 1917 and a similar number of Serbs, Italians, Romanians and Ruthenes incarcerated in the Habsburg empire.[43]

Over and beyond this, treatment of civilians varied from country to country and camp to camp based on a number of factors, notably the existence of independent monitoring of diet and conditions, and the importance governments attached to looking after the interests of their own subjects in enemy hands.[44] In our case it will be argued that the relatively favourable conditions enjoyed by the men at Ruhleben derived more from their nationality than their status as civilians. The Germans did not mistreat them because of the much larger number of German civilians in British captivity (around 26,000 compared to 4,000) and because Ruhleben's geographical location made conditions there easier to monitor. In other words, they had too much to lose. At the same time, pressure from public opinion at home also gradually forced the British government to do more for British internees at Ruhleben, in spite of their status as civilians, whom government officials often regarded as 'shirkers' and 'pro-Germans'. Negative attitudes towards civilian prisoners gradually gave way to more positive ones in the British press from 1916–17 onwards, only for the Ruhleben detainees to be swiftly marginalised again after 1919. In this sense their experience was not so dissimilar from that of returning prisoners of war in general.

The scope of this book

This book does not set out to provide a comprehensive account of civilian internment during the First World War, although such a book is desperately needed. Rather, it aims to illuminate certain key aspects of the experience of internees through focusing on one specific example, British civilian prisoners at the Ruhleben camp in Germany. Ruhleben has been chosen because of all the prison camps in Germany it generated by far the most publicity during and after the war, at least in the English-speaking world, and has thus left behind a significant trail of sources. It is hoped nonetheless that the evidence presented here will stimulate further enquiry into the experiences of other internees in other parts of the world during the 1914–18 period.

Like all authors of studies on POW camps, I have found myself confronted with a dilemma, namely how to present the exciting parts of the Ruhleben story – the moment of arrest and transportation to Berlin, the first days in the camp, the various escape attempts (actually relatively few in number), and the final point of release and return to Britain – while at the same time doing justice to the sheer boredom and monotony of life in captivity. One way around this dilemma is to recognise that internment was a process with many layers of meaning, for both the prisoners and for their captors and helpers; by no means does it represent a final, unalterable text communicable through a single, consensual narrative. Even the individual's interpretation of their experience was subject to change over time (as can be seen when comparing accounts written in 1914–18 with accounts by the same person in the inter-war period or even in the 1960s and 1970s); and no two Ruhlebenites held identical opinions about the significance of their time in the camp.

According to Hayden White, 'competing narratives' about the past necessarily rely on a limited range of 'generic plot types' linking events, causes and outcomes within an overarching discourse or ideological framework – romance, tragedy, comedy, farce and so on.[45] Most classic portrayals of POWs in the Second World War tend to be cast in the romantic and/or comic mode, especially those that deal with escape attempts and other heroic antics.[46] A similar trend can also be detected in some of the early memoirs written about Ruhleben, although after 1945 it was more often the tragic and ironic that came to win out over the comic or romantic. Consider, for instance, the following passage from John Davidson Ketchum's posthumously published work, which appeared in 1965:

> Why were the pioneer internees at Ruhleben condemned to four years' imprisonment? Not for anything they had done or even thought of doing, but as an 'act of reprisal' by one government against another. And a few months later, in a counter-reprisal, 20,000 further unfortunates were put behind barbed wire in Britain. Trifling hardships, these, in comparison with the cruelties of the last war [i.e. the Second World War] and the worse ones now being sedulously prepared. But the same ominous facts underlie them all ... If this is the price we must pay for 'national security' its cost will be disastrous.[47]

In more recent years, however, scholarship on the First World War has become far less reductionist in its approach to matters of language, culture and memory, and there is now a common recognition of the much deeper and more complex 'presence' of that conflict in all aspects of European and world history, from 1914 through to the present.[48] This in turn inevitably raises the question of competing methodologies and approaches. For those working on new themes, such as religious practices and superstitions, childhood narratives, war atrocities, or images of motherhood and sacrifice, for instance, the story of the Great War cannot be confined to a handful of plot types or artistic representations. Rather, the 'cultural turn' in historical research and writing has shown how the war 'seeped into every area of domestic life', engulfing families, communities, religious institutions, schools and universities, and so on.[49] Or, as Pierre Purseigle and Jenny Macleod put it, it is no longer simply the 'sheer size' of the war and its 'industrial and technical dimensions' that make it stand out as a momentous turning point in human affairs, but also its vast and largely unexplored impact on supra-national, regional and local identities and on 'definitions and assertions of self'. Understanding the 'intimate dimension of the war' thus becomes a key task, bringing together as it does collective and individual experiences, local, national and international perspectives, and the often shared or at least inter-linked experiences of civilians and combatants.[50]

These new insights also raise important questions for current and future scholarship on prisoners of war. What impact, for instance, did POWs in the Great War imagine their incarceration would have on themselves personally and on their families? When they dreamt of release, what sort of home-coming did they envisage? When they tried to understand and make sense of their internment, who or what did they blame for their misfortune? When they sought to define themselves in relation to the war, did they share the same feelings towards the 'enemy' as soldiers at the front or civilians back at home? And when they looked for material help and spiritual support, what expectations did they have of outside bodies, whether individual state governments, the churches, their own families, or international organisations like the ICRC and the Young Men's Christian Association (YMCA)?

One of the most effective attempts to recapture the story of First World War captivity from the perspective of the 'new cultural history' is Alon Rachamimov's study, *POWs and the Great War. Captivity on the Eastern Front* (2002). His interest, as he writes, is in prisoner 'experiences' and in 'how reality is subjectively perceived and interpreted by non-elite groups'.[51] Methodologically speaking, Clifford Geertz's model of 'thick description' is deployed as a means of widening the field of inquiry to include different perspectives from those uncovered by conventional military or social histories while at the same time avoiding the extreme relativism of Hayden White and other post-modernists. In particular, by looking for a 'multiplicity of voices' and identities among ordinary rank-and-file Habsburg prisoners captured on the eastern front, Rachamimov poses new questions about prisoner loyalties and political attitudes at a time of great upheaval in eastern and central Europe.[52]

The experience of the Ruhleben prisoners was very different to the experience of those interned in Russia between 1914 and 1918. However, the methodological problems in seeking to understand and reconstruct these experiences are broadly similar. Rachamimov was able to draw, at least in part, on thousands of letters sent by ordinary prisoners to their families via the POW censorship office (*Gemeinsames Zentralnachweisbureau*) of the Habsburg army. In the case of Ruhleben, however, no central censorship records exist, owing to the destruction of the relevant archives.[53] Instead, we have to rely on fragments of information, much of it coming from the memoirs, diaries and letters of elite groups within the camp which have been published or otherwise preserved for posterity by their families. Ketchum, whose above-mentioned study is based largely on such sources, lists forty-nine books and articles dealing with Ruhleben, none of which were written by black prisoners or by sailors, and most of which were written by the members of the white educated elite which dominated the internal structures and cultural life of the camp.[54] In addition there were the views of outsiders, men like US ambassador in Berlin, James W. Gerard, and Bishop Herbert Bury, who again came from the ranks of the privileged and powerful.[55] Occasionally neutral journalists from countries like the USA and Sweden, as well as members of the Danish Red Cross, were given access to the camp. Only one Jewish prisoner, the British journalist Israel Cohen, was able to publish an account of Ruhleben highlighting incidents of racism and anti-semitism, although he again belonged to the more fortunate group of prisoners and was released over two years before the end of the war, in June 1916.[56]

The preponderance of middle- and upper-class voices among the Ruhleben memoirists stands in marked contrast to their actual share among the internees. Thus, according to the figures given by Ketchum, the number of 'permanent' prisoners in the camp on 11 March 1915 was 4,098. Of these, only 18% could be classified as 'professionals' (academics, students, musicians and others). The largest group by far was the sailors and fishermen (34.5%), followed by businessmen and clerks (24%). Workmen (skilled, semi-skilled and unskilled) accounted for 16.5%, and the remainder, including jockeys, waiters and domestic servants, for 7%.[57]

Accounts written by the non-elite groups (i.e. those who fell outside the category 'professionals') are few and far between, although not entirely non-existent. Peter Liddle, for instance, has collected many items of interest for his collection in the Brotherton Library at the University of Leeds, including oral history interviews. There is also a large volume of newspaper clippings, together with various camp magazines and other memorabilia, held in the Ettinghausen collection at the Harvard Law Library in Cambridge, Massachusetts. By and large, however, if one wishes to broaden the social base of the Ruhleben experience, one has to seek out alternative sources of information and/or be prepared to read existing sources 'against the grain'. For instance, there is a great deal of unpublished information on the wives and children of internees in the Society of Friends Library in London and the Evangelisches Zentralarchiv in Berlin, which holds the records of Dr Elisabeth Rotten's relief organisation for stranded enemy aliens in Germany. There is also more limited material in Grimsby Central Library on and by local fishermen who were interned at Ruhleben after being captured at sea, including items used in an exhibition held in the town in 1978 to mark the sixtieth anniversary of the end of the war. Poverty, ill-health and resentment were central to the experience of many of these people, and in writing a history of Ruhleben I am also conscious that I am writing about the profound disillusionment which they felt after the war, when they returned home to a Britain that refused to recognise their contribution or their suffering.

At the same time, investigating the prisoner of war experience 'from below' does not necessarily rule out examining the view 'from above'. The records of the ICRC in Geneva, for instance, provide valuable insights into the way this organisation operated in the face of the new and unexpected phenomenon of civilian internment. With some recent and important exceptions, few scholars have used this archive before.[58] In Britain and Germany, on the other hand, voluntary relief societies were obliged to work in ever-closer association with official government bodies, changing the meaning of 'relief' in the process. The documents in the National Archives at Kew (formerly the Public Record Office) are particularly revealing about the challenges faced by those attempting to assist internees and their families, as well as about links between Ruhleben and the home front more generally. Likewise the German federal archive (Bundesarchiv) in Berlin contains material dealing with the initial internment decision and with the treatment of enemy nationals between 1914 and 1918. For the German Foreign Office in particular internment was an unmitigated disaster which tarnished Germany's image abroad and yet failed to have the desired effect of ensuring the release of substantial numbers of Germans from British captivity. Even on the home front the voices condemning conditions in Ruhleben grew louder as time went on, causing growing discomfiture to the government. Small wonder, then, that studious efforts were made to bring internment to an end, especially in the last two years of the war.

Finally, this work seeks to contribute to the growing body of literature on the relationship between war and remembrance in the twentieth century. The question of what is remembered and how is indeed of perennial interest to social and cultural historians of modern warfare.[59] Ruhleben was the setting for some of the most curious episodes of the First World War, including the staging of a mock parliamentary by-election in July 1915 so that the 'borough of Ruhleben' might be properly represented in the House of Commons, and the declaration of brotherhood between Germans and Englishmen, which took place on 8 November 1918 when the soldiers guarding the camp deposed their officers and hoisted the red flag before setting the prisoners free.[60] The Ruhlebenites were in a unique position to observe the deteriorating conditions on the home front in Germany, or at least in Berlin, in the final two years of the war. The fact that so many of them were fluent German speakers set them apart from British prisoners in other camps. Their testimonies had much to offer to the contemporary observer of politics and society in Germany on the eve of defeat and revolution. Photography was one of the key commercial activities in Ruhleben, and the pictures made of the prisoners (there are literally hundreds to be found in the Liddle Collection and elsewhere) provide an astonishingly broad-ranging visual record of life in the camp. Interestingly, some of these pictures have today been placed on internet sites, or have become collectors' items.[61]

As a 'site of memory', Ruhleben had a very short history, however. Lord Newton, the British minister responsible for POW issues who visited the abandoned camp in August 1919, noted that already the place had fallen into such disrepair 'that it is rather difficult to form a correct opinion' of it.[62] For a short time it was used to house former Russian POWs awaiting repatriation to the Baltic States and the Soviet Union, and then briefly it was used as a racecourse again, but fixtures were suspended from 1939 and today nothing is left of the camp in terms of physical remains. In Germany, the word Ruhleben is usually associated with the end station on the U–2 underground line in Berlin, built in 1929. Few Berliners know that there was once an internment camp, where now there is a sewage processing plant, the *Klärwerk* Ruhleben. In general the horrors of the Nazi concentration camps have overshadowed everything that came before, including the imprisonment of 'enemy aliens' in the years 1914–18. Nonetheless, as will be argued in more detail below, the story of the Ruhleben prisoners offers some extremely important insights into the First World War, the contested ways in which it was managed, experienced and represented, and the psychological devastation that followed in its wake.

Notes

1 'Ergebnis der weiteren Besprechung über die Behandlung der in Deutschland sich aufhaltenden Angehörige feindlicher Staaten', 17 October 1914, in Bundesarchiv (BA) Berlin, R 1501/112363, Bl. 15.

2 Cf. John Horne and Alan Kramer, *German Atrocities 1914. A History of Denial* (New Haven and London, 2001).

3 For evidence see 'Ergebnis der Besprechung über die weitere Behandlung der in Deutschland sich aufhaltenden Angehörige feindlicher Staaten', 30 September 1914, in BA Berlin, R 1501/112362, Bl. 145–8.

4 Christoph Jahr, 'Zivilisten als Kriegsgefangene. Die Internierung von "Feindstaaten-Ausländern" in Deutschland während des Ersten Weltkrieges am Beispiel des "Engländerlagers Ruhleben"', in Rüdiger Overmans (ed.), *In der Hand des Feindes. Kriegsgefangenschaft von der Antike bis zum Zweiten Weltkrieg* (Cologne, 1999), pp. 303 and 318.

5 'Imagined' here does not mean 'fictitious' or 'invented', but rather culturally 'constructed' by means of language, gestures and symbols. See Matthew Stibbe, 'A Community at War: British Civilian Internees at the Ruhleben Camp in Germany, 1914–1918', in Jenny Macleod and Pierre Purseigle (eds.), *Uncovered Fields. Perspectives in First World War Studies* (Leiden, 2004),

pp. 79–94 and, more generally, Benedict Anderson, *Imagined Communities. Reflections on the Origin and Spread of Nationalism*, revised edn (London, 1991).

6 Fred J. Melville, *The British Prisoners' Stamps of Ruhleben* (London, 1980). See also 'Die Lagerpost des Engländerlagers Ruhleben', *Berliner Briefmarken-Zeitung*, 20 (1915), p. 436. Copy in Harvard Law Library, Cambridge, Massachusetts, Ettinghausen Collection (henceforth HLL-EC), box 4, file 9.

7 See e.g. 'Im Gefangenenlager Ruhleben', *Berliner Illustrierte Zeitung*, 21 November 1915, p. 652.

8 'An Old Friend in a New Guise', *The Strand Magazine* (1916), p. 729.

9 Peter H. Liddle and S. P. MacKenzie, 'The Experience of Captivity. British and Commonwealth Prisoners in Germany', in John Bourne, Peter Liddle and Ian Whitehead (eds.), *The Great World War, 1914–45. Vol. 1. Lightning Strikes Twice* (London, 2000), p. 315.

10 For further details see Chapters 4 and 5 below.

11 See Tim Cole's review article, 'Scales of Memory, Layers of Memory: Recent Works on Memories of the Second World War and the Holocaust', *Journal of Contemporary History*, 37/1 (2002), pp. 129–38.

12 See Matthew Stibbe, 'The Internment of Civilians by Belligerent States during the First World War and the Response of the International Committee of the Red Cross', *Journal of Contemporary History*, 41/1 (2006), pp. 5–19.

13 Benjamin Madley, 'From Africa to Auschwitz: How German South West Africa Incubated Ideas and Methods Adopted and Developed by the Nazis in Eastern Europe', *European History Quarterly*, 35/3 (2005), pp. 429–64; Jürgen Zimmerer, 'The Birth of the "Ostland" out of the Spirit of Colonialism. A Postcolonial Perspective on the Nazi Policy of Conquest and Extermination', *Patterns of Prejudice*, 39/2 (2005), pp. 197–219.

14 For an early attempt to document the global nature of First World War internment see James W. Garner, 'Treatment of Enemy Aliens. Measures in Respect to Personal Liberty', *American Journal of International Law*, 12/1 (January 1918), pp. 27–55.

15 Very useful here is Jürgen Osterhammel and Niels P. Petersson, *Globalization. A Short History* (Princeton, NJ, 2005), esp. pp. 81–98.

16 On this theme see John Horne and Alan Kramer, 'War Between Soldiers and Enemy Civilians, 1914–1915', in Roger Chickering and Stig Förster (eds.), *Great War, Total War. Combat and Mobilization on the Western Front, 1914–1918* (Cambridge, 2000), pp. 153–68; and Marc Michel, 'Intoxication ou "brutalisation"? Les "represailles" de la grande guerre', *14–18 aujourd'hui today heute*, 4 (2001), pp. 175–97.

17 Richard B. Speed III, *Prisoners, Diplomats and the Great War. A Study in the Diplomacy of Captivity* (New York, 1990), pp. 141–53.

18 Annette Becker, *Oubliés de la grande guerre. Humanitaire et culture de guerre. Populations occupées, déportés civils, prisonniers de guerre* (Paris, 1998); Tristan

Robert, 'Les prisonniers civils de la grande guerre. Le cas de la Picardie', *Guerres mondiales et conflits contemporains*, 190 (1998), pp. 61–78; Helen McPhail, *The Long Silence. Civilian Life under the German Occupation of Northern France, 1914–1918* (London, 1999).

19 Cf. the interview with Annette Becker in the *Times Higher Education Supplement*, 22 November 2002, p. 20. Also Jean-Claude Farcy, *Les camps de concentration français de la première guerre mondiale, 1914–1920* (Paris, 1995).

20 See Jahr, 'Zivilisten als Kriegsgefangene', passim; Jahr, 'Keine Feriengäste. "Feindstaatenausländer" im südlichen Bayern während des Ersten Weltkrieges', in Hermann J. W. Kuprian and Oswald Überegger (eds.), *Der Erste Weltkrieg im Alpenraum. Erfahrung, Deutung, Erinnerung/La Grande Guerra nell'arco alpino. Esperienze e memoria* (Innsbruck, 2006), pp. 231–45; and Sebastian Tripp, 'Kommunikation und Vergemeinschaftung. Das "Engländerlager" Ruhleben, 1914–1918', unpublished Masters dissertation, University of Marburg, 2005.

21 Rainer Pöppinghege, *Im Lager unbesiegt. Deutsche, englische und französische Kriegsgefangenen-Zeitungen im Ersten Weltkrieg* (Essen, 2006).

22 Odon Abbal, *Soldats oubliés. Les prisonniers de guerre français* (Bez-et-Esparon, 2001); Gerald H. Davis, 'National Red Cross Societies and Prisoners of War in Russia, 1914–1918', *Journal of Contemporary History*, 28 (1993), pp. 31–52; Niall Ferguson, *The Pity of War* (London, 1998), pp. 339–88; Uta Hinz, *Gefangen im Großen Krieg. Kriegsgefangenschaft in Deutschland, 1914–1921* (Essen, 2006); Giovanna Procacci, *Soldati e prigionieri italiani nella Grande Guerra (con una raccolta di lettere inedite)* 2nd edn (Turin, 2000); Alon Rachamimov, *POWs and the Great War. Captivity on the Eastern Front* (Oxford, 2002). See also the PhD thesis by Heather Jones, 'The Enemy Disarmed. Prisoners of War and the Violence of Wartime: Britain, France and Germany, 1914–1920', Trinity College, Dublin, 2005.

23 Uta Hinz, 'Internierung', in Gerhard Hirschfeld, Gerd Krumeich and Irina Renz (eds.), *Enzyklopädie Erster Weltkrieg* (Paderborn, 2003), pp. 582–4.

24 Joël Kotek and Pierre Rigoulot, *Das Jahrhundert der Lager. Gefangenschaft, Zwangsarbeit, Vernichtung* (Berlin, 2001) [French original, Paris, 2000], pp. 87–97.

25 See e.g. David Cesarani and Tony Kushner (eds.), *The Internment of Aliens in Twentieth Century Britain* (London, 1993); and Panikos Panayi (ed.), *Minorities in Wartime. National and Racial Groupings in Europe, North America and Australia During the Two World Wars* (Oxford, 1993).

26 Cf. Osterhammel and Petersson, *Globalization*, p. 89.

27 *Ibid.*, p. 97.

28 Panikos Panayi, *Immigration, Ethnicity and Racism in Britain, 1815–1945* (Manchester, 1994), pp. 105–6. Cf. Panayi, 'An Intolerant Act by an Intolerant Society. The Internment of Germans in Britain During the First World War', in Cesarani and Kushner (eds.), *The Internment of Aliens*, pp. 53–75.

29 Robert, 'Les prisonniers civils de la grande guerre', pp. 61–2.

30 Stéphane Audoin-Rouzeau and Annette Becker, *1914–1918. Understanding the Great War* (London, 2002).

31 *Ibid.*, p. 80.

32 *Ibid.*, p. 75, n. 1.

33 *Ibid.*, p. 156.

34 Bernice Archer, *The Internment of Western Civilians under the Japanese, 1941–1945. A Patchwork of Experiences* (London, 2004), p. 3.

35 This is clearly demonstrated in the German case by Hinz, *Gefangen im Großen Krieg*, passim, and on a comparative level by Pöppinghege, *Im Lager unbesiegt*, passim.

36 Wolfgang Sofsky, *Die Ordnung des Terrors. Das Konzentrationslager* (Frankfurt/M, 1993), p. 62.

37 The same point is made in Jay Winter and Antoine Prost, *The Great War in History. Debates and Controversies, 1914 to the Present* (Cambridge, 2005), p. 102.

38 See the figures in Rachamimov, *POWs and the Great War*, pp. 39–42, and Hinz, *Gefangen im Großen Krieg*, p. 238. As Heather Jones has pointed out, all figures, and particularly those for 1918, are suspect, not least because they do not include prisoners who died (or were killed) in camps and forced labour battalions in occupied territories. Record-keeping procedures also broke down in the final months of the war, especially in the case of Germany and Russia. But even taking this into account, mortality rates were nowhere near as high as on the eastern front in the Second World War. See Jones, 'The Enemy Disarmed', pp. 1–5, 371–2 and 440.

39 Cf. Abbal, *Soldats oubliés*, p. 119.

40 For an excellent summary see Alan Kramer, 'Kriegsrecht und Kriegsverbrechen', in Hirschfeld *et al.* (eds.), *Enzyklopädie Erster Weltkrieg*, pp. 281–92. Also very useful is Daniel Marc Segesser, 'The International Debate on the Punishment of War Crimes during the Balkan Wars and the First World War', *Peace & Change*, 31/4 (2006), pp. 533–54.

41 See in particular Uta Hinz, 'Humanität im Krieg? Internationales Rotes Kreuz und Kriegsgefangenenhilfe im Ersten Weltkrieg', in Jochen Oltmer (ed.), *Kriegsgefangene im Europa des Ersten Weltkriegs* (Paderborn, 2006), pp. 216–36; and Hinz, *Gefangen im Großen Krieg*, passim. On the Second World War see S. P. MacKenzie, 'The Treatment of Prisoners of War in World War II', *Journal of Modern History*, 66/3 (1994), pp. 487–520.

42 André Durand, *From Sarajevo to Hiroshima. History of the International Committee of the Red Cross* (Geneva, 1984), p. 83. On the Hague peace conferences of 1899 and 1907 see also Jost Dülffer, *Regeln gegen den Krieg. Die Haager Friedenskonferenzen von 1899 und 1907 in der internationalen Politik* (Frankfurt/M, 1981).

43 Stibbe, 'The Internment of Civilians', pp. 7–8. See also Eric Lohr, *Nationalizing the Russian Empire. The Campaign Against Enemy Aliens during*

World War I (Cambridge, MA, 2003), p. 127.

44 Stibbe, 'The Internment of Civilians', pp. 16–17.

45 Hayden White, 'Historical Emplotment and the Problem of Truth', in Saul Friedlander (ed.), *Probing the Limits of Representation* (Cambridge, MA, 1992), pp. 34–53.

46 For a critical look at this genre see S. P. MacKenzie, *The Colditz Myth. British and Commonwealth Prisoners of War in Nazi Germany* (Oxford, 2004).

47 John Davidson Ketchum, *Ruhleben. A Prison Camp Society* (Toronto, 1965), p. xviii.

48 For an excellent example see Adrian Gregory, *The Silence of Memory. Armistice Day, 1919–1946* (Oxford, 1994).

49 Winter and Prost, *The Great War in History*, p. 164.

50 Pierre Purseigle and Jenny Macleod, 'Introduction: Perspectives in First World War Studies', in Macleod and Purseigle (eds.), *Uncovered Fields*, pp. 16–17. For a very interesting attempt to examine the impact of the war on the intimate sphere see also Nicoletta F. Gullace, 'Friends, Aliens and Enemies. Fictive Communities and the Lusitania Riots of 1915', *Journal of Social History* (Winter 2005), pp. 345–67. As will become clear below, however, I disagree with Gullace's description of internment camps as 'liminal and communitiless environment[s]' (*ibid.*, p. 357), not only because this flies in the face of empirical evidence, but also because it undermines her otherwise very eloquently put case for placing human agency at the centre of the new social and cultural history of warfare.

51 Rachamimov, *POWs and the Great War*, p. 17.

52 *Ibid.* Cf. Clifford Geertz, 'Thick Description: Toward an Interpretive Theory of Culture', in *The Interpretation of Cultures. Selected Essays by Clifford Geertz* (New York, 1973), pp. 3–30.

53 The Reichsarchiv, which contained (among other things) the records of the Prussian Ministry of War and the Prussian deputy military commands, was destroyed at the end of the Second World War, creating on-going problems for military historians. For further details see Hinz, *Gefangen im Großen Krieg*, pp. 33–4.

54 Ketchum, *Ruhleben*, pp. xxi–xxiii.

55 James W. Gerard, *My Four Years in Germany* (London, 1917); Herbert Bury, *My Visit to Ruhleben* (London, 1917).

56 Israel Cohen, *The Ruhleben Prison Camp. A Record of Nineteen Months' Internment* (London, 1917).

57 Ketchum, *Ruhleben*, p. 23.

58 The exceptions are Becker, *Oubliés de la grande guerre*, passim; Hinz, *Gefangen im Großen Krieg*, passim; and Bruno Cabanes, *La victoire endeuillée. La sortie de guerre des soldats français (1918–1920)* (Paris, 2004). Heather Jones also uses the ICRC archive in her PhD thesis, mentioned in n. 22 above.

59 For major contributions to the debate see Jay Winter, *Sites of Memory, Sites of Mourning. The Great War in European Cultural History* (Cambridge, 1995); and

Jay Winter and Emmanuel Sivan (eds.), *War and Remembrance in the Twentieth Century* (Cambridge, 1999).

60   See Chapters 3 and 5 below.
61   See e.g. Chris Paton's website on Ruhleben at http://ruhleben.tripod.com/index.html.
62   Lord Newton, *Retrospection* (London, 1941), p. 275.

1

The politics of alien internment in Germany

Internment camps were a universal phenomenon in the First World War. They could be found in every continent and were used to imprison men, women and children of all ages and all nationalities.[1] In Germany alone, over 111,000 enemy civilians had been interned by October 1918, according to the German army's own figures.[2] Most of them were deportees from the occupied parts of Belgium, France and Russia, although some, like the prisoners at Ruhleben, were 'enemy aliens' stranded on German territory when the war began. In general, conditions in the other internment camps were much worse than in Ruhleben. This applied in particular to camps in occupied territories where Red Cross officials and diplomats from neutral states were not granted access. Internment was also an on-going process; while some prisoners were released or exchanged, others could be simultaneously arrested and deported in a seemingly endless cycle. An ICRC report in October 1918 complained:

> Every week we are supplied with new lists, some of them relating to very particular groups: English civilians held in Finland, French, Belgian and Portuguese diplomatic personnel expelled from neutral Ukraine and interned in Germany, etc. ... Some civilian detainees in Germany appear to have been transferred to prisons in Belgium and occupied France, where they can neither communicate with their families in unoccupied France, nor receive aid parcels, nor have visits from representatives of the neutral powers charged with their protection. We regret that up till now it has proved impossible to obtain any kind of information on the conditions these prisoners are being held in.[3]

Ruhleben, however, stood out for a variety of reasons. Firstly, most of the Ruhleben prisoners were held in one mass act on 6 November 1914, and the turnover of inmates was relatively low compared to other camps.[4] Secondly, they were not required to work for the German economy and economic motives played no role in the decision to intern them. By contrast deported Belgian, French and Russian civilian prisoners were often used not only as hostages but also as a source of cheap labour, especially after 1916.[5] Thirdly, while there were over 175 prison camps in Germany during the war, only one – Ruhleben – was used exclusively for holding civilians. The remainder held both civilian and military prisoners, albeit usually in separate compounds.[6] And, finally, Ruhleben's geographical location close to Berlin ensured that it was much more in the public eye than other camps. It thus came to symbolise German internment policies to the English-speaking world, even though in reality it was not typical of most German internment camps at this time.[7]

The focus of this chapter will be on the internment decision itself. The archival records suggest that, in addition to straightforward retaliation for the poor treatment of Germans in Britain, the main driving force behind German policy was political and propagandistic.[8] In brief, the German government hoped to draw international attention to alleged British misdeeds in its conduct of the war while at the same time restoring confidence in victory in the face of rising casualty lists and the first signs of food shortages on the home front. On top of this there were some security concerns regarding spying and acts of sabotage by enemy aliens within Germany, although these concerns were probably exaggerated. Last, but not least, the German government intended to use British internees as bargaining counters in any future negotiations over the fate of German nationals in Britain, some (but only a minority) of whom had been interned in the first months of the war. This policy, while having a veneer of rationality, was doomed to failure from the start, because the British government saw no advantage in exchanging the 26,000 Germans of military age it had retained in August 1914 in return for only 4,000 or so of its own subjects. Nor, indeed, was it deterred from enacting a wholesale internment of Germans and Austrians within its borders after May 1915.

Before we go on to analyse this further, however, it is first necessary to consider the status and profile of the British community in Germany in greater detail.

British subjects in Germany

The most accurate figure for the number of Britons in Germany in the autumn of 1914 comes from police lists drawn up for each *Bundesstaat* and each province of Prussia at the behest of the Reich Office of Interior, which in turn acted on behalf of the Reich Chancellor.[9] According to these lists, which were presented to the Reich Chancellor's Office in a final, composite form on 18 December 1914, there were 9,103 British nationals known to be resident on German soil. Of these 4,436 were women and girls, 3,191 were men of military age, 954 were boys under seventeen years of age and 522 were men over fifty-five years of age.[10] The figure includes so-called *Kolonialengländer* (i.e. nationals of British colonies and dominions) but excludes British merchant seaman held prisoner in Hamburg and at other German ports from the outbreak of the war. The latter numbered 1,065 on 14 October 1914, according to the protocols of the Hamburg senate,[11] so that at the time of internment (6 November 1914) just over 10,000 British civilians were in German hands, of whom around 4,200–4,300 were men aged seventeen to fifty-five.[12]

Even allowing for the outbreak of war, this figure is still surprisingly small, especially given the substantial economic, cultural and familial ties that had arisen between Germany and Britain from the 1850s onwards. Britain, for instance, had over 70,000 German and Austrian nationals resident within its shores at the end of 1914, and France 60,000.[13] Germany itself had fewer French residents, again probably about 10,000 in all,[14] but made up for this by relying heavily on migrant labour from other parts of Europe. The official records of the German labour exchange revealed the figures in Table 1 for foreign workers in Germany in the year 1913/14.

In addition to this there were an estimated 50,000 Russians in Germany who were not seasonal labourers but migrants of longer standing (including non-naturalised Baltic Germans) and visitors on short-term trips, for purposes of study, business, or recuperation. Most of them were from the 'better-off' classes and could fend for themselves, at least in the first weeks of the war, although as they ran out of money their situation became less tolerable.[15] The same applied to all other foreigners in Germany, numbering some 1.2 million in total.[16]

In terms of planning and policy, the German government's top priority was to maintain control over poorer migrants from the east in the event of war with Russia. In fact, Russian–Polish seasonal workers had already been subject to severe restrictions on their movements before 1914.[17] However, the key dilemma in July 1914 was not whether to expel or intern them, but

Table 1 *Foreign workers in Germany by country of origin, 1913–14*

Country of origin	Nos. working in agriculture	Nos. working in industry	Total
Russia	286,413	35,565	321,978
(incl. Russian Poland)	(269,000)	(22,538)	(291,538)
Austria-Hungary	135,868	188,991	324,859
(incl. Austrian Poland)	(58,244)	(17,266)	(75,510)
(incl. Ruthenia)	(68,236)	(46,017)	(114,253)
Italy	45	64,992	65,037
Netherlands and Belgium	9,633	46,245	55,878
Total	**436,736**	**346,122**	**782,858**

Source: Ulrich Herbert, *Geschichte der Ausländerbeschäftigung in Deutschland, 1880 bis 1980. Saisonarbeiter, Zwangsarbeiter, Gastarbeiter* (Bonn, 1986), p. 100. Copyright © Verlag J.H.W. Dietz Nachfolger, Bonn.

how to prevent them from leaving their jobs, either to return home or to seek more lucrative contracts elsewhere. Indeed, their contribution to the German war economy was considered crucial, especially in rural areas which were bound to experience serious labour shortages following the call-up of German men. As early as 27 July 1914 the Reich Office of Interior wrote to the Prussian Ministry of War requesting that seasonal workers be exempted from any deportation measures against 'enemy aliens' to be applied after the outbreak of war 'so long as they are in possession of one of the identity cards issued by the labour exchange'.[18] Following on from this, the deputy general staff issued a series of decrees between 4 August and 10 October 1914 which prohibited the departure of Russian–Polish agricultural and industrial workers from Prussia and more or less forced them to stay in their jobs under threat of severe penalties. This also applied to additional workers 'recruited' in occupied Poland after 1915, so that in total some 500,000–600,000 Russian–Polish migrants played an on-going, and largely involuntary, role in the German war economy.[19]

Compared to this, the number of British subjects in Germany was very small, and at first little interest was shown in them. True, a handful of suspected spies were arrested for questioning in the early part of August, but apart from this there were no immediate plans for internment, and significantly the Reich Office of Interior did not even set about compiling a complete list of Britons held in German territory until early October 1914.[20] This in turn reflected the limited influence that the Reich had in relation to determining policies towards foreigners under Germany's complex federal constitution, which left matters largely in the hands of the individual states. Even the Prussian Ministry of War and its Bavarian, Saxon and Württemberg equivalents had no powers to issue orders to the acting commanders of Germany's twenty-four army corps districts, who enjoyed almost unlimited authority within their respective fiefdoms under the state of siege laws.[21] The latter in turn introduced a variety of ad hoc measures ranging from freedom to leave for all enemy nationals, including men of military age (practised in Württemberg in the first weeks of the war) to selective internment for some and voluntary repatriation for others (the experience in southern Bavaria) and limited freedom without internment or repatriation (the policy by and large adopted in Baden, Prussia, Saxony and the remaining German states).[22]

Who were these British nationals trapped in Germany by the outbreak of war? Geographically, they came from all over Britain and the British empire, and were to be found in all parts of Germany. The largest concentration was located in Hamburg, where there were still 1,182 British subjects registered with the police in November 1914, excluding merchant sailors.[23] Of these, 322 were taken to Ruhleben including thirty-two who were born in Hamburg, ten who had been born in other parts of the Reich and one who had been born in Vienna. The remainder were born outside Germany and Austria, mostly in the UK or other parts of the British empire. The police records also reveal the occupations of those removed from Hamburg to Ruhleben. Predictably they were nearly all merchants, bankers, insurance clerks and stock exchange traders, reflecting the city's historic commercial ties with London and other British ports.[24] The 1,065 merchant sailors docked in Hamburg when the war broke out were also taken *en masse* to Ruhleben. Unlike other British nationals, they were treated as prisoners of war from August 1914 onwards and were held from October in cramped and uncomfortable conditions on board three abandoned hulks in the Hansahafen.[25] Their home towns were British ports like Grimsby, Hull, Sunderland and Leith, and few could speak any German before the war took them first to Hamburg, and then to Ruhleben. There were also around 100 black sailors who originally came from British West Africa or the West Indies and were serving on British-registered ships.[26]

Apart from Hamburg, there were relatively large but disparate British communities in other major German cities, especially Berlin, Potsdam,

Frankfurt-am-Main, Düsseldorf, Hanover, Kiel, Bremen, Munich and Dresden (see the appendix at the end of the book for rough figures drawn from police records). Significantly, when internment was finally introduced, the Social Democrat newspaper *Vorwärts* reported the arrest of around 1,500 British subjects in Hamburg, 800 in Berlin, 600 in Frankfurt-am-Main, 140 in Munich and 100 in Dresden. These figures combined come to 3,140, suggesting that three-quarters of the internees were either resident in or travelling through the five major financial, commercial and cultural cities of Imperial Germany when the war broke out.[27]

Other places where Britons could be found included important manufacturing towns in Saxony like Leipzig and Chemnitz, where the textile and knitting machinery industries had developed strong links with their British counterparts, and holiday resorts like Baden-Baden and Bad Nauheim, where the very rich went to take their rest cures. In general, however, Britons in Germany were integrated into society and did not live in isolated communities with other Britons. With the partial exception of Hamburg's commercial, insurance and banking sector, they were not over-represented in any particular profession or trade, nor did they stand out in terms of appearance, mannerisms or outlook. Some did not even consider themselves as British, having spent most or all of their lives in Germany. This applied in particular to the German-born wives and children of British nationals. Under the German citizenship law of 1870, and its revised version in 1913, German women who married foreign nationals lost their legal status as Germans except under certain limited circumstances, and the same applied to their children and grandchildren.[28] Around 600–800 German men fell into the latter category, including some who had lived virtually their entire lives in Germany. Before the war some had used their status as British nationals to avoid military service in the German army or to secure preferential treatment in business or commercial dealings. However, after 4 August 1914 it made them liable to restrictions as aliens, and eventually led to their internment as enemy nationals. Often they were referred to as 'Formalengländer' or 'Scheinengländer' – British nationals in a technical sense only. Some were released early from Ruhleben but others spent the entire war in captivity.[29]

The term 'Scheinengländer' could also be used in a completely different sense, however, to describe Russian-born Jews who had acquired British nationality while resident in Germany, or who claimed to have relatives living in Britain or a British colony who had applied for or intended to apply for British nationality on their behalf, or who had been turned down for naturalisation in Germany and had declared themselves stateless, having renounced their Russian nationality.[30] The numbers involved were small, probably less than 100 and certainly not more than 200. Most of these 'Russians' had been resident in Berlin prior to their internment, but some came from Hamburg and at least one from Cologne. A group of them were removed to Havelberg camp in early 1915, but the majority remained in Ruhleben until the end of the war.[31]

Finally, some of those eventually interned at Ruhleben were simply unfortunate tourists or businessmen who had been on short-term trips to the continent in the weeks before the war broke out. Foreign travel was a favourite pastime of teachers and university professors, for instance, who had the time, and perhaps the money, to venture abroad in the summer months. Jerome K. Jerome had of course already popularised this kind of tourism in his comic novel *Three Men on the Bummel*, published in 1900. There were also a number of professional football players, including the former British internationals Steve Bloomer and Fred Pentland, who were in Germany coaching local teams.[32] Musicians and actors, waiters and jockeys, writers and journalists, language teachers and travel agents, students and academics, not to mention professional criminals and con artists, could all find themselves suddenly trapped by the outbreak of the war and no longer free to travel as they wished. Some were able to keep their jobs in Germany, or had German relatives and in-laws willing to help them out financially, but others faced immediate difficulties once they had been cut off from their usual channels of support. Those unable to pay their rent or hotel bills were forced to rely on the charity of other Britons, or on the goodwill of their German hosts. Their plight only grew worse over time.[33]

At first the German authorities seemed at a loss to know what to do with stranded British subjects caught on German territory after the outbreak of war, and there is certainly no evidence of any immediate plans for mass internment. In the view of the Reich government and deputy general staff in Berlin, enemy civilians would eventually be allowed to go home, but only after the army had completed its mobilisation. Meanwhile, the main responsibility for supervising enemy aliens lay with the acting commanders of Germany's twenty-four army corps districts, who were responsible to the Kaiser only and rarely acted in unison. Concerns were raised by some officials at state level about the obligations Germany might have towards foreigners in distress. If they were to be prevented from leaving Germany indefinitely, should they be treated as prisoners of war under the 1907 Hague convention, with a right to be fed, housed and clothed? If they were not prisoners of war, what responsibilities, if any, did the German authorities have in relation to their welfare and repatriation? And what steps should be taken to taken to ensure that there were no spies or saboteurs among them?[34]

Immediate answers were not forthcoming. Instead, the Reich Office of Interior, after consultation with Prussian Interior and War Ministries, the Foreign Office and representatives of the federal states, issued a vague set of guidelines on 18 August 1914. For the time being, no citizen of an enemy state could leave the police district in which he or she was living without the express consent of the local deputy military commander. A curfew should also be imposed. Nonetheless, the guidelines also urged moderation:

> As a rule there should be only a mild supervision of foreigners. Any attempts to make their situation more difficult should be avoided – not least in consideration of the interests of Germans living in enemy countries.[35]

This broadly complied with a set of instructions issued by General von Kessel, the supreme commander in the marches (i.e. the acting military commander for Berlin and the surrounding province of Brandenburg), on 10 August 1914:

> Enemy aliens living within the police district of Berlin, as long as they are not suspected of any crimes, and as long as they have a fixed address or a regular job, are to be placed under police supervision (enforcement of registration requirements and surveillance of post), but are otherwise to be left to get on with their lives.[36]

In spite of this, regional variations in the treatment of enemy aliens continued, particularly, as we have seen, in the case of Bavaria, where a policy of selective internment was introduced, and in Hamburg, where British sailors were detained indefinitely along with their vessels in violation of the 1907 Hague convention relating to the status of enemy merchant ships at the outbreak of hostilities.[37] Occasionally over-zealous officials ordered the detention of individuals for alleged offences such as 'Majestätsbeleidigung' (insulting the Kaiser) or more generally, for mocking the German war effort. In Leipzig, thirty-five British men were rounded up as 'suspects' on 5 September, moving in an unenviable cycle from the local prison to temporary release on bail to incarceration in the *Leipziger Arbeitsanstalt*. Six of them were still being held at the end of October.[38] In north west Germany, male enemy nationals caught attempting to cross the Dutch border without proper permits were also arrested, detained overnight in local police stations or army barracks, and then sent on to Hanover, much to the dismay of the local police and military authorities there.[39] However, only in the late autumn of 1914, following the failure to achieve rapid victory on the continent, did the Reich government and deputy general staff come to favour the internment of all British males aged seventeen to fifty-five, regardless of their occupation, past police record or place of residence. How and why did this change of policy occur? To understand more we have to look at the changing domestic situation inside Germany in the months between early August and early November 1914, as well as at the developing international context.

The decision for internment

The Ruhleben racecourse was situated between the boroughs of Charlottenburg and Spandau, about two miles to the west of Berlin in its pre-1920 boundaries. It was hired from its owners by the Prussian Ministry of War in September 1914 to house Russian and Russian–Polish prisoners from the Berlin area who were retained as indented labour, as well as a handful of Japanese citizens temporarily taken into custody after the Japanese entry into the war on 23 August 1914. A few Britons arrested as suspected spies or miscreants were also held there, rising to eighty-six by 22 October.[40] However, until the beginning of November 1914 there are no indications of any plans to use this site as a place to house British internees in general. Indeed, in a memorandum dated 1 September 1914 the Reich Office of Interior made it clear that enemy nationals, including men of military age, would be allowed to return home as soon as reciprocal arrangements were in place:

> On the basis of discussions with the relevant Prussian ministries, the deputy general staff and the admiralty, I have the honour to report the following: as soon as the railways are given the go ahead to resume normal passenger traffic, the subjects of enemy states who are currently in Germany will be given permission to leave the territory of the Reich, provided that Germans living abroad are also allowed to return to their homeland.[41]

Exchanges of trapped civilians, in other words, were the preferred solution, but only under guarantee of reciprocity arranged through traditional diplomatic channels. Indeed, this was the one consistent element in German policy towards enemy aliens resident within its own borders (but not towards enemy civilians in occupied territory, whose fate was determined solely by the army high command). Thus agreements were negotiated with Japan and Serbia in the autumn of 1914, and later with Italy, which granted freedom to leave Germany and/or exemption from internment to all civilians, including men of military age, unless or until they had been found guilty of specific criminal offences.[42]

By contrast, Britain and France both took the decidedly more 'modern' line that every enemy civilian within their jurisdiction was a potential spy, traitor, criminal or combatant, whose release would be militarily disadvantageous, even under conditions of reciprocity. The fact that both countries held relatively large numbers of Germans (especially in comparison to the number of their own nationals in Germany) also conditioned their attitude. Thus the British War Office argued in a memorandum on 19 August 1914 that any arrangement for the exchange of civilian prisoners would

> from a purely military view... be detrimental to the interests of this country, as British subjects, so exchanged, might not be available to serve in the Army, while the German subjects would probably be liable for military service.[43]

The British Foreign Office, on the other hand, was inclined to believe that a deal might be possible with Germany on the basis of an exchange of equal numbers of civilians, regardless of liability for military service or previous military training (the 'man for man' rather than 'all for all' approach).[44] The Home Office concurred, while the admiralty was prepared to approve the release of prisoners who would be 'of no military use, such as invalids, doctors and ministers of religion', but argued for the retention of 'those prisoners liable for military service'. This included captured German merchant seamen, whom Winston Churchill, as first lord of the admiralty, insisted on treating as POWs, even in cases where they were seized from neutral ships.[45]

In September and early October 1914 a variety of agreements were in fact reached for the exchange of women, children and the elderly, as well as doctors and priests.[46] However, no such agreement was forthcoming in relation to men of military age, largely because of the continued objections raised by the British War Office and admiralty. In a new twist, the War Office even claimed to have discovered evidence that men as old as fifty-five were being called up into the German army, an assertion which turned out to be wholly unfounded.[47] There were also rumours, cited by the British Foreign Office and in the British press, that German forces had been deporting as prisoners of war all British male civilians of military age captured in Belgium and northern France.[48] The German authorities countered with accusations of their own, particularly regarding the alleged arrest of German reservists returning home from various parts of the world on board neutral ships, some of whom had indeed been held in British ports and others taken on the high seas on Churchill's orders.[49] As a result of these claims and counter-claims, Britain now made it known that it would countenance the exchange of men over fifty-five only, whereas the original agreement had also included men aged between forty-five and fifty-five. Each side accused the other of bad faith, while American diplomats, particularly the two ambassadors in Berlin and London, tried their best to mediate in difficult circumstances. By the middle of October it was clear that the negotiations had stalled, and in fact there was no further progress on prisoner exchanges for the rest of the year.

In the meantime, from 12 October 1914 onwards the military and political authorities in Berlin came under a sustained campaign from the right-wing press at home demanding the internment of British men in retaliation for the alleged abuse of German and Austrian citizens in Britain. This campaign developed a momentum of its own and was directly linked to news of developments in Britain, in particular the violent anti-German riots in Deptford, south London, on 18 and 19 October which were widely reported in the German papers.[50] Even before this, articles began appearing on a daily basis detailing the 'appalling' conditions in Newbury and other British camps where, it was alleged, German civilians were being held in tents and wooden shacks. On 16 and 17 October, for instance, the disgraced German colonialist Carl Peters caused a sensation by publishing an article in the *Tag* in which he gave a lurid account of his own treatment and that of his fellow nationals in British hands:

Germans are no longer able to own weapons of any kind, signalling equipment, photographic apparatus, cars, motorcycles, pigeons, atlases, telephones etc. A young German lady recently got six months in prison because she was found to be in possession of a camera. Every day countless numbers of Germans are sent to jail because they unwittingly breached the five-mile exclusion zone [around their places of residence] ... In London every restaurateur, hotel owner and boarding house keeper has been told that they face imprisonment if they do not immediately dismiss their German employees or if they hire new ones.[51]

The only legitimate response, he argued, was retaliation against British nationals living in Germany, as 'we cannot wait until the end of the war in order to settle accounts'.[52]

Prominent figures inside the German military shared views similar to those of Peters. For instance, the acting commander of the 7th deputy general command in Münster (Westphalia) wrote to the Reich Chancellor Bethmann Hollweg on 12 October 1914:

> It has come to my knowledge, via various complaints I have received from business and industrial circles, that there is considerable disquiet among the population that all unsuspicious British subjects – i.e. the vast majority of those living in Germany – are at liberty, while in Britain all Germans aged 17 to 45 have been interned. The last detail is at any rate reported in the local papers. I would urge Your Excellency to investigate this matter, and if England really is proceeding in the manner reported, I would also recommend ordering the arrest of *all* British subjects in Germany who are of military age.[53]

In Berlin, the press department of the Reich Naval Office actively encouraged sensationalist newspaper reporting on the anti-German outrages in Britain, while keeping a close eye on the Social Democrat newspaper *Vorwärts*, which ran a series of more sober accounts. In its view, the *Vorwärts* articles were clearly written by British spies masquerading as Germans.[54] The supreme military commander in the marches, General von Kessel, was equally determined that British nationals in Germany should be expelled from their jobs in response to similar measures allegedly taken against Germans in Britain.[55] Finally in Hamburg-Altona, the acting commander of the 9th deputy general command, General von Roehl, even threatened to order a local round-up of British citizens in a telegram sent to the German Foreign Office in Berlin on 27 October 1914:

> Unless we receive official confirmation from the American ambassador in London by 5 November that the German prisoners in England, especially those being held at Newbury, are being treated humanely, the local deputy general command recommends: the arrest of all English males aged 16 and over within this army corps district and their internment in the Lockstedter Lager. Reply requested by telegram.[56]

However, the most forceful advocates of harsher measures against British civilians were the deputy general staff and deputy admiralty staff in Berlin. A close reading of government files reveals that their representatives had already pushed for the radical option of wholesale internment during official meetings with representatives of the Prussian Minister of War and the Reich Naval, Interior and Foreign Offices held on 12 and 17 October 1914.[57] According to Christoph Jahr, their motives were three-fold: fear of spying, preventive prisoner-of-warhood (i.e. depriving the British army and navy of manpower) and finally, the potential for using the internees as bargaining counters in talks on the status of prisoners of war more generally.[58] The subsequent investigations of the Reichstag committee of inquiry into the causes of the war and of Germany's defeat, which also had access to the relevant documents, emphasised all of these motives, but above all the need for increased security at home:

> The freedoms granted to English subjects in Germany ... led to a situation which left us wide open to the risk of continued and extensive espionage. The observations made by English sailors in our harbours, the visits made by English insurance brokers to wharves and warehouses, the exact knowledge of our troop transports, the deliberate sabotaging of one of our air ships at its base in Düsseldorf – all of these things were evidence of a continuation of spying on a grand scale. The mysterious fires that broke out in several grain depots in the countryside also lent force to the suspicion that England was hell bent on putting its intention to destroy us economically into practice.[59]

In contrast to Jahr, however, I would argue that preventive prisoner-of-warhood, while relevant in other contexts and at other times, was not a serious issue here. Indeed, at first the German military authorities estimated that only 1,200–1,500 British men would be eligible for arrest, hardly a large enough tally to present a real threat to the German war effort.[60] Of far greater importance was the use that could be made of internment in propaganda terms. Thus at home, public support for the war would be given a much-needed boost by a policy which demonstrated Britain's vulnerability to counter-measures in the form of 'legitimate' retaliation for the riots and anti-German measures taken in Britain. And at the same time, the British government's apparent refusal to negotiate over the fate of its own subjects in enemy hands could be used to illustrate its alleged contempt for human rights and the rule of international law more generally. In particular, Sir Edward

Grey, the British foreign secretary, was portrayed in German publications as a blood-thirsty warmonger for whom war was a 'business like any other'.[61] The only language he understood, as Carl Peters wrote in an influential pamphlet published shortly after his articles in the *Tag*, was the language of naked self-interest:

> Those who think otherwise only demonstrate their complete lack of understanding of the British character ... The only thing that impresses them is power and the sentiment: 'they are not afraid of us.' They are also given to sober calculation, much more so than we Germans, who are always influenced by our emotions, whether zest, passion or jealousy.[62]

The Kaiser evidently agreed with this assessment too, for in marginal comments on the second of Peters' *Tag* articles (published on 17 October) he vented his anger against the 'hair-raising' British excesses and demanded that plans be presented to him *'immediately'* for the adoption of new measures 'against English subjects living in Germany'.[63] Since the deputy general staff and the deputy admiralty staff were already pushing for wholesale internment, the Kaiser's intervention came just at the right moment to overcome the resistance of more cautious elements in the Foreign Office. As the legal department of the Foreign Office warned in a telegram to general headquarters on 26 October:

> With regard to retaliatory measures against England we have always adopted the principle that the measures should follow the English precedent exactly and should only be undertaken after certain proof that England has acted so. In the current circumstances we would recommend sticking to this principle even more rigidly, especially given that more German subjects and German property are currently under England's control than [vice versa], so that anything done in excess of what is a proportionate response could do incalculable damage to German interests.[64]

The Foreign Office also wished to draw the Kaiser's attention to evident exaggerations in Peters' account of events in London:

> In general Peters' allegations are... not be trusted without further corroboration, especially as we are in possession of more reliable reports, some of them even quite favourable ones. At the very least

it seems that there is no indication that employers have been banned from hiring Germans on pain of imprisonment. As far as retaliatory measures are concerned, we would therefore recommend awaiting the outcome of our on-the-spot investigations, which we have asked the American ambassador in London to conduct in person.[65]

In the end, however, these objections were overcome when a decision was made at general headquarters not to proceed directly to internment but rather to send an ultimatum to the British government which stated that unless all the interned Germans in England were released by 5 November, then all the Englishmen of military age living in Germany would be immediately arrested and interned. On this basis, the chief of the general staff issued instructions on 31 October to begin preparations for the arrest of all British males aged seventeen to fifty-five if, as expected, the British government failed to meet the German deadline.[66] This in turn gave the German internment measures a veneer of legality and satisfied the Foreign Office doubters. The plan as it now stood was to take all internees into military custody on the morning of 6 November, although for the time being the 309 *Kolonialengländer* in Germany enjoyed immunity, as did doctors and priests.[67] The deputy general staff in Berlin, in conjunction with the police and deputy general commands, were responsible for the arrest and transfer of the prisoners to Ruhleben, while the camp itself came under the authority of the supreme command in the marches and the Berlin *Kommandantur*. A later inquiry from the Prussian Ministry of Interior revealed that this was a Reich measure which had been undertaken 'in the interests of the German war effort', and was therefore being paid for from Reich funds.[68]

The role of public opinion

What role did popular hostility towards Britons living in Germany play in this decision? In Britain in 1914–15, according to Panikos Panayi, 'the strength of public opinion … forced the government to adopt Draconian measures against enemy aliens, notably wholesale internment and repatriation'.[69] Colin Holmes is more cautious, noting that 'the [British] government's own propaganda against Germany – the exaggeration of German atrocities in Belgium for instance – reinforced popular anti-Germanism'.[70] Was this the same in Germany?

Certainly the early weeks of the war were characterised by a marked shift from anti-Russian to anti-English feeling in the German press, so much so that by the end of October 1914 only the Social Democrat newspaper

Vorwärts was taking a principled stand against internment.[71] There is also
some evidence that this press campaign had had an impact on public opinion.
The archives, for instance, are littered with letters from 'outraged' citizens
denouncing British maltreatment of German prisoners and demanding a
rigorous response from the German government.[72] In Hamburg the anger
seems to have been particularly acute because so many of the internees in
Britain were 'sons of Hamburg', as one advert in a local newspaper put it.[73]
In Cologne, newspaper reports of the alleged abuse of German merchants in
Hong Kong and other British colonies seem to have had a particular impact.
The National Liberal *Kölnische Zeitung* claimed to speak for the whole of
Germany when it argued, on 23 October 1914, that British nationals must
be treated as prisoners of war:

> Today ... when England and the English seek to slander the good name
> of Germany throughout the world, when they trample Germany's
> rights under foot, rob German firms and employees in the most
> perfidious manner, in short, when they stoop to the lowest means in
> order to mistreat and do harm to Germans, then we must finally stop
> treating the 'gentlemen' with kid gloves and instead be resolved to
> protect ourselves ... This is all the more important when we consider
> that the continuance of uncontrolled networks of communication
> [between England] and the Englishmen living in our midst represents
> a danger to our national defence.[74]

In Berlin, several police reports for the week ending 2 November 1914 noted
an upsurge in popular anglophobia. The police president, Traugott von Jagow,
even claimed that the anti-German measures in England had aggravated the
'underlying and deeply-rooted hatred of the English' to the point where 'a
policy of retaliation ... is demanded from all sides'.[75] Likewise in Stuttgart
a concerned citizen wrote to the acting military commander drawing his
attention to the 'righteous anger and resentment of the people towards the
English, especially as our German brothers and sisters in England are being
interned and mistreated in such an inhumane way'. In his view:

> A sigh of relief would be heard throughout the nation if our government
> would at least take equivalent measures and intern all the foreigners
> in question and do this without any further delay.[76]

The evidence for a sudden growth in popular hostility towards British
nationals is not overwhelming, however, and it is notable that interest in the

internment question appeared to be much greater in big cities like Hamburg or Stuttgart than in small towns and villages.[77] Certainly there were ugly scenes outside the British embassy in Berlin in the first days of the war, including smashed windows and verbal assaults on embassy staff. Even after this there were parts of the capital where it was not safe, even for Americans, to speak English in public.[78] There are also clear signs that British prisoners captured on the battlefield and paraded through German towns and villages in the autumn of 1914 were treated with greater hostility by onlookers than their French and Russian counterparts, as Heather Jones has recently shown.[79] However, little of this seems to have spilled over towards 'ordinary' non-combatants, and in most parts of Germany the worst a civilian British national experienced in the autumn of 1914 was exposure to some one-sided public criticism of Sir Edward Grey or a cursory insult thrown out across the street.[80] Some observers were struck by the relative normality of everyday life as an 'enemy alien', while others remembered the remarkable acts of kindness they experienced from strangers as well as friends. V. V. Cusden, an English teacher working in Giessen at the outbreak of the war, later recalled the following incidents:

> My brother and I both had a dentist's bill to pay. We asked for our bills. None came. At long last the bills arrived considerably reduced. By that time it was too late. We had no money left. 'Never mind', he said. 'Pay me after the war. I know I'll get my money.' I also had a small bill owing to my bookseller. He refused to accept payment saying I might need the money before I could get away and also told me to pay after the war. Kindnesses such as these cannot easily be forgotten. Nor were they. We were able after the war to repay them in kind.[81]

Meanwhile, in Berlin too opinion was also less clear-cut than the weekly reports from police president von Jagow suggest. Information collected by police spies and informers did indicate a widespread sense of anger towards the British, but this was also mingled in with a growing anti-war feeling caused, in the main, by rising food prices.[82] In some Social Democrat pubs the mood was openly hostile towards internment, since a 'policy of reprisals' [*Vergeltungspolitik*] was considered to be 'incompatible with the principles of international socialism', as one informer put it.[83] In Hamburg, too, the local Social Democrat newspaper, the *Hamburger Echo*, sounded a note of caution over internment, noting that an indiscriminate policy of retaliation would inevitably lead to injustices:

'Englishmen' who are not really English must be protected from the effects of these war regulations ... It makes no sense to intern these people. And the current need to take reprisals does not mean that we should make the internees themselves pay for the sins committed by the cultural Pharisees on the other side of the North Sea. They are mostly harmless people who have nothing in common with the jingoistic dogs over there; we should treat them accordingly.[84]

Interestingly, the government itself was keen to present the case for internment in a manner which would appeal to as broad a section of the population as possible, rather than appearing to address the right-wing or anglophobe press alone. This was absolutely necessary in order to maintain the domestic political truce (*Burgfrieden*) between the warring political parties in the Reichstag, which was an essential part of Bethmann Hollweg's domestic political strategy in 1914–15.[85] On 6 November the semi-official *Norddeutsche Allgemeine Zeitung* adopted a fairly restrained tone which emphasised above all the need for balance and moderation:

Wanton acts of cruelty against Germans are by and large not in evidence as far as the English are concerned. But cases of unnecessarily harsh and unworthy treatment have come to light which at the very least indicate some degree of negligence on the part of agents of the British crown. Full redress cannot be sought through revenge against innocent people, nor through an exchange of letters, nor through the intervention of neutrals, nor through referring the matter to a court of arbitration. These matters are part of the stubborn arrogance with which England has offended against everything German, and we must include them in the balancing of accounts which we are determined to carry through against this island nation that insists on its unassailable position.[86]

Finally, internment was part of the military's attempt to create a common belief in Germany's invincibility while compensating for the failure to achieve swift victory on the continent. The Allies, it was suggested, could still be beaten, and in the meantime the prison camp at Ruhleben was one of several bargaining tools which would force Britain into a more reasonable treatment of German prisoners of war. Even *Vorwärts* accepted this argument in an article published on 7 November 1914, while still regretting the move towards internment.[87] Academics and legal experts also agreed that Germany had a right in international law to take action to protect the interests of its citizens living abroad.[88] Only much later in the war, in 1916, did Social Democrats like Wolfgang Heine and Oskar Cohn publicly denounce internment as an aggressive move on the part of Germany, rather than as a defensive reaction to British and French policies.[89] By then, however, conditions on the home front had also changed quite radically and there was little left of the original *Burgfrieden*.

Arrest and transfer

The actual process of internment took place reasonably smoothly and was completed within a three-week period. All over Germany British civilians were arrested, usually in their homes, and held in local police stations or prisons before being taken by train to Berlin. According to a note issued by the Reich Chancellor (Reich Office of Interior), the internees were to be handled 'firmly' [*mit der erforderlichen Festigkeit*], but 'without unnecessary brutality' [*ohne unnötige Härte*]. They were allowed to take with them a handful of personal items, including 'one bed sheet, one pillow case and two light blankets'. All the rest of their property was to be held separately until such time as they were released or allowed to return home to England. Apart from women, children and men over fifty-five, only doctors, priests and those certified as being too ill to travel were excluded from the new measures; the necessary information had already been gathered some weeks before.[90]

Some of those arrested on 6 November clearly found their first night in a German police station a deeply humiliating and/or frightening experience. This was particularly the case for those who had not expected arrest, namely the 600 or so Scheinengländer who had lived in Germany all their lives and regarded themselves as German but now, because of their formal legal status as British nationals, found themselves suddenly thrown into jail. Frank Stockall, a British national arrested in Chemnitz, Saxony, remembered sharing a cell with a badly shaken young man 'who could speak English only with a pronounced German accent':

His father was English, had married a German girl and settled in Germany. The son had been registered at birth at the British consulate and so was British by nationality ... The poor lad wept like a child – he wouldn't be more than seventeen and had never been separated from his family before. I cheered him up as best I could and as the darkness fell at about 3 p.m. I suggested that we should sing to keep ourselves cheerful. The only songs in English that he knew were songs from the

Boer war – Goodbye Dolly etc. and curiously enough a Negro spiritual about 'The Lord delivering Daniel from the Lions' Den'.[91]

In another case, a man from Stuttgart was so incensed by the arrest of his brother-in-law, a German who had emigrated to England some years before but was visiting his family when the war broke out, that he wrote a letter of protest to the local deputy general command:

> It surely cannot be the intention to use these measures to punish our own people who have been spreading German customs, German manners, German character and German industry beyond our borders and have merely lost their German nationality in a legal sense, but not their German way of feeling and thinking.[92]

Children occasionally came out onto the streets or railway stations to jeer at the internees. Sir John Balfour, for instance, recalled 'being spat at and reviled the whole journey up' from Baden-Baden to Berlin, while even members of the German Red Cross refused to hand out food and drinks.[93] Frank Stockall likewise remembered that the train carrying him and other internees from Saxony 'pulled up at one station where the young boys who sell hot sausages from a container strapped around their middle came to each window and showed the sausages all steaming and very desirable – then walked away shaking their fists at us and shouting "English Pig-Dogs" [*Schweinhunde*]'.[94]

In spite of these and similar complaints, most of the individual testimonies from internees bear witness to the politeness of the police officials sent to arrest them, and the efforts made to preserve their dignity. For instance, the prisoners were allowed to buy in meals and tobacco for consumption in local police stations and prisons. While in transit they were not handcuffed to their captors, and were allowed to travel in relative comfort, albeit often in third class carriages.[95] Occasionally, as in Stockall's case, the guards were even willing to share their food, and did their best to protect the prisoners from the unwanted attentions of curious onlookers.[96] There were some exceptions, however. For instance, Edward Morris Falk remembered the chaos in Hanover when British prisoners were temporarily brought to the city's police headquarters:

> There were whites and blacks, Boers, Canadians, Australians and oddments from outlying corners. There were merchants and mechanics, artists and invalids, and members of every calling from

the owner of large estates to the alleged keeper of a brothel, a lion tamer and the person pointed out to me as a notorious international thief.[97]

The guards sent to take them to Berlin were clearly nervous and therefore 'charged magazines in our presence ... we were informed that we should be fusiladed if there were any attempts to escape'.[98] There were also unpleasant scenes in Hamburg, especially as the police authorities there decided to cram even more people onto the already overcrowded prison ships in the Hansahafen as a temporary measure while trains were prepared to take them to Berlin.[99] Later a British resident in Hamburg claimed to have been pushed down some steps during disembarkation for failing to respond quickly enough to an order given by a harbour police official. It was also alleged that one British seaman was sent to Ruhleben on 8 November 1914 in spite of having a serious lung infection; he died in a Berlin hospital on 15 November. A subsequent investigation ordered by the Prussian Ministry of War in March 1915 nonetheless exonerated the harbour police in Hamburg and found their conduct to have been exemplary.[100]

Although the final destination of the internees was Ruhleben, many were taken first to the *Stadtvogtei* jail, one of the largest criminal prisons in Berlin, which now functioned (against the wishes of its governor) as a clearing house for all internees. Others were taken to a different jail at Plötzensee. Over the next few days they were forced to march from these prisons to the railway station at Alexanderplatz on full view to the Berlin public, who had been informed about the internment measures in the press and turned out in large numbers to view the spectacle. Israel Cohen, a British journalist who wrote for *The Times* and other British newspapers, later remembered:

> The crowd that was lined up on either side was remarkably undemonstrative, but among the onlookers were weeping wives or mothers of some of the prisoners who were domiciled in Berlin.[101]

Similar scenes were also reported in the *Berliner Tageblatt*, which noted that many of the wives looked 'totally dejected' [*niedergeschlagen*] as they walked alongside their husbands. The internees and their wives were to be pitied as victims of the British government's anti-German policies, the paper continued; many had been heard cursing Sir Edward Grey as they were led into captivity.[102]

Other sources recalled a greater degree of hostility from the crowd, with incidents of spitting and fists being shaken.[103] In general, however, the atmosphere was calm and the crowd 'well-behaved' [104] – unlike in Britain, where German shopkeepers in several towns were subjected to verbal and physical assaults in October 1914 (and on a larger scale in May 1915). Some sympathetic Berliners even offered to help the internees with their luggage, and others prayed for their early release. Another internee, Edward J. Hales, remembered that 'there was no ill-feeling at all. In fact many [in the crowd] were the friends of those passing by'.[105]

From Alexanderplatz the internees were taken by train to the emigrants' railway station (*Auswanderer Bahnhof*) in Spandau, so called because in peacetime this was a stop-off point where Russian and Polish emigrants were forced to disembark and wash themselves with disinfectant before travelling on to Hamburg or Bremen, and then to North America.[106] At the emigrants' railway station the civilian prisoners were again lined up in fours and marched the short distance to the racecourse at Ruhleben. For many of them this was to be their last view of the outside world for the next four years. In effect they were now pawns in the larger game of international diplomacy, and while some were freed in exchange agreements, others were released only at the end of the war.

Notes

1 Audoin-Rouzeau and Becker, *1914–1918*, pp. 72–3.
2 The exact figure was 111,879. See Wilhelm Doegen (ed.), *Kriegsgefangene Völker. Bd. 1: Der Kriegsgefangenen Haltung und Schicksal in Deutschland* (Berlin, 1919), p. 29.
3 *Bulletin International des sociétés de la Croix-Rouge*, 196 (October 1918), p. 496.
4 There were exceptions, firstly in relation to so-called *Kolonialengländer* who were not interned until January and February 1915, and secondly in relation to British civilians captured in occupied territory and on the high seas, who were brought to Ruhleben in small numbers throughout the war. But in general the Ruhleben population was more stable and permanent than the population of other camps: at least 2,000 people were there for the full four years (November 1914–November 1918), and only a handful were removed to other camps. By contrast, as Abbal, *Soldats oubliés*, p. 56, points out, regular displacement from one camp to the next was a common experience for French (and British) military POWs in Germany. Evidence from German files on the civilian camp at Rastatt, which was mainly used for holding French civilians, also indicates a high inmate turnover, particularly among female prisoners – see BA Berlin, R 901/84415.
5 Ulrich Herbert, *Geschichte der Ausländerbeschäftigung in Deutschland, 1880 bis 1980. Saisonarbeiter, Zwangsarbeiter, Gastarbeiter* (Bonn, 1986), pp. 82–

113; Jochen Oltmer, 'Zwangsmigration und Zwangsarbeit – Ausländische Arbeitskräfte und bäuerliche Ökonomie im Ersten Weltkrieg', *Tel Aviver Jahrbuch für deutsche Geschichte*, 27 (1998), pp. 135–68.

6 Apart from Ruhleben, the following camps also had facilities for holding substantial numbers of civilians: Havelberg, Holzminden, Limburg and Sennelager (all in Prussia), Rastatt (in Baden) and Traunstein (in Bavaria). Smaller groups of civilian prisoners could be found in virtually every other camp in Germany. For further details see Doegen (ed.), *Kriegsgefangene Völker*, pp. 12–25, and on Traunstein, Jahr, 'Keine Feriengäste', pp. 237–40.

7 Descriptions of life in other camps can be found in Becker, *Oubliés de la grande guerre*, pp. 27–88; and McPhail, *The Long Silence*, pp. 158–85. A detailed study of all internment camps still remains to be undertaken.

8 See also Matthew Stibbe, 'A Question of Retaliation? The Internment of British Civilians in Germany in November 1914', *Immigrants & Minorities*, 23/1 (2005), pp. 1–29.

9 See the instructions sent out by the Reich Chancellor (Reich Office of Interior) on 8 October 1914, and the various lists delivered, in BA Berlin, R 1501/112376–112377, which form the basis of the appendix at the end of this book.

10 'Übersicht über die im Deutschen Reiche vorhandenen Engländer', c. 18 December 1914, in BA Berlin, R 1501/112364, Bl. 134–6.

11 'Auszug aus dem Protokolle des Senats', 14 October 1914, in Staatsarchiv (StA) Hamburg, Senatskriegsakten 111–2, Lz38.

12 This corresponds to the high point of 4,273 prisoners held at Ruhleben in February 1915. Admittedly a handful of these were British civilians deported from German-occupied Belgium and Northern France, but they can be offset against the small number of prisoners released in the first weeks of internment on health or other grounds. See Jahr, 'Zivilisten als Kriegsgefangene', p. 303; BA Berlin, R 1501/122365, Bl. 21–2.

13 Speed, *Prisoners, Diplomats and the Great War*, p. 147; Farcy, *Les camps de concentration*, p. 129.

14 The final figure arrived at by the Reich Office of Interior in mid-November 1914 was 9,625 including 1,803 men of military age (seventeen–sixty years). French civilians deported from occupied territory and French merchant mariners were not included. See 'Übersicht über die im deutschen Reiche vorhandenen Franzosen', in BA Berlin, R 1501/112364, Bl. 17–22.

15 Dr James Simon to the Auswärtiges Amt (henceforth AA), 13 August 1914, in BA Berlin, R 1501/112361, Bl. 27.

16 Oltmer, 'Zwangsmigration und Zwangsarbeit', p. 141.

17 Herbert, *Geschichte der Ausländerbeschäftigung*, pp. 15–81.

18 Reich Chancellor (Reich Office of Interior) to the Prussian Ministry of War, 27 July 1914, in BA Berlin, R 1501/112361, Bl. 2–3.

19 Oltmer, 'Zwangsmigration und Zwangsarbeit', p. 143.

20 See n. 9 above.

21 For a succinct summary of the system of military government in Germany after the declaration of the state of siege on 31 July 1914 see Wilhelm Deist (ed.), *Militär und Innenpolitik im Weltkrieg, 1914–1918*, 2 vols. (Düsseldorf, 1970), vol. 1, pp. xl–li.

22 For further details see Stibbe, 'A Question of Retaliation?', and Jahr, 'Keine Feriengäste'.

23 'Verzeichnis der in Deutschland befindlichen englischen Staatsangehörigen, Bundesstaat Hamburg', 2 November 1914, in StA Hamburg, Senatskriegsakten 111–2, Lz1.

24 *Ibid.*

25 Cf. 'Auszug aus dem Protokolle des Senats', 14 October 1914, in *ibid.*, Lz38. Conditions on the hulks in Hamburg are also described in the personal account of John Green, Skipper of the Grimsby trawler *St Cuthbert*, which was captured on 20 August 1914, in Grimsby Central Library (henceforth GCL), Ruhleben Collection, File 3.

26 Ketchum, *Ruhleben*, p. 6.

27 'Weitere Vergeltungsmaßnahmen gegen Ausländer', *Vorwärts*, 8 November 1914.

28 On the German citizenship laws see Eli Nathans, *The Politics of Citizenship in Germany. Ethnicity, Utility and Nationalism* (Oxford, 2004), esp. pp. 169–98.

29 For further details see Chapter 4 below.

30 See e.g. Oskar Cohn's use of the term '*Scheinengländer*' in the Reichstag on 7 April 1916, in *Verhandlungen des Reichstags* (Berlin, 1916), vol. 307, p. 915.

31 On the Russian Jews in Ruhleben see Cohen, *The Ruhleben Prison Camp*, esp. Chapters 6 and 21.

32 Peter Seddon, *Steve Bloomer. The Story of Football's First Superstar* (Derby, 1999), esp. pp. 132–46.

33 Plentiful evidence of this can be found in the records of the National Archives (henceforth NA), FO 369/712.

34 See e.g. Minister of Interior of the Grand Duchy of Baden to the deputy general command of the 14th army corps, 19 August 1914, in Generallandesarchiv (GLA) Karlsruhe, Bestand 456/F8, no. 269.

35 Reich Chancellor (Reich Office of Interior) to all federal governments, 18 August 1914, in BA Berlin, R 1501/112361, Bl. 39–40.

36 Supreme commander in the marches, 10 August 1914, in Niedersächsisches Hauptstaatsarchiv (NHStA) Hanover, Hann. 122a, no. 7010, Bl. 44.

37 Merchant sailors had traditionally been viewed as 'legitimate prisoners of war in European maritime conflicts', and were not usually regarded as civilians – see Gavin Daly, 'Napoleon's Lost Legions: French Prisoners of War in Britain, 1803–1814', *History*, 89/3 (2004), p. 363. Nonetheless, article 1 of the 1907 Hague Convention relating to the status of enemy merchant ships at the outbreak of war (Hague VI) stated quite clearly that 'when a merchant ship belonging to one of the belligerent Powers is at the commencement of hostilities in an enemy port, it is desirable that it should be allowed to

depart freely, either immediately, or after a reasonable number of days of grace, and to proceed, after being furnished with a pass, direct to its port of destination or any other port indicated'.

38 Unpublished notes by Jack Griggs on his experiences in Leipzig in 1914 prior to internment at Ruhleben, no date. I am grateful to Elizabeth Beasley for permission to use this source. See also letter from three British citizens in Leipzig to the Foreign Office, 31 October 1914, in NA, FO 369/714.

39 Stibbe, 'A Question of Retaliation?', pp. 9–10.

40 'Verzeichnis der in Deutschland befindlichen englischen Staatsangehörigen', Berlin, 22 October 1914, in BA Berlin, R 1501/112376, Bl. 61. Interestingly, the camp is described here as the 'Russenlager Ruhleben-Spandau'. Cf. the appendix at the end of this book.

41 Reich Chancellor (Reich Office of Interior) to the Baden Ministry of Interior, 1 September 1914, in GLA Karlsruhe, Bestand 456/F8, No. 269. Same document in BA Berlin, R 1501/112361, Bl. 86–7.

42 Information about these agreements can be found in BA Berlin, R 1501/112362 and 112365. See also Garner, 'Treatment of Enemy Aliens', pp. 49–55; Jahr, 'Keine Feriengäste', pp. 235–7; and Rolf-Harald Wippich, 'Internierung und Abschiebung von Japanern im Deutschen Reich im Jahr 1914', *Zeitschrift für Geschichtswissenschaft*, 55/1 (2007), pp. 18–40. Nonetheless, the German government did intern Portuguese, Romanian and Siamese nationals after the breakdown of diplomatic negotiations in 1916 and 1917, respectively. See the relevant documents in BA Berlin, R 1501/112369–70.

43 War Office to Foreign Office, 19 August 1914, in NA, FO 369/713.

44 Foreign Office to War Office, 17 September 1914, in *ibid*.

45 Home Office to Foreign Office, 28 September 1914, and admiralty to Foreign Office, 29 September 1914, both in *ibid*.

46 The text of these agreements, and similar agreements between the French and German governments, can be found in BA Berlin, R 1501/112361.

47 Acland to Page, 3 October 1914, in NA, FO 369/713. In fact, only men born between 1869 and 1900 were liable to conscription during the years 1914–18, i.e. those aged eighteen to forty-five. See Benjamin Ziemann, *War Experiences in Rural Germany, 1914–1923* (Oxford, 2007), p. 31.

48 See e.g. the Foreign Office memorandum, 'Arrest of enemy subjects on board neutral ships', 23 September 1915, citing evidence gathered twelve months previously, in NA, FO 383/76.

49 In addition to the British Foreign Office memorandum cited above, see e.g. German Minister in the Netherlands to Bethmann Hollweg, 4 October 1914, in BA Berlin, R 901/82969. Also the testimonies collected in StA Hamburg, Senatskriegskaten 111–2, Lz16a, and the evidence later presented by the Reichstag committee of inquiry into the causes of the war and of Germany's defeat – *Das Werk des Untersuchungsausschusses, 1919–1928* (henceforth WUA), *Reihe 3: Völkerrecht im Weltkrieg, Bd. III/2: Gutachten des Sachverständigen Geh. Rates Prof. Dr. Meurer. Verletzungen des Kriegsgefangenenrechts* (Berlin, 1927), p. 726.

50 On the Deptford riots see Panayi, *The Enemy in Our Midst*, pp. 225–28.

51 Carl Peters, 'Englische Verlogenheit', in *Tag*, 16 and 17 October 1914. Copy in BA Berlin, R 8034 II/8721, Bl. 102. Peters, who had lived in London since 1898 and returned to Germany in October 1914, was clearly attempting to atone for past crimes committed in Africa.

52 *Ibid.* Both the above quotations are taken from the concluding part of the article, published on 17 October 1914.

53 The deputy general command of the 7th army corps to Bethmann Hollweg, 12 October 1914, in BA Berlin, R 901/82969.

54 The news department of the Reich Naval Office to Traugott von Jagow, 3 December 1914, in Landesarchiv (LA) Berlin, Rep. 30, Tit. 95, No. 15808, Bl. 158.

55 The supreme commander in the marches to the Reich Office of Interior, 26 October 1914, in BA Berlin, R 1501/112363, Bl. 47.

56 The deputy general command of the 9th army corps to the AA, 27 October 1914, in StA Hamburg, Senatskriegsakten 111–2, Le.

57 Minutes of these meetings can be found in BA Berlin, R 1501/112362, Bl. 196–201, and R 1501/112363, Bl. 11–18.

58 Jahr, 'Zivilisten als Kriegsgefangene', p. 303.

59 WUA, Reihe 3, Bd. III/2, p. 727. This is lifted almost word for word from a letter sent by the chief of the deputy general staff to the chief of the general staff on 20 October 1914 asking him to approve the internment measures. Copy in BA Berlin, R 901/82969.

60 See the minutes of the two meetings mentioned in n. 57 above. Also the evidence in Tripp, 'Kommunikation und Vergemeinschaftung', pp. 16–17 and 19.

61 This was a common theme of German anti-English propaganda. Cf. Matthew Stibbe, *German Anglophobia and the Great War, 1914–1918* (Cambridge, 2001), esp. pp. 10 ff.

62 Carl Peters, *Das deutsche Elend in London* (Leipzig, 1914), pp. 43–4.

63 Kaiser's marginal comments in BA Berlin, R 901/82969.

64 AA (Abteilung III: Rechtsabteilung) to Gottlieb von Jagow, 26 October 1914, in *ibid.*

65 *Ibid.* The Social Democrat newspaper *Vorwärts* also ran an article on 27 October 1914 reporting, accurately as it turned out, that in London the wave of arrests and anti-German rioting was now over and that plans for mass internment were in abeyance. Indeed, as we have seen, wholesale internment was not introduced in Britain until after the Lusitania riots in May 1915. Cf. Panayi, *The Enemy in Our Midst*, p. 73.

66 The chief of the general staff to the Reich Office of Interior, 31 October 1914, in BA Berlin, R 1501/112363.

67 Doctors and priests who fell into enemy hands were not to be regarded as prisoners of war under article 9 of the 1906 Geneva convention, to which Germany was a signatory. *Kolonialengländer*, it was decided, were to lose

their immunity only if and when it had been ascertained that internment had been introduced in their respective lands of origin. Subsequently all but the Australians were interned at Ruhleben in January 1915, and the Australians followed in February 1915. See the instructions issued by the chief of the deputy general staff on 22 January and 6 February 1915, in NHStA Hanover, Hann. 122a, no. 7011, Bl. 107 and 117.

68 Prussian Ministry of War to the Prussian Ministry of Interior, 20 December 1914, in *ibid.*, Bl. 102. Cf. the Prussian Ministry of War memorandum of 9 August 1915, 'Verrechnung der Kosten für festgenommene feindliche Ausländer', which again confirmed that the cost of maintaining Ruhleben was being met from Reich funds. Copy in BA Berlin, R 1501/112368, Bl. 100–1.

69 Panikos Panayi, 'Anti-German Riots in London, 1914–1918', *German History*, 7 (1989), p. 185.

70 Colin Holmes, *John Bull's Island. Immigration and British Society, 1871–1971* (London, 1988), p. 97.

71 'Ende der Deutschen-Verhaftungen in England', *Vorwärts*, 27 October 1914. On the move from russophobia to anglophobia in the German press see also Stibbe, *German Anglophobia*, pp. 12–16.

72 See the evidence in Jahr, 'Zivilisten als Kriegsgefangene', p. 301, n. 18 and Tripp, 'Kommunikation und Vergemeinschaftung', pp. 11–12.

73 Advert in the *Hamburger Nachrichten*, 28 October 1914.

74 'Unsere lieben Engländer: Sollen wir Vergeltungsmaßregeln ergreifen?', *Kölnische Zeitung*, 23 October 1914. For similar newspaper reports calling for retaliation see e.g. 'Vergeltung gegen die Engländer', *Deutsche Tageszeitung*, 27 October 1914; 'Gegenmaßregeln zum Schutz der Deutschen in Feindeshand', *Neue Preußische (Kreuz-) Zeitung*, 29 October 1914; 'Auge um Auge', *Leipziger Neueste Nachrichten*, 30 October 1914.

75 Traugott von Jagow, 14. Stimmungsbericht, Berlin, 2 November 1914, in LA Berlin, Rep. 30, Tit. 95, No. 15807, Bl. 238. Cf. the further reports in *ibid.*, Bl. 242–7.

76 Eugen Häcker to the deputy general command of the 13th army corps, 6 November 1914, in HStA Stuttgart, M77/1, no. 860.

77 For evidence that anti-English feeling was not as strong in rural areas and in small and middle-sized towns see also Ziemann, *War Experiences*, esp. pp. 15–27 and 138–9; and Christian Geinitz, *Kriegsfurcht und Kampfbereitschaft. Das Augusterlebnis in Freiburg. Eine Studie zum Kriegsbeginn 1914* (Essen, 1998), pp. 109–10.

78 Joseph C. Grew, diary entries for 4–11 August 1914, in Grew papers, Houghton Library, Harvard University, MS Am 1687, vol. 5.

79 Heather Jones, 'Encountering the "Enemy": Prisoner of War Transport and the Development of War Cultures in 1914', in Pierre Purseigle (ed.), *Warfare and Belligerence. Perspectives in First World War Studies* (Leiden, 2005), pp. 133–62.

80 I make this point after reading scores of individual accounts from the Liddle Collection, the Imperial War Museum and other sources.

81 V.V. Cusden, 'Lingering Rays' (n.d.), typescript recollections, pp. 29–30, in Liddle Collection, RUH 14.

82 On food shortages and the effect on public opinion from October 1914 see Belinda J. Davis, *Home Fires Burning. Food, Politics and Everyday Life in World War I Berlin* (Chapel Hill and London, 2000), esp. pp. 34 ff.

83 Report of the 4th Kommissariat, 7 November 1914, in LA Berlin, Rep. 30, Tit. 95, No. 15807, Bl. 247.

84 'Die Engländer in Deutschland', *Hamburger Echo*, 8 November 1914.

85 On the importance of the *Burgfrieden* to Bethmann Hollweg's domestic strategy see Jeffrey Verhey, *The Spirit of 1914. Militarism, Myth and Mobilization in Germany* (Cambridge, 2000), esp. pp. 139–46.

86 *Norddeutsche Allgemeine Zeitung*, 6 November 1914 [evening edn].

87 'Das Schicksal der Zivilgefangenen', *Vorwärts*, 7 November 1914.

88 Franz von Liszt, *Das Völkerrecht*, 10th edn (Berlin, 1915), p. 461.

89 See Chapter 4 below.

90 Prussian Minister of Interior to all provincial governors, 5 November 1914, in NHStA Hanover, Hann. 122a, No. 7011, Bl. 81. Cf. Tripp, 'Kommunikation und Vergemeinschaftung', p. 18.

91 Frank Stockall, unpublished memoirs (1961), pp. 26–7. I am grateful to Norman Stockall for permission to quote from this source.

92 Emil Lang to the deputy general command of the 13th army corps, 10 November 1914, in HStA Stuttgart, M77/1, no. 860.

93 Sir John Balfour in an interview with Peter Liddle, March 1976, in Liddle Collection, RUH 02.

94 Stockall, unpublished memoirs, p. 38.

95 Francis Gribble, *Seen in Passing. A Volume of Personal Reminiscences* (London, 1929), pp. 286–7.

96 Stockall, unpublished memoirs, p. 39.

97 Edward Morris Falk, 'My Experiences During the Great War, 1914–1915', transcript recollections (1920), p. 11. Copy in Liddle Collection, RUH 22.

98 *Ibid.*, p. 12.

99 'Die Gefangenensetzung in Hamburg', *Hamburger Fremdenblatt*, 6 November 1914 [evening edn].

100 For further details see the reports in StA Hamburg, Senatskriegsakten 111–2, Ly.

101 Cohen, *The Ruhleben Prison Camp*, p. 27.

102 'Die Internierung der Engländer in Groß-Berlin', *Berliner Tageblatt*, 6 November 1914 [evening edn].

103 H. Richard Lorenz, interview with Peter Liddle, October 1977, in Liddle Collection, RUH 31.

104 Phrase used by the internee Sumner F. Austin. See his typescript recollections, n.d., in Liddle Collection, RUH 01.

105 Edward J. Hales, interview with Peter Liddle, April 1978, in Liddle Collection, RUH 25.
106 Cohen, *The Ruhleben Prison Camp*, p. 28. See also Tobias Brinkmann, '"Grenzerfahrungen" zwischen Ruhleben und Ellis Island. Das System der deutschen Durchwandererkontrolle im internationalen Kontext, 1880–1914', *Leipziger Beiträge zur jüdischen Geschichte und Kultur* 2 (2004), pp. 209–29.

2

Inside Ruhleben I: administration and physical conditions

According to Stéphane Audoin-Rouzeau and Annette Becker, civilian and military prisoners experienced captivity during the First World War as a 'double exile, an exile far from their country and far from their country *at war*':

> For them, the predicament of imprisonment entailed shame, a feeling of being abandoned, and constant misery ... They had lost the sense of material and emotional comfort to which they were accustomed, the feeling of continuity with their past. Theirs was an uprooting that could only have meaning if it was provisional, if there would be a future elsewhere. But the continuance of the war, and hence of captivity, quashed even the most tenacious hopes, the more so since real or false news of the captors' victories was deliberately spread within the camps as propaganda.[1]

Certainly, much of this rings true when considering the experience of the Ruhleben prisoners. Thus like civilian and military detainees elsewhere they had to cope with the boredom, lack of privacy and ever-present sensual, sexual, spatial and material deprivation that went with life behind barbed wire. They had no way of knowing how long their incarceration would last, and were entirely dependent on friends and supporters back at home to send them relief parcels. The absence of reliable and regular news about the progress of the war meant that the camp thrived on hearsay and false stories, so much so that one of the earliest camp publications carried a mock advert for a private detective agency which promised, for a small fee, to 'trace all rumours to source'.[2] Some prisoners, especially those aged forty and over, suffered permanent damage to their physical health while others fell victim to a severe form of mental incapacity later known as 'barbed wire disease'.[3] Even those who remained relatively fit were in 'a constant state of great mental anxiety as to the fate of their businesses... and their families', as the American ambassador James W. Gerard later noted.[4]

Having said this, the Ruhleben prisoners were an extremely diverse group of people and some were better able to adapt than others. Differences in class, ethnicity and cultural background, as well as age and marital status, all helped to determine how they would experience their time in captivity. The result was neither as monolithic, nor as crushing as Audoin-Rouzeau and Becker's description suggests, although by arguing this I do not wish to understate the extent of human suffering caused by wartime captivity. Clearly it was traumatic, frustrating, boring, stifling, oppressive and at all times extremely uncomfortable. Even so, beneath the surface there was also a great deal of stability within the Ruhleben community, a point made by Ketchum in his 1965 study.[5] In particular the relatively low turnover of prisoners, at least during the first three years of internment, helped to foster a gradual sense of solidarity which over time was combined with a weary fatalism about the future. This, as well as the near complete absence of women and the sheer length of confinement, was a factor in explaining the difficulties which some inmates found in readjusting to 'normal' life after their release and repatriation in 1918.

In what follows we will identify some of the key aspects of life in Ruhleben while attempting to do justice to the multiplicity of voices within the camp.

The Ruhleben camp structure

The Ruhleben camp consisted of eleven 'barracks' (horse stables), three grandstands, a boiler-house and a restaurant (the 'Tea-house') to which further barracks and a YMCA hut were added at later stages (Figure 1). Excluding the racecourse itself (which was out of bounds to prisoners until March 1915) it was no more than ten acres in size and took less then ten minutes to cover on foot end to end.[6] It was run by a dual system of administration, part military and part civilian, with the prisoners also establishing communal organisations of their own to run alongside the formal political structures. In agreement with the German authorities, the site was visited regularly both by representatives of the protecting power (first the USA, and then from February 1917 the Netherlands) and by private

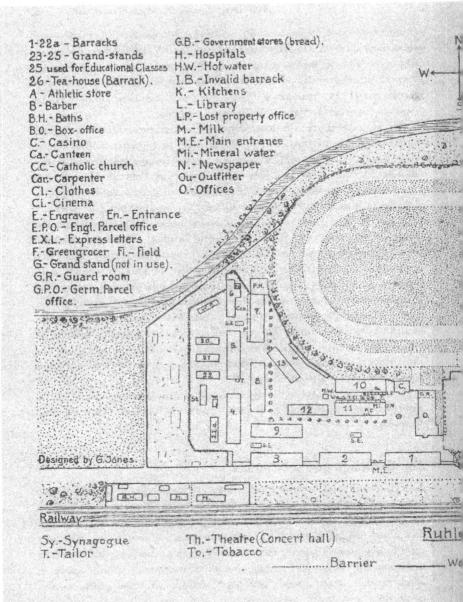

1-22a – Barracks
23-25 – Grand-stands
25 used for Educational Classes
26 – Tea-house (Barrack).
A – Athletic store
B – Barber
B.H. – Baths
B.O. – Box- office
C. – Casino
Ca. – Canteen
C.C. – Catholic church
Car. – Carpenter
Cl. – Clothes
Ci. – Cinema
E. – Engraver   En. – Entrance
E.P.O. – Engl. Parcel office
E.X.L. – Express letters
F. – Greengrocer   Fi. – field
G – Grand stand (not in use).
G.R. – Guard room
G.P.O. – Germ. Parcel
    office.

G.B. – Government stores (bread).
H. – Hospitals
H.W. – Hot water
I.B. – Invalid barrack
K. – Kitchens
L. – Library
L.P. – Lost property office
M. – Milk
M.E. – Main entrance
Mi. – Mineral water
N. – Newspaper
Ou – Outfitter
O. – Offices

Designed by G. Jones.

Railway

Sy. – Synagogue
T. – Tailor

Th. – Theatre (Concert hall)
To. – Tobacco

.... Barrier

Ruhl

1   The Ruhleben camp, 1915

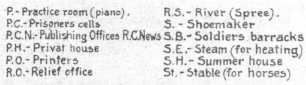

P.- Practice room (piano).
P.C.- Prisoners cells
P.C.N.- Publishing Offices R.C.News
P.H.- Privat house
P.O.- Printers
R.O.- Relief office

R.S.- River (Spree).
S. - Shoemaker
S.B.- Soldiers barracks
S.E.- Steam (for heating)
S.H.- Summer house
St.- Stable (for horses)

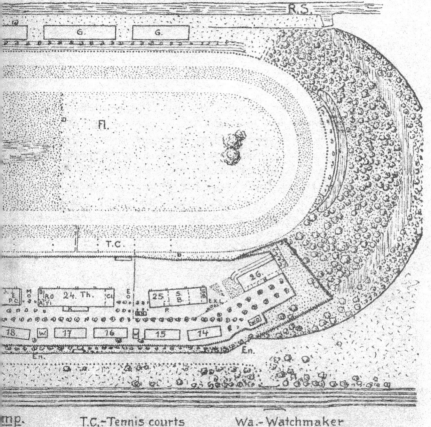

mp.

T.C.-Tennis courts
W.- Wash houses
High wire fence

Wa.- Watchmaker
W.C.- Public lavatory

charity organisations like the German branch of the American YMCA. The Reverend H. M. Williams, Anglican chaplain at Berlin, and Pastor Friedrich Siegmund-Schultze, a leading figure in the German ecumenical movement, were also granted access for the purpose of holding services, their appearances averaging about one a fortnight.[7] Undoubtedly it was these visits by outside observers, as well as considerations of social class, that explain why the Ruhleben prisoners were not exposed to the harshest sides of the German camp system, although they were occasionally given reminders of their relatively privileged position through the stories told by new arrivals from other camps.

The military administration

The military administration comprised the elderly commandant, Count Schwerin, his younger deputy, Baron von Taube, a staff of officers and a company of soldiers who performed guard duties (Figure 2). In practice the day-to-day running of the camp was in Taube's hands, and Schwerin took a back-seat role, as did his successor in 1916, Lieutenant-Colonel von Reichenbach. The primary purpose of the military administration was, as Israel Cohen put it, to 'prevent us from escaping'.[8] The camp was indeed heavily guarded, with a 200-strong detachment of reservists and

2   Baron von Taube and his staff, 1915

convalescents on leave from the front allocated to patrol the perimeter fence. At first one officer and two or three soldiers were also attached to each individual barrack. However, on 16 September 1915 they were withdrawn with the agreement of the Berlin *Kommandantur*, and thereafter German military personnel rarely entered the camp enclosure itself except during the morning roll call (*Appell*) presided over by Taube as *Lageroffizier*.[9]

Censorship of outgoing and incoming post was another important task of the military administration, carried out by Baron von Mützenbecher and his assistant, the Prince of Thurn and Taxis, both of them fluent English speakers. Mützenbecher in particular was highly popular with the prisoners, partly because he turned a blind eye when English newspapers were smuggled into the camp but also because he sometimes wrote to the families of internees on their behalf.[10] At first the prisoners were allowed to write two postcards and one four-paged letter per month, and could use either English or German as the language of correspondence.[11] Later this was increased to one postcard per week and two letters per month, or two postcards per week.[12]

Far less popular than Mützenbecher was Lieutenant Rüdiger, the officer in charge of forwarding petitions for release and leave of absence to the higher authorities. Several accounts agree that he was the most hated and feared man on the German staff at Ruhleben, mainly because he seemed to take a malicious delight in building up prisoners' hopes of imminent release, only to destroy their dreams of freedom at the last minute. It was also rumoured that he kept a card-index of all the prisoners in his office and used this information to ensure that those who had crossed him were never considered for exchange schemes.[13] Eventually he was removed after a series of complaints from the US embassy and a statement by Matthias Erzberger before the Reichstag Main Committee, who noted that '[Rüdiger's] dismissal is also to be recommended on foreign policy grounds'.[14]

At the more senior level, the military administration at Ruhleben was responsible to the *Kommandantur* in Berlin, which in turn reported to General von Kessel, the supreme commander in the marches, in whose army corps district the camp lay.[15] Guidelines on specific themes like accommodation and diet were also provided by the Prussian Ministry of War, whose *Unterkunftsdepartement* played a coordinating role but did not command individual camps.[16] Indeed, there were times when both Schwerin and Taube actively ignored directives from above in the interests (as they saw it) of 'their' prisoners. Thus an attempt by the *Unterkunftsdepartement* to halt the supply of army cigarettes to allied POWs, because all the tobacco was needed for the front, was successfully resisted by Schwerin on the grounds that this was 'the one little bit of *Gemütlichkeit* permitted to the prisoners'.[17]

Prisoners later remembered that Taube was a frequent visitor to the camp, and that he could often be seen walking about on his own or in the company of his wife or adjutants. He had an unpleasant side to his character, which sometimes manifested itself in short outbursts of anger. On one occasion in January 1915, for instance, he confined the whole camp to sudden barrack arrest after receiving a complaint from a pro-German prisoner that inmates regularly referred to the German people as 'the bloody Germans', a phrase, which when translated into German, came out as 'bloodthirsty Germans'. It was the British, not the Germans, he declared, who were the 'bloodthirsty nation'.[18] However, in general he was seen as a reasonable man who was willing to introduce whatever reforms were possible given his limited powers and influence. The American embassy official charged with making regular visits to Ruhleben, Ellis Loring Dresel, certainly blamed those higher up the chain of command for the poor dietary and housing conditions at the camp, and absolved both Schwerin and Taube of any blame.

> Their attitude towards the interned civilians has been constantly humane and considerate, and they have spared no pains to render the camp life as endurable as possible and to make such improvements as were practical within their power.[19]

One of Taube's first acts was to nominate a 'barrack captain' for each barrack. The nominees had to speak both German and English fluently, and had to have the confidence of their fellow barrack inhabitants, but they were not always put up for democratic election, a source of some discontent later on. The barrack captains in turn formed a 'captains' committee' chaired by the overall 'captain of captains' or *Oberobmann des Lagers*. The first 'captain of captains' was E. M. Trinks, but he was released in January 1915 and replaced by his deputy, Joseph Powell, who held the position until the dissolution of the camp in November 1918. The barrack captains, and Powell personally, were not always popular, particularly with the more upper-class prisoners, and were sometimes criticised for being pro-German or unduly secretive in their handling of camp affairs.[20] The fact that Powell was allowed to leave the camp for a few hours each week to visit the American embassy and carry out other errands added to these resentments, but all attempts to oust him were stubbornly – and successfully – resisted. Some barrack captains admittedly won respect in other ways, for instance Wallace Ellison, who was dismissed and placed in detention for five weeks in April 1915 after daring to speak out against an alleged abuse of camp funds committed by some of the German staff officers. After this he became a hero among the prisoners, and made several escape attempts, finally succeeding in the autumn of 1917.[21]

Earlier in the camp's history there had been a rather nasty incident involving anti-semitism among the German guards. On 12 November 1914 the Jews in the camp were asked to step forward and identify themselves. They were then told that they would be rehoused so that they could be supplied with *kosher* food from a soup kitchen run by the Berlin Jewish community. At first they were taken to the overcrowded waiting room of the emigrants' railway station, where they had to sleep on the floor, and later to barrack 6 at the end of the camp, which according to Israel Cohen, was the 'oldest and dirtiest stable in the compound'. The guards sent to escort them to their new quarters forced them to carry bedsteads and wooden planks to the accompaniment of taunts such as 'Verdammter Judenpack!' and 'Saujuden!'[22] Regular raids were organised on this barrack in search of contraband goods, since it was assumed, quite wrongly, that the Jewish prisoners, many of whom spoke only Russian or Yiddish, were behind all forms of illicit trading, gambling and smuggling.[23] Eventually barrack 6 was closed down after a direct protest from the US ambassador Gerard to Count Schwerin in March 1915, and its inmates were either transferred to other barracks or, in the case of the Russians, to Havelberg camp. To say that this episode was in any way similar to the German treatment of Jews in the 1930s and 1940s would be a gross exaggeration. Nonetheless, isolated cases of petty harassment continued, and were given a form of official legitimation when the deputy Prussian Minister of War General von Wandel referred disparagingly to the presence at Ruhleben of 200 'international Jews of British nationality' [*internationale Juden englischer Staatszugehörigkeit*] in a speech before the Reichstag on 7 April 1916.[24]

Two further groups were also placed in separate barracks: the pro-Germans (housed in barracks 14–15 and in the 'Tea-house' from April 1915) and the black sailors, who were accommodated in a newly built wooden barrack (barrack 13) when they arrived from Hamburg in December 1914. The fact that the German military authorities had decided to house black prisoners in Ruhleben at all, albeit in separate quarters, was interpreted as a hostile act by some of the white prisoners, who saw it as a deliberate attempt to undermine morale. For instance, those who read the German newspapers on sale in the camp suspected that reports about the alleged mistreatment of German civilians in the African colonies were being used to justify the counter-view that 'anything was good enough for Englishmen', including putting them on the same level as 'coloureds'.[25] Certainly there are signs that the German government was becoming increasingly concerned about the fate of its nationals who had fallen into enemy hands following the British and French occupations of Togoland, Cameroon and South-West Africa. Accusations were made that German men, women and children had been placed in concentration camps or deported under the guard of black colonial troops, and conditions in the French camp at Dahomey were said to be particularly bad.[26] However, there is nothing to indicate that either Schwerin or Taube were personally inclined to organise Ruhleben as if it was a new front in the 'cultural war' or 'war of reprisals' against the Allied forces. Nor is there any evidence that they sought to stir up racial tensions within the camp as a form of 'divide and rule'; on the contrary, the barrack system was deliberately designed to avoid such possibilities.

From time to time the prisoners were made uncomfortably aware of the much harsher regimes in other POW camps in Germany, where up to 500 British civilians were still languishing in conditions well below those at Ruhleben.[27] In the autumn of 1915, for instance, a number of British fishermen were transferred to Ruhleben from the naval camp at Sennelager near Paderborn and brought with them tales of routine humiliation and violence. Some of the arrivees had a red triangle and a large letter 'Z' for 'Zivilgefangene' (civilian prisoner) painted on their clothing, and had had their heads shaved as if they were convicts. Others alleged that during their time at Sennelager local women were brought to jeer at them.[28] But nothing like this ever happened at Ruhleben itself, and at least one prisoner wondered whether this was connected with the fact that General von Kessel had a son in British captivity (rather than the fact that the Ruhlebenites were civilians).[29] The geographical proximity of Ruhleben to Berlin clearly made a difference, too, as the quotation at the beginning of this book makes clear. But these factors notwithstanding, it was the personality of the camp commandant and his staff of officers and non-commissioned officers (NCOs) that often determined the nature of the environment that the prisoners lived in, and the types of treatment they were exposed to.[30] In this regard the Ruhleben prisoners were undoubtedly well off, and most of them knew it.

Communal organisation

At the heart of Ruhleben's communal life lay the barrack, led by a nominated (and at later stages sometimes elected) barrack captain. The latter's duties included not only representing the barrack on the captains' committee, but also maintaining a basic level of internal discipline and overseeing the work of various sub-officials, including the barrack vice-captain, postman, fireman, cashier and laundryman. He also made decisions on applications for transfer to and from other barracks, a powerful position to be in when competition for space was so tight. Responsibility for cleaning barracks lay with all prisoners, but in many cases the captain raised a small levy and used it to pay a prisoner or prisoners to do this work on the others' behalf. Larger work parties were formed to carry out heavy labour duties around the camp, or to perform tasks shunned by others, like cleaning the camp latrines or emptying the rubbish bins, with the wages averaging 5 marks per week. Finally, from February 1915 barrack captains were placed in charge of distributing relief money issued to destitute prisoners via the US embassy and were obliged to maintain receipts for presentation to the camp finance committee.[31]

Within the barracks themselves there was a certain amount of borrowing from military forms of social organisation, with members of each horse-box or loft space agreeing to 'mess together', i.e. to share out the contents of their parcels from home and their purchases from the German-run camp canteen. This system began to break down, however, for a number of reasons. Firstly, while from March 1915 thousands of parcels entered the camp each month, the system of delivery was far from perfect and there were often periodic droughts caused by postal or other delays. Secondly, the unregulated system of British POW relief, which lasted until the formation of the government-backed Central Prisoners of War Committee at the end of 1916, gave rise to a great deal of duplication and unnecessary waste, so that members of the same horse-box or loft space often found that they had too much of one thing, and not enough of another.[32] Thirdly, a small but significant minority of prisoners received no parcels at all. And finally, those prisoners who received gifts of cash from home were limited by the military authorities to spending only 10 marks per week at the camp canteen, a move which was intended to preserve stocks and prevent hoarding of tobacco in particular, but also inevitably encouraged the growth of a parallel trade in contraband goods smuggled in by the guards.[33]

'Messing' therefore did not last very long on its own, and was soon eclipsed by a rudimentary free market system with some intervention by the state where necessary. In the beginning, for a few pfennigs or a packet of cigarettes, wealthy inmates could hire a fellow prisoner to polish their shoes or fetch parcels or stand in the queue for hot water at the boiler-house.[34] Later a sophisticated 'exchange and mart' service was established so that prisoners from different barracks could swap all kinds of goods from mattresses and pillows to reading lamps and batteries. To this was added a privately run lending library, a cinema and an internal mail system, the Ruhleben Express Delivery (RXD).[35] Some of the more enterprising inmates also set up businesses offering hairdressing, tailoring, engraving or shoe mending services, all at competitive prices. Others were allowed to cultivate small vegetable patches as a means of supplementing their rations. Finally a regular camp store was brought into being by the captains' committee to sell all manner of things made available to it from communal parcels sent from Britain. At this store luxury items were sold at inflated prices (a form of value added tax, or VAT) and the profits were absorbed into the camp fund which was used to pay for the police force, medicines, dentistry, stationary, cleaning utensils, funeral expenses and other essential items. The laundry and boiler-house were also 'state-owned' enterprises and kept up a healthy surplus through sale of passes and hot water for bathing and tea-making.[36]

The evidence suggests that most prisoners were satisfied with the development of these communal arrangements,[37] although there were near-constant attempts by a group of disgruntled inmates to accuse the captains' committee, or Powell personally, of misusing camp funds.[38] Some of these complaints eventually made their way to London via exchanged prisoners, and were investigated by the Foreign Office, but were discovered to be without foundation.[39] The camp treasurer and chair of the finance committee, J. P. Jones, presented his accounts to the captains' committee and the American ambassador on a quarterly basis, and these were also forwarded on to London at the Foreign Office's request. No irregularities were ever found in these financial statements.[40] From September 1915 they were even published in the camp magazine for inspection by the prisoners themselves.[41]

The German military authorities were also happy to allow the system of self-government to continue. Thus when Schwerin was replaced as commandant by Lieutenant-Colonel von Reichenbach in 1916 the latter told Powell that he had been instructed by the Berlin *Kommandantur* and the War Ministry to keep things exactly as they were:

> His one desire seemed to be that the camp should be quiet and orderly; and I think it can be said with truth that the English prisoners gave him far less trouble than the German soldiers, and were punished far less frequently.[42]

The one down-side of this arrangement, from the prisoners' point of view, is that they could address individual complaints to the military authorities only through their barrack captain. Any direct approach to a German officer was strictly forbidden and could invoke harsh penalties.[43] The only other course of action was to try to speak to one of the American embassy officials, but getting an appointment was not always easy, especially when their visits were often of short duration and taken up with other business.[44]

Material conditions

In all the sources on Ruhleben there is a clear agreement that conditions were at first very bad, but later improved. This applied in particular to accommodation and washing facilities, where considerable progress was made by the middle of 1915, although lapses in the quantity and quality of food and medical care continued into 1916 and beyond. However, any account of these changes has to proceed on the basis that appearance and perception were often just as important as reality. Indeed, over time the 'war of words' over material conditions at Ruhleben was waged not only between the prisoners and the German military authorities, but also, on a much fiercer level, between the prisoners and the US embassy, and between the US embassy and the German military authorities. This in turn reflected a growing sensitivity among the prisoners about how their plight was being portrayed to the government and the people back home, and at the same time a growing anger within the German government about how their treatment of prisoners was being presented to the outside world. Thus one released British prisoner recalled that Gerard was known in Ruhleben as the 'pro-German ambassador' because of his favourable reports on the camp,[45] while later in the war the former *Lagerkommandant* Count Schwerin complained that the US embassy, and in particular the officials Dresel and Taylor, had not acted impartially but 'entirely for the English cause' [*in echt englischem Sinne*].[46] Significantly, these arguments over Ruhleben often led British and American propagandists (including Gerard in his post-1917 publications) to overlook the much harsher conditions prevailing in other camps for French and Russian civilians in Germany and German-occupied territory.

Accommodation

As we saw in Chapter 1, the German military authorities initially expected 1,200–1,500 British subjects to be eligible for internment. It is not surprising, therefore, that they were overwhelmed when faced with numbers that were in excess of 4,000. The overcrowding in the first few weeks of internment was indeed shocking, although it is worth noting that conditions were much better than at Münster and other places, where military prisoners were expected to live in the open while building their own prison barracks.[47] By February 1915 the population of Ruhleben had reached 4,273, in spite of the early release of some men found to be too old or sick for life in a prison camp environment.[48] At first they all had to be crammed into the original eleven barracks. This meant expecting men to live six to a horse-box (there were usually twenty-seven such boxes in a barrack), or, worse still, up to 200 in the sloping-roofed loft spaces above each stable, which were reached by means of outer stairs (Figures 3 and 4). Both types of 'accommodation' had inadequate lighting and ventilation, and only the boxes had access to heating from hot water pipes. Two descriptions of the stench-filled atmosphere, mingled in with the cold and frost, should suffice to paint a picture of life inside the lofts and boxes during the winter of 1914–15. Geoffrey Pyke, a reporter for the *Daily Chronicle* who arrived at Ruhleben in January 1915, remembered that in his loft

> there were two hundred people in four rows; two back to back in the centre, and one on each side. The people on the side, if tall, were unable to stand upright ... The floor could not be seen for huddled forms that covered it. The atmosphere was thick and misty, but through it could be seen an avenue of clothing and personal belongings hanging from the low roof and beams, fading away into the darkness in the far distance ... Occasionally a word or so of conversation drifted up from the other end, and all night long the doors at the end banged, with people going out to the latrines, and every time great flakes of wind-borne snow would rush in and swirl about, finally settling down evanescent and wet on some huddled form ... So close were we all that there was hardly any gangway ... and all the while the discordant hum of vibrating tonsils form[ed] the background to every other noise. Nearly two hundred forms, just animate, lay there, each with two square yards in which to live, to eat [and] to sleep.[49]

John Davidson Ketchum also wrote about the cold and crowded conditions in his barrack, but what struck him in particular was the lack of electric lighting:

> The twilight in which much of life had to be lived was so depressing in itself, and such a hindrance to any effort to pass the time constructively, that a real 'light-hunger' resulted. Every evening a score of men crowded under each lamp in the [stable] corridors, huddled together on stools and suitcases, poring over books, playing checkers, mending their clothes, or trying to write home. Every inch

3 Inside one of
the loft spaces

4 Inside one of
the horse-boxes

on which a beam fell was occupied in spite of the freezing draughts
that swept the passage, and exasperated groans arose as someone's
shadow fell for the twentieth time across the page. Some gave up the
struggle and sought their beds in the darkness, but others could be
seen, even on the coldest nights, reading under the arc lamps that
always burned in the compound.[50]

The constant feeling of being wet and never being able to get dry was made worse by the fact that the stable yard between the barracks was not paved, creating the ideal conditions for heavy rains to turn the ground beneath the prisoners' feet into a sea of mud. By March 1915 a pool of water reckoned to be 130 feet long and 25 feet wide had emerged to completely surround the German-run kiosk (the Casino) in the middle of the camp, which was henceforth known as the 'Pond Stores'. For a joke some inmates made rods and pretended to fish, while others announced the opening of a private boat club. In the summer, on the other hand, the pond dried up and the hot weather created clouds of dust and dirt kicked up by the prisoners as they walked about the camp, causing eye infections and other ailments.[51]

A final complaint concerned the particularly poor conditions in the loft of barrack 6, the Jews' barrack, which was used as an overspill for all new arrivals, whether Jewish or not, from February 1915. According to Israel Cohen this part of the camp became 'so crammed and crowded with prisoners, all sleeping on straw sacks packed close to one another, that the place, with its low-lying roof, its little windows, its stifling atmosphere, its dismal light and its fetid smells, gave the impression of a veritable "Black Hole of Calcutta"'.[52] Other prisoners gave barrack 6 a wide berth, resulting in further isolation for its inmates. Indeed, rumours were soon spread that the food given to the Jews was better than that provided to the camp as a whole, thus aggravating existing tensions and resentments.[53]

This is the situation which greeted Ambassador Gerard on his first visit to Ruhleben on 3 March 1915. He was forced to observe some of the overcrowding in the stables, and 'recoiled with an angry shudder' after climbing the stairs to peer into the loft of barrack 6.[54] Later he was criticised by some prisoners for not coming to Ruhleben earlier, although members of his staff had visited the camp on previous occasions. The fact that they reported nothing amiss was held as further evidence of their alleged 'negligence' or pro-German bias. Whatever the truth behind these claims and counter-claims, Gerard was clearly shocked by what he saw in March 1915 and made his views known at the time and in follow-up letters to Schwerin and Kessel.[55] This had an immediate impact, for Gerard's inspection was followed three days later by a visit from representatives of the Berlin *Kommandantur*, and shortly after this a decision was made, presumably on the authority of the Prussian War Ministry, to build several new barracks outside the original compound. By June 1915 nine new wooden barracks had been completed (see barracks 14–19 and 20–22a in Figure 1) at a cost of 140,000 marks. The new barracks had room for around 120 men each, and as a result many (but not all) of the prisoners could be moved out of the

overcrowded loft spaces into horse-boxes of their own.[56] Although far from
ideal, this was a substantial improvement on conditions prevailing in the first
weeks of the camp. The problem of 'light-hunger' was also partially solved
by the sale of small accumulators in the camp which could be recharged at a
low cost.[57] Even so, overcrowding and lack of privacy continued to blight the
lives of the prisoners. In July 1916, a year after the new barracks had been
built, and with the number of inmates now down to around 3,700 as a result
of early releases, the American diplomat Dresel still wrote that:

> The overcrowding of barracks, both stone and wood, is now as
> noticeable as at any time in the history of the camp, as certain barracks
> are now used for other than sleeping purposes, for example, the loft
> of barrack 1 is used for storage purposes ... and the loft of barrack 6
> is used for school purposes.[58]

Indeed, it was only when the population got down to less than 2,500,
after a spate of fresh releases in the early part of 1918, that the problem of
overcrowding was finally resolved.

Washing and toilet facilities

Like the accommodation, the washing and toilet facilities were at first entirely
inadequate to cater for the needs of over 4,000 men living in cramped and
dimly lit horse-stables.[59] Francis Gribble noted that in his barrack:

> There was one tap ... for the use of about three hundred men, and
> hot water was not to be had for love or money. Soap, too, was not
> provided, though most of us had bought some for ourselves; and there
> were no mirrors, so that shaving was out of the question, and we had
> to guess whether our hair was parted straight.[60]

Those who wanted a warm shower were at first allowed just one a fortnight
at the emigrants' railway station, which had the necessary facilities but in
small quantity only. Percy Hull, who entered Ruhleben on 28 November,
was taken for his first shower on 9 December, and this seems to have been
the normal waiting time.[61] Meanwhile hot water for shaving was made
available from the new boiler-house which opened for business in February
1915. By June 1915 warm showers were available once a week for the
prisoners, and cold showers could be had at any time.[62] Later, in August 1915,
a purpose-built shower block and wash-house were erected on the site of
the old latrines, but in winter frozen and burst pipes and/or coal shortages

often interrupted the supply of hot water and thus rendered these facilities unusable for all but the most intrepid.[63]

The old latrines were field army standard issue and after a few months the stench was hard to bear. In March 1915 they were described by the American ambassador as 'a danger not only to the camp but to Berlin', and clearly the War Ministry agreed, because new latrines were constructed in June 1915 with a supposedly more adequate drainage system.[64] Nicknamed 'Charlottenburg' and 'Spandau' they were to be found at either end of the camp, which necessitated a brisk walk in the snow for those caught short during the long winter nights. They also gave off a terrible odour and occasionally broke down completely.[65] In the end, though, it has to be admitted that there were no uncontrollable typhus, typhoid or cholera epidemics in Ruhleben caused by lice, contaminated water or unhygienic toilet facilities, as there clearly were in other POW camps in Germany in 1914–15.[66]

Food

Of all the issues surrounding conditions in Ruhleben, the question of food – both quantity and quality – was by far the most controversial. The early months of the war, when most prisoners were reliant on the standard German rations, were the worst. According to John Masterman:

> The menu was not appetizing; breakfast consisted of dry bread and acorn coffee, the midday meal was soup, in which the advertised meat was seldom to be found, the evening meal a piece of blood sausage with skilly or cocoa. The bread ration was soon cut down to one-fifth of a loaf a day ... many of the prisoners were hungry men during that winter.[67]

On 27 November 1914 there was a 'skilly riot', i.e. a spontaneous demonstration by sailors protesting against the soup provided by the German authorities.[68] Later when Gerard paid his first official visit to Ruhleben on 3 March 1915, his guided tour of the camp was continually interrupted by shouts from ordinary prisoners such as 'Let's have some bread, not sawdust!' and 'We want bread!' Written messages of similar content were thrown into his car as he left, despite the efforts of the German soldiers to prevent this.[69]

Under article 7 of the 1907 Hague convention (Hague IV) the German government was obliged to provide the same daily ration to enemy soldiers in captivity as it did to its own soldiers, and the indications are that the

Prussian Ministry of War initially intended to meet this requirement in respect to British internees, too. However, the problem at Ruhleben was that the authorities there hired in an outside contractor, a man called Griese, who turned out to be corrupt and incompetent (allegedly he was jailed after the war for embezzlement of military funds).[70] Griese's reign came to an end on 7 March 1915 when he was sacked four days after Gerard's first visit. Thenceforth the camp kitchen was handed over to the prisoners, who formed a staff of four inspectors and thirty cooks, their wages and uniforms being paid for out of the camp fund. Indeed, by the time General von Kessel inspected the camp on 20 March, the new regime was already in place and one prisoner noted in his diary: 'kitchens whitewashed, men in clean aprons, taps clean + all alleyways put in special order.'[71] During the remainder of 1915 the food situation improved considerably, largely because of the increased volume of Red Cross parcels, while clothing and footwear needs were also generally met by gifts sent from home.

However, the controversy did not end here. Only a minority of the prisoners, mostly pro-Germans, were totally reliant on German supplies to meet their needs. Most of the others, when they were in receipt of regular parcels sent from home, were choosy about what they took from the Germans.[72] This applied in particular to the infamous German *K-brot* (*Kommissbrot* or military bread), which was made either from rye, or from a mixture of rye, wheat and potatoes, and was considered to be vastly inferior to the white doughy loaves baked and sent in to the camp from British Red Cross depots in Switzerland and Denmark.[73] When deliveries from outside Germany failed, however, as they did from time to time, the prisoners were again forced to rely on the German military fare or go hungry, taking them back to the position before March 1915. Some prisoners also chose to subsist on German rations alone, either on 'patriotic' principle or because they did not wish to burden their families.[74] This meant that opinion inside the camp about the quality and quantity of food was subject to variation, and it was difficult for outside observers to assess whether there was a problem or not.

Further difficulties arose when the Prussian Ministry of War began looking at ways of saving money by reducing prisoners' rations to a level equivalent to the daily intake of German civilians rather than (as required by international conventions) to German soldiers.[75] To the prisoners' consternation, nobody at first seemed to notice (indeed in London both the Foreign Office and War Office were surprisingly reluctant to encourage sensational press reporting on this issue, not least because they suspected that 'a large portion of the civilian population of Germany is but little, if any, better off than our people at Ruhleben').[76] However, suddenly in the early summer of 1916 the issue heated up when the American embassy filed a series of new reports by its expert nutritionist Dr Alonzo Taylor casting serious doubt on whether the rations supplied by the Germans were adequate in terms of quantity and quality, and indicating that they might be as low as half of the amount given to their own soldiers.[77] When the reports were finally debated on the floor of the House of Commons in early July 1916 there was, as predicted, an outcry among MPs and in the British press which the government could not ignore. Probably against its better judgement it therefore felt obliged to pre-empt the parliamentary discussion by issuing in advance a public warning to Berlin threatening reprisals against German internees in Britain if the situation did not improve.[78]

The German government responded angrily to both the American reports and to the British reactions. The prisoners at Ruhleben, it asserted, were 'adequately fed according to tried and tested rules, in the same way as all prisoners of war are'. Furthermore:

> If the British Government should reduce the rations provided to German civilian prisoners as a form of retaliation, then the German military administration would not only find itself obliged to withdraw its consent to the dispatch of communal parcels [from British Red Cross depots], but would also place a ban on the entry of all individual packages, and reduce the diet in the camp to the levels then prevailing in England.[79]

After a further round of diplomatic correspondence the German authorities gave way and under protest agreed to make minor adjustments to the quantity and quality of food delivered to Ruhleben in spite of the ever-tightening allied economic blockade.[80] However, even after this, as Ketchum observed, 'the bread supplied was often uneatable; several men made museum collections of the straw, stones, potato peelings and other objects found in the sour, soggy loaves'.[81] At least 250 prisoners, and possibly more, remained reliant on German rations alone, although some of their fellow inmates took pity and gave them occasional 'gifts' of food and clothes. By the second half of 1916, of course, many basic foodstuffs like meat, eggs and potatoes had become unprocurable, even for middle-class Germans, and with prices rising and supplies running out, rations were cut across the board, including (again) for prisoners.[82] It is therefore probably no exaggeration to say that without food parcels from home the Ruhlebenites would have been seriously underfed; but with the food parcels they were better off than most Germans on the home front during the last two years of the war.

Medical and dental services

Like the accommodation and washing facilities at Ruhleben, medical and dental provision was at first inadequate but gradually got better.[83] However, in this case it was British money channelled through the American embassy, and later the Dutch legation, that funded the improvements, not the Prussian Ministry of War. In the early months of internment the prisoners were forced to rely on the official German hospital or *Lazarett*, situated in the emigrants' railway station just outside the camp, where sick inmates were kept waiting for hours in a draughty corridor for treatment and were then usually palmed off with a couple of aspirins, whatever their symptoms were. Only rarely would one of the German doctors actually come inside the camp itself, and then only if a patient had been unable to sit up unaided for more than two days.[84] Following Ambassador Gerard's second visit to the camp in June 1915, however, one of the new barracks, no. 19, was designated as a convalescent barrack with bed space for forty patients. It was run by a prisoner, Stanley Lambert, who was assisted by a team of orderlies and cleaners paid for from the camp fund.[85] Lambert was responsible for procuring and allocating medical supplies, blankets, bandages and other essential objects through the Red Cross and other sources, a task which he performed with considerable success. He also acted as official interpreter for the German doctors who now agreed to visit regularly each morning. Between June 1915 and July 1916 some 640 patients were treated here.[86]

Meanwhile those prisoners who needed long-term care were sent to Dr Weiler's private sanatorium at Nussbaumallee 38 in Charlottenburg (100–140 beds) under a special arrangement negotiated by the US embassy. Those who could afford it paid for an upgrade to private rooms at 10–12 marks daily, while those who could not had their fees of 7–8 marks per day met by the British government. For this they got a bed in a sparsely furnished dormitory shared by four or five others.[87] Also in August 1915 a fully equipped dental surgery, run by two American dentists, was set up inside the camp to replace the incompetent German practitioner initially supplied by the military authorities.[88] At the same time a fully qualified German oculist was brought in to treat eye complaints caused by the dust and dirt inside the camp and by the strain of nighttime reading without adequate electric lighting.[89]

In general the health of the prisoners bore up remarkably well in the aftermath of these improvements. Camp records indicate that there had been

seventeen deaths among the internees in the period down to July 1915, rising
to fifty by the end of 1917.[90] Assuming a probable final death tally of around
sixty out of a total of 5,500 prisoners passing through Ruhleben between
1914 and 1918, this represented a rate of just over 1%, i.e. well below that
experienced by military and civilian prisoners in other camps in Germany
and elsewhere.[91] Admittedly this was helped by periodic agreements between
Britain and Germany to repatriate invalids and those deemed permanently
unfit for military service.[92]

Even so, many of the prisoners expressed profound dissatisfaction at the
medical and dental services on offer. For instance, when their equipment
was finally delivered in August 1915, the two American dentists at Ruhleben
had to deal with a backlog of almost 500 cases, and due to prior neglect the
majority of their patients were already suffering from serious forms of dental
decay when their turn came around. One prisoner complained in a letter
to his father in March 1916: 'I have been waiting for a month for the dentist
to attend to my teeth. They profess to attend only to those suffering actual
pain and [say] that they have more on their hands ... than they can attend
to. Meanwhile some of my few remaining teeth are going and if not soon
looked to will be beyond salvation.'[93]

Dr Weiler's sanatorium also received mixed reports. Some were
positive[94] but others were not. According to one exchanged prisoner:

> The sanatorium was nothing short of a fraud. It was a private
> lunatic asylum, situated a few miles from the camp. Dr Weiler, the
> proprietor, enlarged it by renting a few untenanted houses in the
> immediate neighbourhood for keeping destitute prisoners (some of
> them not even British subjects) in this "Sanatorium". The British
> taxpayer has to pay M. 7 per day per man, and that at a time when in
> that same neighbourhood board and residence could be got in good
> boarding houses at M. 5 per day.[95]

Another released prisoner alleged that Weiler was stockpiling Red Cross
parcels sent from Ruhleben for his own use rather than distributing them
to his patients: 'there is very good reason for thinking that Weiler is not
a man to be trusted in any way to act fairly.'[96] Meanwhile even the US
embassy itself admitted in a report in November 1915 'that the proprietor
of this sanatorium cares more for pecuniary gain than the humanitarian side
of his work'.[97]

Dr Weiler's institution was also in no position to perform surgical
operations, and when these were needed the prisoners had to be treated at

the *Kriegsgefangenen-Lazarett* in Berlin-Alexandrinenstrasse, where medical facilities and food supplies were extremely rudimentary. Complicated negotiations were needed each time a prisoner was admitted to this hospital, and the waiting times could be life-threatening. One black prisoner whose leg was amputated in 1916 was reportedly sent back to Ruhleben, even though he was clearly no longer fit for military service.[98] The same thing happened to another prisoner, Thomas Cornford, after he was admitted as a private patient to the Krankenhaus-Westend in Charlottenburg in July 1918.[99] In a separate incident, a prisoner referred to the *Kriegsgefangenen-Lazarett* for minor surgery died after contracting diphtheria and erysipelas, and other inmates sent there were allegedly exposed to great risk by being forced to act as orderlies on the diphtheria ward.[100]

Such cases apart, all, or nearly all, the prisoners felt the general physical and mental strain of internment, and most succumbed to ill-health at one time or another during their captivity at Ruhleben. Age was an important determinant here, with those over forty-five faring noticeably worse than their younger comrades. Even Ellis Loring Dresel of the US embassy, who was generally inclined to praise the medical provision at Ruhleben, sounded a note of caution in a report in July 1916:

> There are many men from forty-five on who look ten years older, and who appear to be on the point of physical and mental breakdown, or both. Extreme nervousness, amounting in some cases to hysteria, is often present, and great depression, loss of power of concentration, and impairment of memory are to be observed. In some men, especially those over fifty, the actual mental decay is still more marked. It is no wonder that all in the camp look with apprehension on the prospect of another winter.[101]

As we shall see in Chapters 4 and 5, it was eye-witness accounts such as these which first led the British and German governments to sit up and take notice of the effects of long-term imprisonment on older internees in particular. But even within this age group the number of deaths was comparatively low, another tribute to the efforts of the prisoners and their supporters in getting sufficient food and medical supplies into the camp.

Notes

1 Audoin-Rouzeau and Becker, *1914–1918*, pp. 80–1.
2 *Ruhleben Camp News*, no. 2, 27 January 1915. Copy in HLL-EC, box 9, file 2. The former internee Ketchum devotes a whole chapter of his book

on Ruhleben to exploring the social significance of camp rumours and their impact on morale – see Ketchum, *Ruhleben*, Chapter 4.

3   Adolf Lukas Vischer, *Die Stacheldraht-Krankheit* (Zurich, 1918), translated into English as *Barbed Wire Disease. A Psychological Study of the Prisoner of War* (London, 1919).

4   Gerard, *My Four Years*, p. 132.

5   Ketchum, *Ruhleben*, especially Chapter 3.

6   Stockall, unpublished memoirs, p. 67.

7   See the archival materials in Evangelisches Zentralarchiv (EZA) Berlin, Bestand 51 C II b 1/1–2. Also Ketchum, *Ruhleben*, p. 29. The spiritual needs of other religions and denominations were met by chaplains in residence, i.e. religious ministers who chose to stay in the camp rather than accept repatriation as they were entitled to under international law.

8   Cohen, *The Ruhleben Prison Camp*, p. 51.

9   Ketchum, *Ruhleben*, p. 101. Cf. Gerard to Page, 11 October 1915, in NA, FO 383/69.

10   Powell and Gribble, *The History of Ruhleben*, pp. 48–9 and 144–7.

11   Cohen, *The Ruhleben Prison Camp*, p. 61.

12   See the new postal regulations issued by the Prussian Ministry of War, 22 February 1915, in HLL-EC, box 4, file 9.

13   Cohen, *The Ruhleben Prison Camp*, pp. 215–16; Powell and Gribble, *The History of Ruhleben*, p. 50.

14   *Der Hauptausschuß des Deutschen Reichstags, 1915–1918*, 4 vols. (Düsseldorf, 1981–83), vol. 2, p. 452 (sitting on 4 April 1916).

15   Powell and Gribble, *The History of Ruhleben*, p. 23.

16   Hinz, *Gefangen im Großen Krieg*, pp. 71–3.

17   Powell and Gribble, *The History of Ruhleben*, p. 43.

18   This incident is referred to so many times in other publications that it does not need repeating again here in any detail. See e.g. *ibid.*, pp. 27–30; Ketchum, *Ruhleben*, pp. 119–20.

19   Ellis Loring Dresel, untitled 55 page report on Ruhleben camp, dated 22 July 1916, in NA, FO 383/142, p. 55.

20   Gerard, *My Four Years*, pp. 122–3; Jahr, 'Zivilisten als Kriegsgefangene', p. 311–12.

21   On Ellison see the material in Liddle Collection, RUH 20 and NA, FO 383/76, and Chapter 6 below. Also Ketchum, *Ruhleben*, p. 176.

22   Cohen, *The Ruhleben Prison Camp*, p. 48.

23   *Ibid.*, pp. 205–6.

24   *Verhandlungen des Reichstags*, vol. 307, p. 918. Also cited in Jahr, 'Zivilisten als Kriegsgefangene', p. 307.

25   Powell and Gribble, *The History of Ruhleben*, p. 10.

26   See e.g. the German Foreign Office memorandum 'Die Behandlung der deutschen Bevölkerung seitens französischer und englischer Truppen in den von diesen besetzten Teilen der deutschen Kolonien', n.d. [November 1914]

in BA Berlin, R 1501/112364, Bl. 83–6.

27 The figure of 500 is given as an estimate in the *Note from the US ambassador transmitting a report, dated June 8, 1915, on the conditions at present existing in the internment camp at Ruhleben* (London, 1915).

28 Percy Hull, diary entry for 29 October 1915, in Liddle Collection, RUH 26. Significantly there is also a cartoon featured in one of the camp publications, *Prisoners' Pie*, in January 1916, which depicts a man wearing a striped uniform with a triangle and the letter 'Z' on his back. A similar cartoon appears in the *Ruhleben Camp Magazine*, no. 2, April 1916, p. 2, this time of a new arrival from Celle camp who has a triangle but no 'Z' on his back.

29 Percy Hull, diary entries for 11 March and 20 March 1915, in *ibid.*

30 Hinz, *Gefangen im Großen Krieg*, pp. 74–5. The same point is also made by Gerard, *My Four Years*, pp. 121 and 135.

31 Ketchum, *Ruhleben*, p. 101.

32 On the Central Prisoners of War Committee of the British Red Cross and Order of St John, to give it its full title, see also Chapters 4 and 5 below.

33 Ketchum, *Ruhleben*, p. 101.

34 *Ibid.*, pp. 27–8.

35 See the various memorabilia items in HLL-EC, boxes 3 and 4.

36 Advertisements for these services can be found in the camp magazine, *In Ruhleben Camp* (henceforth IRC).

37 See e.g. Stockall, unpublished memoirs, p. 66.

38 See e.g. letter to editor by L.E. Filmore, IRC, no. 3, 11 July 1915, pp. 38–9, and similar letter in IRC, no. 6, 29 August 1915, pp. 41–2. Also Ketchum, *Ruhleben*, pp. 282–3.

39 See the evidence in NA, FO 383/140.

40 For examples of financial statements see HLL-EC, box 5, files 5–8. For a useful explanation of the different camp funds see the interview with Jones in IRC, no. 2, 27 June 1915, pp. 3–7.

41 See the finance committee's report on the accounts to 30 June 1915, in IRC, no. 7, 12 September 1915, pp. 43–5.

42 Powell and Gribble, *The History of Ruhleben*, p. 46.

43 See the list of military regulations for 1914–15 in HLL-EC, box 5, file 10.

44 See the rather one-sided, but nonetheless at least partly representative criticisms of the US embassy made by various exchanged prisoners in interviews with FO officials in NA, FO 383/68, 69 and 141.

45 Francis Gribble, 'The Conditions at Ruhleben. A Memorandum for the British Red Cross Society', n.d. [October 1915]. Copy in NA, FO 383/69.

46 Count Schwerin to the Prussian Ministry of War, 19 March 1917, in BA Berlin, R 901/84424. Evidence from the papers of Joseph C. Grew and Ellis Loring Dresel in the Houghton Library, Cambridge, MA, also indicates serious disagreements among US embassy staff themselves over how to represent conditions at Ruhleben and other camps, with both men accusing Jackson, head of the British section, of pro-German bias. See in particular

Grew's diary entry for 10 July 1916, in Houghton Library, MS AM 1687, vol. 7.

47 Hinz, *Gefangen im Großen Krieg*, p. 93.
48 Jahr, 'Zivilisten als Kriegsgefangene', p. 303.
49 Geoffrey Pyke, *To Ruhleben – and Back. A Great Adventure in Three Phases*, first published 1916, new edn with an introduction by Paul Collins (New York and San Francisco, 2002), pp. 108–9.
50 Ketchum, *Ruhleben*, p. 17.
51 Cohen, *The Ruhleben Prison Camp*, pp. 85–6.
52 *Ibid.*, p. 50.
53 Tripp, 'Kommunikation und Vergemeinschaftung', p. 26.
54 Cohen, *The Ruhleben Prison Camp*, p. 85. Cf. John Alexander Lloyd's diary entry for 3 March 1915, in Liddle Collection, RUH 30. Here Gerard is said to have described the scene in the loft of barrack 6 as 'eine Schande und menschenunwürdig'.
55 See Gerard to Schwerin, 18 March and 17 April 1915, and Gerard to Kessel, 25 March 1915. Copies of all these letters were forwarded by the US embassy in London to the British government in May 1915. See NA, FO 383/42.
56 The figure of 140,000 marks was given by Schwerin to Pastor Siegmund-Schultze during one of his visits to the camp – see Pastor Siegmund-Schultze's unpublished notes, 'Antwort auf den Artikel eines Korrespondenz vom 8. März', in EZA Berlin, Bestand 51 C II b 1/2. On the new barracks see also the *Note from the US ambassador* (as n. 27 above).
57 Ketchum, *Ruhleben*, p. 156.
58 Dresel, untitled 55-page report on Ruhleben camp (as n. 19 above), p. 11.
59 This is also made clear by Pastor Siegmund-Schultze in his unpublished notes 'Antwort auf den Artikel eines Korrespondenz vom 8. März' (as n. 56 above).
60 Gribble, *Seen in Passing*, p. 298.
61 Percy Hull, diary entry for 9 December 1914, in Liddle Collection, RUH 26.
62 Schwerin to Siegmund-Schultze, 23 June 1915, in EZA Berlin, Bestand 51 C II b 1/2. See also IRC, no. 1, 6 June 1915, p. 26.
63 Ketchum, *Ruhleben*, pp. 156, 160, 315 and 329.
64 *Ibid.*, p. 18. Cf. the *Note from the US ambassador* (as n. 27 above).
65 Cohen, *The Ruhleben Prison Camp*, p. 124; Tripp, 'Kommunikation und Vergemeinschaftung', p. 32; notes made by Lord Robert Cecil on an interview with released prisoner Mr G. A. Cohen, 15 September 1915, in NA, FO 383/69.
66 Ketchum, *Ruhleben*, p. 163. On the typhus epidemic of spring 1915 which hit several camps in Germany, in particular Wittenberg, Kassel-Niederzwehren and Gardelegen, and led to allied accusations of criminal negligence against the German military, see Hinz, *Gefangen im Großen Krieg*, pp. 102–6 and Jones, 'The Enemy Disarmed', pp. 118–33.

67 J. C. Masterman, *On the Chariot Wheel. An Autobiography* (Oxford, 1975), pp. 100–1.

68 Ketchum, *Ruhleben*, p. 19.

69 Cohen, *The Ruhleben Prison Camp*, p. 85.

70 Stockall, unpublished memoirs, p. 49. According to Hinz, *Gefangen im Großen Krieg*, p. 94, private companies often supplied food to POW camps, at least in the early part of the war.

71 Percy Hull, diary entries for 7 March and 20 March 1915, in Liddle Collection, RUH 26.

72 Cf. Alonzo E. Taylor, *Report on the conditions of diet and nutrition in the internment camp at Ruhleben* (= misc. No. 18) (London, 1916). According to this report, over a week-long period from 14 to 20 April 1916 the number of prisoners eating the German food at the camp kitchen varied from 1,676 to 2,480 out of a total camp population of 3,700 (*ibid.*, p. 5).

73 Ketchum, *Ruhleben*, p. 160.

74 Taylor, *Report on the Conditions*, p. 3.

75 Hinz, *Gefangen im Großen Krieg*, pp. 209–12.

76 Sir Herbert Belfield to Lord Robert Cecil, 22 June 1916, in NA, FO 383/141.

77 See Taylor's follow-up reports in *Further correspondence respecting the conditions of diet and nutrition in the internment camp at Ruhleben* (= misc. no. 21) (London, 1916). For a further discussion see also Tripp, 'Kommunikation und Vergemeinschaftung', pp. 35–7.

78 Sir Edward Grey to Walter Hines Page, 23 June 1916, in NA, FO 383/141.

79 AA to Gerard, 2 July 1916, in BA Berlin, R 901/83953.

80 *Further correspondence respecting the conditions of diet and nutrition in the internment camp at Ruhleben and the proposed release of interned civilians* (= misc. no. 25) (London, 1916); *Further correspondence with the United States Ambassador respecting the treatment of British prisoners of war and interned civilians in Germany* (= misc. no. 26) (London, 1916).

81 Ketchum, *Ruhleben*, p. 157.

82 On food shortages in Berlin see Davis, *Home Fires Burning*, pp. 140–8 and passim; and on cuts made to POW's rations see *ibid.*, p. 187 and Hinz, *Gefangen im Großen Krieg*, pp. 213–14.

83 Cohen, *The Ruhleben Prison Camp*, pp. 183–6; Powell and Gribble, *The History of Ruhleben*, pp. 97–106.

84 Cohen, *The Ruhleben Prison Camp*, p. 183.

85 Powell and Gribble, *The History of the Ruhleben Camp*, pp. 110–16.

86 Dresel, untitled 55-page report on Ruhleben Camp (as n. 19 above), p. 47.

87 Tripp, 'Kommunikation und Vergemeinschaftung', p. 41.

88 See the copy of the agreement to establish a dental surgery at Ruhleben, 24 August 1915, with covering letter from Gerard to Page, 3 September 1915, in NA, FO 383/69.

89 Ketchum, *Ruhleben*, p. 164; Cohen, *The Ruhleben Prison Camp*, pp. 186–7; Powell and Gribble, *The History of Ruhleben*, pp. 106–8.

90 See the medical records in HLL-EC, box 5, files 9 and 14.

91 For comparative figures see Rachamimov, *POWs and the Great War*, pp. 39–42, Hinz, *Gefangen im Großen Krieg*, pp. 235–46; and Jones, 'The Enemy Disarmed', pp. 1–5.

92 See Chapters 4 and 5 below.

93 J. L. Steinke to R. Steinke, 9 March 1916. Copy in NA, FO 383/140. The figure of nearly 500 dental cases dealt with since August 1915 can be found in Lord Robert Cecil's notes on an interview with exchanged prisoners Beaumont (vice-captain) and Hawkins, 7 April 1916, in *ibid*.

94 See Beaumont's description in *ibid*.

95 F. W. Hanson to FO, 7 June 1916, in NA, FO 383/141.

96 Lord Robert Cecil's notes on an interview with exchanged prisoners Boss, Cohen and Cailleau, 10 June 1916, in *ibid*.

97 Tripp, 'Kommunikation und Vergemeinschaftung', p. 41.

98 Lord Robert Cecil's notes on an interview with exchanged prisoner Moresby White, 13 July 1916, in NA, FO 383/141.

99 Minutes of barrack captains' committee, 25 July 1918, in HLL-EC, box 5, file 15.

100 Powell and Gribble, *The History of Ruhleben*, p. 122.

101 Dresel, untitled 55-page report on Ruhleben camp (as n. 19 above), pp. 54–5.

3

Inside Ruhleben II: the prisoner community

> Understanding a people's culture exposes their
> normalness without reducing their particularity.
> (Clifford Geertz[1])

While the physical conditions gradually improved for most inmates, the main enemy in Ruhleben was boredom, particularly as the weeks turned into months and then into years. The life of an internee could be very frustrating, and there were occasional bouts of violence, fighting and drunkenness, especially among the sailors. Other prisoners experienced periods of prolonged depression or lethargy. The worst times were Christmas and the period just after New Year, when the days were very cold and the nights very long, and it seemed as if the war might last forever. In spite of the more regular flow of Red Cross parcels, the future often looked bleak, particularly for those whose businesses effectively went bankrupt as a result of their internment. The American diplomat Joseph C. Grew, who visited the camp on 1 January 1916, recorded his admiration for the prisoners, who had put on a 'first class' play, but nonetheless confessed that he found it 'all rather depressing ... especially when the crowds wished us a Happy New Year as we departed'.[2]

In part, the various sports clubs, territorial associations and reading circles that made up the cultural life at Ruhleben emerged as a means of forgetting these worries and frustrations. They also acted as a survival mechanism in the broadest sense of the term by enabling the internees to make sense of their feelings and emotions in a context where time, quite literally, seemed to stand still.[3] Last but not least, the prisoners at Ruhleben needed to construct an identity for themselves based on notions of continuity with the past and future and framed within a language and culture that fostered a collective sense of purpose.[4] This was all the more important given that the British identity of the camp was not something which could be taken for granted amid the relatively large number of prisoners with German names or from German or Russian backgrounds. What, then, was the basis of the so-called 'Ruhleben spirit'? In what sense did the camp's inmates constitute a 'community at war'?

Cultural and social life

One of the first things to be organised by the prisoners after their arrival at Ruhleben was a lending library, followed by the establishment of a whole host of other clubs, societies and cultural associations designed to meet the educational and social needs of the inmates. Thus the first camp newsheet, issued in January 1915, carried advertisements for a debating society, a chess association and a rounders league.[5] In the next few weeks this was followed by the formation of a camp theatre and camp orchestra, a camp school, an Arts and Science Union, and a host of cultural 'circles' with specific territorial affiliations – including the Lancastrian association and its Australian, Canadian, French, German, Irish, Italian, Scottish, Welsh and Yorkshire equivalents.[6] Art, literature and politics were frequently discussed in the columns of *In Ruhleben Camp*, an illustrated fortnightly magazine which began in June 1915 and acted as an outlet for a variety of comic sketch writers, graphic artists, caricaturists and budding journalists.[7] Most evident, though, were the personal rivalries and petty in-fighting that became a common feature of associational life in the camp and absorbed the energies of a substantial minority of the inmates. As Timothy Eden later wrote:

> On all sides committees and societies spring up like mushrooms, quarrel among themselves, and disappear in a cloud of smoke and bloom in another corner – under a different name ... Matters of no importance are discussed with a bitterness and righteous indignation worthy of a noble cause. Here within the wooden walls of a shed a trembling chairman is unseated while the whole camp for days is a flutter with whispered scandal ...But ... how could it be otherwise? When the body is concentrated, the mind must gradually become so too, and it is far better to raise enthusiasm over the delinquencies of a member of some temporary committee than to sit and brood over some distant glories or to sigh out for a freedom which may not be.[8]

Of course, not all aspects of Ruhleben culture were unique to Ruhleben, or even to POWs in general. They were part of a much broader wartime culture which allowed a constant stream of communication between the home front and those fighting or living away from home. The cultural historian Andrew Horrall has already identified the importance of 'up-to-dateness' or 'topicality' as a key ingredient in the transformation of popular entertainment and leisure in London during the period 1890–1918.[9] Ruhleben, with its Jews, its Germans, its music-hall artists, its sailors, its Irish comedians and Scottish singers, and its unending obsession with current events, both inside the camp and (to a lesser extent) in the world beyond, in many ways resembled a microcosm of the Edwardian metropolis in its heyday. Football, for instance, was a major pre-occupation from the very beginning of the camp, with impromptu matches played out on a daily basis in the courtyard, often attracting crowds of excited spectators. As the camp magazine *In Ruhleben Camp* put it in an article published to coincide with the start of the new football season in October 1915:

> Cricket may be the 'noble old English pastime' and all that sort of thing, but without doubt this is the football age; something short and strenuous, a buzz of excitement, and a chance to exercise the lungs is the demand made by the English crowd of to-day, and the Ruhleben crowd is no exception.[10]

Periodic 'crazes' also did the rounds, and were commented upon humorously in the various camp publications, while song writers updated well-known lyrics to reflect local happenings and events, as in the following number taken from the 1915 Christmas pantomime *Cinderella*:

> It's a long way to walk to Spandau
> When the snow's lying thick
> It's a long way to walk to Spandau
> When you've got to get there quick.
> When you're dressed in pyjamas
> Overcoat and clogs,
> It's a long long way to walk to Spandau
> To the new Spandau ...[11]

Finally, there was also a constant 'topical cross-over'[12] between different cultural activities, as sportsmen were encouraged to become involved in theatre, actors in music, musicians in sport, and so on. Minor camp

5   The barrack cricket captains, c. 1915; Harold Redmayne is on the back row, third from left, and Steve Bloomer on the front row, far right

celebrities were created in this manner, including the footballers Steve Bloomer and Fred Pentland, and the history don John Masterman, who not only gave popular lectures to the Arts and Science Union, but was also a champion cricket and tennis player and the 'best all-round man in the Camp' (Figure 5).[13] The most frequently mentioned person in camp publications, however, was the dramaturge and arts critic Leigh Henry, who 'dressed eccentrically, wore a beard even in summer, and lectured daringly on [a variety of subjects] from Schönberg to the Italian Futurists'.[14] After the war he worked for the British Council in Rome, and later for the BBC.[15]

Another famous 'celebrity' in the camp was a South African national named Castle who was said to be about 7 ft 6 in. tall and had been arrested while working at a Berlin circus. His father was a Transvaal Boer, his mother a native American, and his unusual height meant that he had to sleep in a specially constructed bed placed in the Tea-house.[16] German newspapers like *Der Weltspiegel* frequently carried pictures of him, and he also appeared in a silent German film of the camp dressed in the full regalia of a 'Red Indian' prince.[17] The film was shot in the summer of 1915 and first screened in the camp on 21 August, to mark the formal opening of the new cinema. *In Ruhleben Camp* commented: 'The ... film has proved very popular and besides giving us some very good pictures of Camp celebrities there are excellent pictures of Baroness von Taube and several officers.'[18]

While the film was made by the Germans for propaganda purposes, and yet was found to be entertaining too, visual culture more generally played a key role in communicating ideas about Ruhleben and forging a sense of belonging and common identity. Thus *In Ruhleben Camp* and its successors contained numerous sketches, illustrations and photographs of the camp and its inhabitants. On a much larger scale, prisoners bought mass-produced photographs of the camp from a licensed Berlin photographer and used them as postcards when writing to their families at home.[19] Some of these postcards contain pictures of the camp grounds (although never the outer perimeter), while others are group portraits, for instance of the barrack cricket captains or the casts of theatrical productions, and others still are of individuals or a pair of friends. This remarkable range of visual imagery indeed bears testimony to the bustling, civilian atmosphere of the camp. Not only are all the figures in civilian dress, but the poses they adopt are decidedly non-military, and even the barracks and grounds are more suggestive of peacetime tranquility than wartime internment. The only hint that this is a prison camp comes with the occasional glimpse of a German officer in full uniform, although even they have something of a music hall quality about them. Small wonder, then, that one prisoner described his fellow inmates in a letter home as 'more like a bank holiday crowd than prisoners', and although this was undoubtedly an exaggeration, at times – particularly during the 'explosion' of cultural activity in the camp in the late spring and summer of 1915 – it seemed as if he might be right.[20]

German propagandists were of course more than willing to advertise Ruhleben culture as an example of the Reich's supposedly 'humane' treatment of prisoners and as a means of countering allied atrocity propaganda.[21] Film and 'family' postcards were one method of achieving this, but so too was the print media. Thus photographic images of Ruhleben began to appear in the daily press alongside claims that Britain would never allow such freedoms to the German civilians it was holding. German efficiency and organisation were also praised, and the period of chaos and improvisation in the first weeks of the war was quickly set to one side. According to Käthe Schirmacher, the radical feminist turned nationalist who was commissioned to write an article about the camp for the illustrated section of *Die Woche* in September 1915:

The good standard of health at Ruhleben is down to adequate diet (for instance 2,000 eggs per day), and German order and cleanliness ... A hospital and respite home have been made available, but are rarely needed. The photographs show a robust and active population, and the scenes remind one simultaneously of life in a wild-west town, a modern bathing establishment and the bustling markets at world exhibitions.[22]

Likewise, the *Berliner Illustrierte Zeitung* informed its readers in November 1915 that:

The prisoners have a relatively large degree of freedom... They organise football and baseball matches ... [and some] have opened up small businesses. Thus there are engravers, tailors, cobblers, and even a shop selling milk has been established. Those with artistic talents have put together musical and theatrical events, for which a small entrance fee is charged. Every day gifts of money arrive at the Ruhleben 'bank', and the prisoners can draw a certain sum each week.[23]

Meanwhile, solidarity among the prisoners manifested itself in other ways. Firstly, the Ruhlebenites created a new hybrid language, which was a strange idiomatic mixture of English with the odd debased German word or phrase thrown in, such as 'Come on, let's hole our Essen'.[24] In 'The Seven Ages of a Kriegsgefangener', a poem published in the first edition of *In Ruhleben Camp*, the student 'seeks the shining morning hours to pass/with irregular verbs and der, die, das', and it is safe to assume that every prisoner gained at least a smattering of German while in the camp.[25] The merchant sailors added their own unique vocabulary which abounded with nautical terms so that, for instance, servants were 'stewards' and the kitchen was the 'galley'.[26] In order to remind themselves of home, the inmates also named the ally ways and squares of the camp after famous sites of London topography, like 'Bond Street', 'Marble Arch' and 'Trafalgar Square', a form of territorial behaviour that was also popular among British soldiers on the western front (Figure 6).[27] Swearing was so commonplace that 'each man selected for release to England was advised by his friends to go into a sort of quarantine before venturing to emerge in the bosom of his family'.[28] Indeed, the problem of bad language was also commented upon in a short poem published in one of the earliest editions of the *Ruhleben Camp News*:

6   Trafalgar Square with barracks 11 and 10 in background

> Wherever I go, I hear men swear:
> 'By G–d' and 'd– n' and 'h–ll' and 'd– v– l'!
> It strikes me, some of our fellows here
> Are far more 'prisoners' than 'civil'.[29]

The local dialect, spoken by men of all classes, was complemented by topical music, including the 'Ruhleben song', written by Cyrus Harry Brooks and set to music by Ernest MacMillan. It was first performed in Ruhleben as part of a revue in eight episodes on 8 May 1915, and became something of an anthem, sung by the audience at the end of each evening at the camp theatre. The words are fairly meaningless today, but the song gives a clear indication of the defiant mood of cheerfulness which, according to one inmate, made even 'the gloomiest man ashamed to indulge in his melancholy':

> Oh, we're roused up in the morning
> When the day is gently dawning,
> And we're put to bed before the night's begun;
> And for weeks and weeks on end

We have never seen a friend,
And we've lost the job our energy had won.
Yes, we've waited in the frost
For a parcel that got lost,
Or a letter that the postmen never bring;
And its not all beer and skittles
Doing work on scanty victuals,
Yet every man can still get up and sing. So –

    Chorus
Line up, boys, and sing this chorus,
Shout this chorus all you can;
We want the people there
To hear in Leicester Square
That we're the boys that never get down-hearted.
Back, back, back again in England,
There we'll fill the flowing cup;
And tell them clear and loud
Of that Ruhleben crowd
Who always keep their pecker up.

Oh, and we send our love and kisses
To our sweetheart or the missus.
And we say the life we lead is simply grand;
And we stroll around the Tea-'us
Where the girls can sometimes see us,
And we say it's just as good as down the Strand.
Yet there sometimes comes a minute
When we see there's nothing in it,
And the tale that we've been telling isn't true;
Down our spine there comes a-stealing
Just that little homesick feeling –
Then I'll tell you, boys, the best thing you can do:
      Repeat Chorus[30]

The appeal of this song can be seen in the references to London, which every inmate, from every corner of Britain and every corner of the empire, would understand, and to the 'sweetheart' waiting back at home. A sense of topicality is also reinforced by the desire for up-to-date news from home, and for home to receive up-to-date news from Ruhleben. Finally, there is the hint of 'darker moments', which could only be overcome through a collective effort to 'keep your pecker up'.

The fact that many of the inmates were fluent German speakers, and steeped in German culture, also allowed for a common understanding of literary allusions, including an up-to-date version of Heinrich Heine's famous mermaid song, *Die Lorelei* (1823), written for another concert party:

Ich weiß nicht was soll es bedeuten,
Daß ich so traurig bin.
Ich sitze hier in Ruhleben
Und werde bedenklich dünn.
Die Suppe – die sollte mehr kräftig
Und nicht halb Wasser sein.
Auch Kaffee und Tee sind so
 wässrig
Das ist meine grösste Pein.
Meine Frau nun zuhause sitzet,
Wie wir, voll Sorg und Qual.

Der Mann in Ruhleben schwitzet,
Blos nicht von der Heizung im
 Stall.
An der Zahl sind's viertausend
 zweihundert
Alt, jung, krank, blind und
 lahm.
Ueber 'Rumours' sind alle
 verwundert –
Wahrheit ist kein daran.

Um sieb'n, zwölf, fünf marschiert
 man
Durch Sumpf, Morast und Dreck
Aus dem großen Kessel bekommt
 dann
Seine Brüh' und geht weiter weg.
Man wäscht sich morgens im
 Gange,
Die Reichen – die Schwarzen, und
 wir.

I don't know what it all means,
Why I'm feeling so sad.
I'm sitting here in Ruhleben
Growing thin and going mad.
The soup should be more hearty –
Half water, it's that bad.
The tea and coffee are little better

The worst torment I've ever had.
My wife at home is sitting,
Like ourselves full of worry and
 pain.

The men in Ruhleben are sweating,
With no heating worth the name.

We are four thousand two hundred
 in number
Old, young, sick, blind and lame.

'Rumours' disturb our slumber –

There's no truth in them all the
 same.

At seven, twelve and five it's 'march
 men!'
Through quagmires, bogs and mud
From a giant cauldron is served
 then
Our broth, and then we're off.
Mornings we wash in passages
 dank,
The rich – the blacks, and the rest.

Es ist daher nichts mit dem Range,	For here we find there's no rank,
Es gibt keinen Unterschied hier.	No difference 'twixt worst or best.
Nun sitzen wir Armen gefangen	Now we poor souls sit imprisoned
Hier in dem Sandlocke fest.	Here in this sand hole jail.
Und allein zwei Karten gelangen	With only two postcards envisioned
Allwöchentlich aus dem Nest.	Our meagre weekly mail.
Unser Blatt: 'Die B.Z. am Mittage'	The newspaper, 'B.Z. am Mittag'
Das ist alt Weibergeschwätz.	Offers nothing but old wives' tales.
Sie schreibt von der glänzenden Lage	It says our conditions are not hard
Und führt gegen uns ein Gehetz.	And tells lies to boost its sales.
Auf Strohsäcken wir uns ja betten,	We bed down on sacks of straw,
Da Federn (und Tinte) sind rar.	For feathers (and ink) are rare.
Wir von unserem Gelde erhalten	With just 10M a week, no more
Nur 10M die Woche in bar.	Of our money left to spare.
Man kaufet auch an der Kantine	Everything to buy in the canteen
Alles – nur nicht was man will	All sorts– except what we will
Und dann noch die schönen Latrine!!!	And then there's the beautiful latrines!!!
Der Anblick, wie traurig und still!!!	The view, how melancholy and still!!! [31]

Gradually the production of musical events and concert parties became more organised through the formation of an entertainments committee which sought to control the pricing of tickets and the distribution of box-office takings. After a protracted battle between the artists and the captains' committee over the make-up of the entertainments committee, a compromise formula was reached in September 1915 and at last the go ahead was given for improvements to the stage and lighting in the hall under grandstand 2.[32] A pivotal figure in this respect was John Roker, who before the war had been ballet master at the famous Metropol theatre in Berlin's west end and after 1915 presided over the Ruhleben dramatic society (Figure 7). He was assisted by the lyricist Cyrus Harry Brooks, the composer Ernest MacMillan, and by a host of volunteer actors, stage-hands, costume- and set-designers and musicians. Thanks to their efforts theatrical productions and concert parties became a permanent feature of camp life and a constant reminder of home. Standard 'high-brow' plays by Galsworthy, Ibsen, Shakespeare, Shaw, Sheridan and Wilde were performed alongside more 'middle-brow' thrillers and farces and Gilbert and Sullivan operettas like *The Mikado* (Figure 8).[33] However, the most popular performances were

7   Behind the scenes
at the Ruhleben camp
theatre: the scenic
artists' studio

8   The cast of *The
Mikado*, Ruhleben camp
theatre, 1916

the musical-comedy revues dreamed up by the prisoners themselves, and pantomimes performed at Christmas, such as *Cinderella* which, as we have seen, was full of 'topical plums' as well as up-to-date references to the war and internment.[34]

German officers and officials from the US embassy were often invited to attend these events, along with their wives and families. Costumes were either made in the camp or hired from a Berlin costumier, while prisoners donated part of their own money and allowances to buy curtains, props and other paraphernalia.[35] Theatre gave the prisoners plenty of opportunities for self-mockery and humorous commentaries on the war, although, unlike soldiers in the trenches, they could not directly insult the Kaiser or other German military leaders. As time went on the various dramatic and musical societies developed their own elaborate sets and painted scenery which, in the words of Frank Stockall, were 'as good as any repertory that I have seen'.[36] Christmas was a particularly poignant time, and on Christmas Eve 1917 some of the internees' children were briefly allowed into the camp to watch a festive pantomime and receive presents sent from Britain, an event made possible through the efforts of the British Red Cross and Elisabeth Rotten's relief organisation in Berlin.[37]

With regard to sports, golf, rugby, cricket and tennis were all part of Ruhleben life, but football stood out in particular as a collective obsession, reflecting its dominance in pre- (and post-) war British popular culture. The diaries and letters of the internees are indeed full of references to the centrality of the game in their lives. One internee noted in his diary as early as 12 November 1914:

> The Germans can't understand our football. They think we should all pull long faces with the exception of the old commander, and he smiles very much when he comes round and sees it... In fact, the whole thing is damn funny.[38]

Football also provided one of the camp's most poignant moments, when Baron von Taube was asked to kick off the first official match on the racecourse on 28 March 1915. According to the same observer, he 'seemed very pleased. A raised seat for his wife and himself was placed near the ground'.[39] When Bishop Bury visited the camp in November 1916 he too was asked to kick off at a match between the 'Bloomers' and the 'Wolstenholmes', a so-called 'ragtime' or non-league game, which ended in a draw.[40]

Boxing was also popular (as it had been in Edwardian London) and spars between rival legends attracted big crowds, including German guards and

9   Boxing match at Ruhleben, 1915

officers who came to watch as spectators (Figure 9).[41] According to Israel Cohen: 'Most of the matches consisted of three bouts of one minute each, and some effective punching was done by men who had figured in boxing rings at home.'[42] Several pictures of boxing matches indeed made their way out of the camp and were published in the German and British press. The London *Daily Sketch* carried as its headline on 6 August 1915: 'Even the German atmosphere cannot kill the old British sport of boxing.' It also published a picture of the camp theatre, which it named 'the Ruhleben Empire'.[43] Likewise a German propaganda brochure issued in French by the Prussian Ministry of War at the end of 1915 included a picture of a boxing match under the caption: 'Les Anglais internés à Ruhleben ne peuvent vivre sans la boxe.'[44]

The desire to 'put on a show' for the Germans could also be seen in two events in particular. The first was the staging of a sports day on 24 May 1915 (Empire Day in Britain since 1904) in which prisoners competed in various races and track events, including the 120 yards hurdles, the three-legged race, the running high jump, the tug-of-war and the relay race.[45] This was indeed a good chance to demonstrate what were seen as the 'British' virtues of fair play and good sportsmanship, combined with a symbolic display of 'effortless' British superiority. Thus when a group of German officers asked if they could compete in the relay race, their offer was taken up.[46] Even those prisoners who did not take part but watched from the side-lines were drawn into the spectacle, thereby demonstrating a sense of 'civic pride' and contributing to what Jim English has described as the 'righteous celebration' of British imperial culture which marked Empire Day in its pre-1918, Edwardian incarnation.[47] A few weeks later, the Baroness von Taube was asked to hand out the prizes at a special ceremony, and was herself presented with a silver cup in memory of the occasion. *In Ruhleben Camp* commented thus:

> The Baroness, who was evidently moved at this little token of the Camp's appreciation, took the Cup amid three cheers – cheers that really did one's heart good and convinced one that after all this IS an English camp. They came from the men's very hearts, and we believe that the Baroness will always have a pleasant memory of those three ringing British cheers.[48]

The second event that appeared to bring the whole camp closer together and reinforced its British identity was the debating society's decision to hold a mock by-election in July–August 1915 to ensure that the 'borough of Ruhleben' was properly represented at Westminster (Figure 10). A total of three candidates stood: Alexander Boss (Conservative), Israel Cohen (Liberal) and Reuben Castang (Votes for Women). A mayor, Walter Butterworth, was

10   A scene from the 'Ruhleben by-election', July 1915

also appointed to act as returning officer for the 'borough'. The campaign, which lasted for two weeks, was a parody of the Edwardian British election, with posters plastered all over the camp, committee rooms set up for each candidate, and open-air meetings held each evening before rowdy audiences. A commemorative booklet was also produced, complete with photographs, illustrations, election songs and a potted history of the campaign.[49] The Conservative candidate, Boss, played on his 'aristocratic' pedigree, and the fact that he allegedly owned a 12,000-acre estate in Surrey, while the Liberal, Cohen, put himself forward as a 'Manchester man' and 'man of the people' who supported old-age pensions from the age of forty and was standing at the behest of various local organisations including 'the Clog Repairers' Union, the Amalgamated Association of Hair-Dresssers, the Casino Vinters' League, the Band of Hope for Discharged Actresses, [and] the Sock Darners' Union'.[50] In the end, however, it was the suffragist candidate Castang who won on the slogan: 'vote for us ... think of your wives and sweethearts and vote for Castang'.[51] The final results were as follows:

> Reuben Castang (Votes for Women) 1,220 (46.7%)
> Israel Cohen (Liberal) 924 (35.3%)
> Alexander Boss (Conservative) 471 (18.0%)

There were also seventy-four spoiled ballot papers, so that in total 2,689 votes were cast, representing a turn-out of just under two-thirds of the 'borough's' electorate.[52]

The German press interpreted Castang's 'victory' as a vote against Britain's continued involvement in the war, although it probably had more to do with feelings of homesickness and of gratitude towards the hundreds of women volunteers in Britain who helped to collect and pack relief parcels for POWs.[53] Nonetheless, the very act of holding a by-election, and the publicity this generated, was to some extent a protest against the British government's inaction on the internment question and its apparent failure to negotiate with Germany for an exchange of prisoners. The implication of attempting to send an MP to Westminster, however far fetched, was that the interests of the internees were not being adequately represented in parliament, in other words that they had largely been forgotten by the politicians back at home.

One final purpose of the by-election was to demonstrate to the German authorities the importance and advantages of the democratic process. This was more than just an attempt to assert the alleged superiority of the British parliamentary system over so-called 'Prussian militarism'; it also had an immediate practical application in that the prisoners were attempting to persuade their captors to allow them to elect their own barrack captains rather than having them appointed from above. In this sense, the organisers of the by-election could claim only a partial success. From the autumn of 1915 some of the barrack captains were indeed elected rather than appointed, but when Mr L. G. Beaumont, the vice-captain of the camp, was released in March 1916, the commandant Count Schwerin rejected a petition drawn up by some of the prisoners' representatives to allow for a camp-wide ballot to elect a successor. As he told a meeting of the barrack captains, elections were all very well in theory, but in practice:

> an [elected] Vice Captain in the Camp could only represent the views of the majority, but would not have the confidence of the minority; and could not therefore be said to have the support of the whole Camp ... The Graf added that he had tried to govern the Camp in a fatherly manner ... and that after careful consideration the best manner in which the question of the Vice Captain could be settled was that he himself should appoint someone who would support the Captain of the Camp in his work.[54]

In other words, Ruhleben was and remained a camp subject to German military discipline and even the captains were hardly 'free agents' when it came to making important decisions. Nonetheless, as we have seen, in September 1915 Schwerin and Taube did agree to grant a form of 'home rule' to the prisoners, an event that led the editors of *In Ruhleben Camp* to call a halt to their regular criticisms of the camp captains and instead to praise 'the present constitution of the civil authority' as 'not merely adequate but in every way successful'.[55] As an earlier editorial put it:

> We all grouse, I.R.C. too, at our Camp Officials, our Ruhleben Supermen ... but please realise that our bark is worse than our bite, that when you do good work we shan't say anything, but when you do bad work, we shall say 'the divil of a lot'. You can't do what you would like, but in working to make Ruhleben life more endurable for some of your fellow-prisoners you are 'doing your bit' and a 'good bit' at that.[56]

Tensions

While the cultural activities described above do seem to indicate that a rough form of solidarity existed among the prisoners, other aspects of camp life were more problematic. For one thing, privacy and personal space were almost non-existent in Ruhleben. It was simply impossible to be alone, and those who did cut themselves off from other inmates were presumed (sometimes correctly) to be on the brink of mental collapse. Friends or 'mess-mates' often fell out and never spoke to each other again, and a malicious rumour or idle piece of gossip could darken the atmosphere of a particular barrack for days on end. Some inmates, like the Irishman William O'Sullivan Molony, deliberately avoided mixing with the same set of people for more than a few days at a time, and instead flitted from one group to the next in a restless and ultimately futile pursuit of distraction. In his view Ruhleben was a 'mock city built on the fringes of madness, and one in which Ibsen would have delighted'.[57] Others simply did not fit in at all, finding nothing to interest them and no like-minded souls to bond with. The fact that over a third of the prisoners decided not to vote in the 'Ruhleben by-election' is in itself a worrying sign.

True, some of the internees did find solace in activities that lay outside the mainstream cultural life of the camp, for instance in art, meditation or gardening, all of which were distinctly minority preoccupations but nonetheless important to those who pursued them. Other internees made it their business to mediate when quarrels broke out, and there were many 'good Samaritans' willing to volunteer as orderlies in the camp kitchen or convalescent barracks. Religion played a central role in at least some prisoners' lives, as seen by the variety of faiths catered for in the camp: not merely Anglicanism (as represented by Williams and Bury) but Non-Conformism, Roman Catholicism, German Lutheranism, Islam, Hinduism and Judaism.[58] However, from March 1915 two other factors helped in part to undermine the solidarity of the camp community.

The first of these was the rapid development of a class society, mimicking the inequalities of wealth and status to be found in Edwardian Britain. In the early months of internment all prisoners faced the same minimalist conditions and class differences seemed irrelevant. However, as Frank Stockall later put it: 'With the coming of parcels came the school tie, the blazer [and] the club badge.'[59] Elitist rivalries soon filled the air, as old Etonians and others vied to create their own exclusive clubs, complete with 'stewards' dressed in white uniforms to serve them drinks.[60] What the 'stewards' themselves felt about this is difficult to say. One prisoner who worked as a valet to the twenty-year-old 'old Etonian' Thomas Cottrell-Dormer asked to have his wages paid into his post office account in England for collection after the war, presumably so he could look forward to better times.[61] However, even he got fed up with being a skivvy and had to be replaced, as Cottrell-Dormer reported in a letter to his mother:

> The only way to make him work was to bully him from morning to night as that was apparently the treatment he had been used to in the army. It got very annoying having to tell him every little thing before he would do it, & we have come off extremely well from the change. Our new man ... Anderson ... performs his work thoroughly & was valet to my cousin Archie Lever. He is the most frank & open person imaginable & will make life in this place quite a different affair, especially in the winter.[62]

The second source of tension was the widespread prevalence of drinking among a certain section of the camp, especially some of the sailors who were actually quite well supplied in terms of parcels and money through the Mercantile Marine Service Association and other organisations. Alcohol was banned but was brought in by the guards or brewed illegally inside the camp. Gambling also took place on a grand scale, and some prisoners built up huge debts, in spite of the half-hearted attempts of the camp captains and the German military authorities to clamp down on this activity. George Merritt, the professional actor who was best known for more than fifty appearances in the camp theatre, later revealed that he was not averse to a bit of poker on a winter's evening: 'With a little skill and innocent cheating I could augment my five marks weekly allowed by the British government. This I think went mainly on cigarettes.' He also helped his guard-escort to smuggle in alcohol during trips to the costumier in Berlin.[63]

Against the prevailing middle-class morality in the camp, it could be argued that gambling and drinking were fairly harmless pastimes which acted as a safety valve and for this reason were at least partly tolerated by the camp authorities. Nonetheless, on occasions levels of violence could get out of hand, and in June–July 1917 eight Ruhleben prisoners (two stokers, a seaman, a mechanic, two tradesmen, an artist and a bookbinder) were transferred to Havelberg camp for what the Prussian Ministry of War described as 'repeated disturbances of the peace, verbal and physical attacks on other prisoners, running around after nightfall and constant noise-making'.[64] Ruhleben also held a number of shady characters with previous convictions for theft, assault and other crimes, and one or two were in Germany in 1914 precisely because they were on the run from the British police. One barrack in particular had a bad reputation, and anyone who crossed the gang that operated there ran the risk of a beating or, even worse, having their faces slashed. Frank Stockall, for instance, recalled the following incident:

> One night a Tyneside stoker and his mates were playing cards, drunk and quarrelsome. They were so objectionable that Percy Brown, a Daily Graphic Reporter, told them to shut up. [The stoker] drew a jack knife, stuck it in the table, and threatened the next man who interfered. That table was at the foot of my bed. Brown again told them to be quiet or he would summon the guard. All I remember is [the stoker] seizing the knife. I lost my nerve and went out of the Barrack in my pyjamas into the freezing cold ... The next morning I went to the German doctor to try to persuade him to move me to another barrack.[65]

On a more mundane level prisoners worried that the growing coarseness of their language would make it difficult for them ever to mix again in 'polite' (i.e. female) company. According to the Swiss expert Adolf Lukas Vischer, this was one of the seven chief symptoms of 'barbed wire disease', the others being 'sexual difficulties', 'a taste for gambling', 'a taste for needless gossip and rumours', 'scrounging and petty quarreling', 'excessive smoking' and 'anxiety about the future'.[66] Even so, it is important not to overplay the extent to which the sailors challenged the middle-class ethos of the camp. Indeed, some prisoners later recalled that, apart from their colourful language, the seamen added a much needed element of domesticity to life in Ruhleben, putting up makeshift washing lines from string inside the lofts (see Figure 3) and taking on sweeping tasks which nobody else would perform.[67] Furthermore, alongside the ratings there were also ships' captains who did their best to keep order and rein in excessive forms of drinking, although under British maritime law they had no authority to issue orders except when on board ship.[68]

There were also racial tensions inside the camp, as we have seen. The worst affected were the pro-Germans. Francis Gribble, for instance, noted that 'the English interned avoided them and they were seldom seen at the English end of the camp. Consequently they soon ceased to have any voice or influence.'[69] Denunciations of individual pro-Germans fill the British Foreign Office files, with exchanged prisoners frequently turning on each other.[70] There is evidence of hostility towards Jewish prisoners too, as

Israel Cohen's memoirs testify. However, it is important not to exaggerate the impact of this. *In Ruhleben Camp* and other publications are admittedly full of cheap anti-semitic jokes at the expense of the inhabitants of barrack 6, including the occasional attempt to conflate 'Jew' and 'pro-German'. Nonetheless, on the whole the Jews were well integrated into camp life and many played an important role in the Ruhleben community, for instance as tailors, cobblers and barbers and also as teachers, musicians and actors. Cohen himself served as the chairman of the Ruhleben Debating and Literary Society for several months, and also featured as the Liberal candidate in the 'Ruhleben by-election', as we have seen. Another Jew, F. Charles Adler, was the conductor of the camp orchestra.[71]

The black and Arab prisoners who inhabited barrack 13, and, later on, barrack 21, were, it is true, much more isolated (Figure 11). Indeed, apart from competing in the barrack football and cricket league, they were usually excluded from the cultural activities of the camp. There were some exceptions, though. 'Peanuts' or 'Jacko', a black sailor seized from a British merchant ship, was something of a local celebrity, his nickname deriving from his occupation as a peanut salesman inside the camp.[72] There was also

11   Members of barrack 13 with their barrack captain, Harold Redmayne, 1916

the case of Sylvester Leon, a Jamaican actor who played more parts on the Ruhleben stage than any other prisoner except George Merritt and also acted as secretary of the Ruhleben Debating and Literary Society.[73] According to Frank Stockall, writing in the early 1960s, Leon

> was studying drama and the stage in Germany, [having been] sent there by the Government to establish a school for West Indian actors on his return to the West Indies. I can still remember his 'Mathias' in 'The Bells' (Sir Henry Irving's part). I was standing in the wings when he came off the stage and it was literally minutes before he divested himself of Mathias and resumed life as Sylvester Leon. He was to my mind the finest actor we had, but seldom seen [outside his barrack] as even then the colour bar was his greatest obstacle.[74]

In general, however, few of the white prisoners seem to have paid much attention to the black British prisoners in their midst, and fewer still ever went inside their barracks, which were seen as strictly off limits.[75] Bishop Herbert Bury, who did venture into this part of the camp during his visit to Ruhleben in November 1916, reported in terms that typify the colonial mentalities of the time:

> The Negroes are in their own barrack, and have two of our best men in charge of them, who just simply love their work. It would never have done to put one of their own number in charge; but as it is they have just what the two races need – the white chivalrously helping the black, giving leadership and sympathy, and the black looking up to the white, confident of getting a really helpful and friendly lead.[76]

For people like Bury, of course, any intermingling between the races on equal terms would have been out of the question. Yet it is also worth noting that the Ruhleben seafaring fraternity 'had long been accustomed to sailing on ships with coloured seamen and foreman', as Harold Redmayne, captain of barrack 13, later remembered. In general it seems that the merchant sailors were more accepting and less prejudiced than the other white prisoners towards their fellow black British subjects.[77]

Last, but not least, a largely hidden set of tensions existed over the issue of (homo-) sexual relations within the camp. In the dominant discourse of the day homosexuality was frowned upon as a perversion which could cripple morale and the 'fighting spirit' of the nation, as the trial and conviction of Oscar Wilde in the 1890s showed. On the rare occasion that its existence in

Ruhleben was admitted, it was used as a means of impressing on the British authorities the importance of making progress on exchange negotiations before more prisoners were drawn towards this 'unnatural vice', as one ex–internee put it.[78] Sexual relations between prisoners, like masturbation, were thus seen as harmful and self-destructive, a theory which continued at least until the 1960s in all accounts of Ruhleben although it was effectively discredited by the leading Berlin sexologist Magnus Hirschfeld and his team of researchers in their 1930 study of moral behaviour during the war.[79] Only in the 1970s, in some of the interviews conducted by Peter Liddle, is a more candid approach to the subject adopted. Thus the shipping clerk Norman Robson told Liddle in 1977

> After twelve months we had only [ships'] officers [in our barrack] but they used to bribe the guards to bring them Schnapps and they used to get themselves roaring drunk and there were a few deck boys about and we had to deal with the awkward thing about homosexuality.[80]

Likewise John Balfour recalled in 1976 that a 'great deal of homosexuality went on' in the camp, albeit mostly 'of a very transitory kind'. Given the absence of women it was 'inevitable', in his view.[81] The prevalence of real as opposed to imagined homosexual encounters remains an open question, however. As the actor George Merritt remembered, 'we were a crowded camp of 5,000 men with little space for proper physical intimacy'.[82] Certainly the prevailing wisdom among most historians and POW memoirists is that lack of privacy and fear of being stigmatised placed restrictions on open homosexuality, while the prisoners who played the female parts in theatrical productions provided more 'acceptable' (if at times highly ambiguous and subversive) objects of desire.[83] Or as Merritt himself put it:

> [T]he boys that were girls, they were wanted a bit you know. They played their courtesan role in the camp to a certain extent. They could get ... free wine and things like that, but I don't think there was anything excessive.[84]

Like most POWs, the Ruhlebenites also spent a lot of their time trying to discover ways of making contact with women outside the camp, especially the Russian and Polish girls who could occasionally be glimpsed marching past the camp on their way to work in the munitions factories in Spandau. Actual liaisons were very rare, however, and were strictly prohibited. Indeed, the only prisoners who seemed to have got close to Russian women

A RUHLEBEN EXCHANGE (OF PHOTOS)

HIS TO HER   HERS TO HIM

12   'A Ruhleben Exchange (of Photos)'

were those who were sent to the much harsher camp at Havelberg after failed escape attempts; here prostitution was said to be rife and the guards relatively easy to bribe.[85] Otherwise, images of women had to remain at the level of fantasy, which again explains the fascination of prisoners with public theatre and female role-playing.[86] Meanwhile, the real women at home in Britain or in Germany soon faded into an unreachable part of the past, to be longed for but not to be idolised in the same way as the prima donna-like female impersonators inside the camp. The whole experience of captivity indeed led to an 'acute sense of masculine disempowerment', as Alon Rachamimov puts it.[87] This was also hinted at in a cartoon published in the *Ruhleben Camp Magazine* in August 1916, in which a prisoner and his sweetheart exchange photographs. Here the prisoner wears a woman's wig and is dressed for a female role in the camp theatre, while his fiancée appears in the uniform of a tram conductor, complete with belt and breeches (Figure 12).[88]

Ruhleben as a community at war

Was Ruhleben, in spite of the tensions outlined above, a community in Benedict Anderson's sense of the term, namely a body of strangers *imagined* as a community?[89] Did its inmates feel and act as part of a broader whole, or were their perceptions of the war and of each other too fragmented to make talk of a common 'Ruhleben spirit' possible?

Christoph Jahr and Sebastian Tripp certainly have a point when they argue that the notions of national solidarity, patriotism and manifest British identity in the camp were cultural constructs created by the educated elite among the ex–internees.[90] Like all artificially created societies, Ruhleben needed legends of its own that could bind its members together in a positive, timeless framework. The communication of a collective sense of purpose based on 'stories' of primordial origins, continuity and tradition was one of the first tasks of journalism inside the camp, and makes the case of Ruhleben comparable with other discourses on nationhood to be found in the modern world.[91] Take, for instance, the following tale published in the second edition of the *Ruhleben Camp News*:

> Many years ago, when Ye Earthe was fyleed with savages and stryfe was in ye lande, there dwelte in a far-off countrie a tribe of men, barabarous and strange and whose custom and habits were yet stranger. They lived in cages behind an encircling wall and their dwellinge-place was called Ruhleben. No one knew whence they had come, for they had appeared from ye East and West, from ye North and ye South – and it was darkly whyspered that they had come from gloomy houses of correction –– which yon tribe in its strange jargon did call 'quodde'. Some said they were prisoners captured in war and stryfe – others, that they were hostages – and still others spoke up and declared them to be ye lost tribes of Israel... and yet still others came and said they were ye sons of Ham and unto this day ye stryfe hath not ceased and ye origin of yon tribe is still unexplayned.[92]

We should also bear in mind Jeffrey Verhey's assertion: 'Nations are less often created in a shared experience than in a shared memory, a shared narrative, a national myth.'[93] This might well apply to the 'Ruhleben spirit', just as it applies to the 'spirit of 1914' in Germany or, to take another example, the 'spirit of the Blitz' in Britain in 1940–41.[94] Nonetheless, my own reading of camp publications, artwork and photography, and my understanding of the concepts developed by the cultural historian Andrew

Horrall, lead me to conclude that there was a certain up-to-dateness or topicality about the cultural life in Ruhleben which gave it an inclusive, vibrant and at times subversive edge not apparent in any of the more staid and jingoistic post-war accounts. Or, to put it another way, the shared living traditions of the Ruhleben prisoners were very contemporary and their main points of reference were Edwardian politics, communal songs, popular entertainments and sport, and not the rabid nationalism and anti-Germanism of the immediate post-war era. Furthermore, these national/imperial reference points were intermixed with more immediate/personal concerns which were both unique to Ruhleben and its particular historical setting and

13 John Paton
(seated) and
friend, Ruhleben,
c. 1916

14 Front cover of *In Ruhleben Camp*, no. 8, September 1915

yet at the same time also draw our attention to the importance of the human and intimate element in the process of community formation more generally. At the micro level, at least, Ruhleben was a real community based on real interpersonal relationships, and not just a post-war construct.[95]

Three examples should suffice to illustrate this. The first of these is the decision of the Ruhleben Debating and Literary Society, one of the most prominent organisations in the camp, to debate controversial issues at its regular gatherings. Among the topics discussed in 1915, for instance, were divorce, universal manhood suffrage, capital punishment, corporal punishment in schools, the cinema, the press versus the pulpit, the degeneracy (or not) of modern English literature, social reform, and votes for women. According to *In Ruhleben Camp*, attendance at these events averaged 600 and at times reached 800. As a rule it was the 'progressive' side that tended to come out on top.[96] Another motion in March 1916, which suggested that 'the abolition of trade unions would *not* be to England's benefit', was carried with a huge majority when put to the vote, and it was generally agreed that the opposing side had failed to establish an effective case.[97]

The second example, from Chris Paton's website on Ruhleben, is a photograph of his great uncle John Paton with a friend, taken shortly after his arrival at the camp in 1916 from German-occupied Belgium (Figure 13). The pose adopted by both men is decidedly civilian in tone, and it is difficult, without knowing the context, to recognise that they are prisoners of war. The standing figure has his hands in his pockets, while the seated figure (John Paton) is reclining in his chair. There is not a hint of military bearing from either man, or of suffering or anguish. The rolled up sleeves and greenery in the background rather give the impression of relaxation on a summer's day. In part photographs such as these were sent home as postcards in order to reassure anxious relatives at home. Yet they also indicate a certain self-mockery and defiance in response to the January 1916 report filed by US ambassador Gerard, which complained that the Ruhleben prisoners were lazy and refused to perform fatigue duties in exchange for wages. Cartoons in the camp magazine also suggest that the deck chair was frequently used as a visual metaphor for the 'quiet life' which the internees were supposedly enjoying.[98]

The third example comes from the front cover of issue no. 8 of *In Ruhleben Camp*, which bears a curious design of a shield depicting various aspects of the life as an internee (Figure 14). Examined more closely, the shield itself is being held up by two prisoners, one black and one white, under the motto: 'Are we downhearted?' The answer, which was given as a form of greeting, was a resounding 'No!' – a final illustration of the intimate sense of community at Ruhleben, and a nod to the seafaring fraternity in particular.[99] The image presented here was once again a form of self-mockery, but not of anger, bitterness or despair. The latter came only towards the end of the war and during its immediate aftermath, as we will see in Chapters 5 and 6.

Notes

1   Geertz, 'Thick Description', p. 14.
2   Grew, diary entry for 1 January 1916, in Houghton Library, Grew papers, MS Am 1687, vol. 7.
3   The phrase comes from Paul Cohen-Portheim, *Time Stood Still. My Internment in England, 1914–1918* (London, 1931). On the importance of meaningful activity in combating the boredom and routine of captivity see also Pöppinghege, *Im Lager unbesiegt*, pp. 11 and ff.
4   On the role of constructed identities in the creation of nations and other fictive communities see Anderson, *Imagined Communities*, passim; Eric Hobsbawm and Terence Ranger (eds.), *The Invention of Tradition*, 2nd edn

(Cambridge, 1992); and Eric Hobsbawm, *Nations and Nationalism since 1780. Programme, Myth, Reality*, 2nd edn (Cambridge, 1992).

5 *Ruhleben Camp News*, no. 1, 9 January 1915. Copy in HLL-EC, box 9, file 1.

6 Ketchum, *Ruhleben*, p. 184.

7 It was replaced at the beginning of 1916 by *Prisoners' Pie* (one issue only) and from March 1916 by *The Ruhleben Camp Magazine* (henceforth RCM) and a smaller circulation journal, *La Vie française de Ruhleben*, produced by members of the French circle.

8 Timothy Eden, typescript recollections, no date, in Liddle Collection, RUH 18.

9 Andrew Horrall, *Popular Culture in London, c. 1890–1918. The Transformation of Entertainment* (Manchester, 2001), pp. 3 and ff.

10 IRC, no. 9, October 1915, p. 9.

11 Programme for *Cinderella*, Christmas Pantomime, 27 December 1915, in LA Berlin, Rep. 129, Acc. 1884, B6c. The reference here is to the latrines, not the town.

12 Horrall, *Popular Culture in London*, p. 4.

13 IRC, no. 8, September 1915, p. 23.

14 Ketchum, *Ruhleben*, p. 259.

15 Stockall, unpublished memoirs, p. 57.

16 W. E. Swale, 'Memories of Ruhleben Camp, Berlin, 1914–1918', unpublished typescript recollections (November 1977), p. 3. Copy in GCL, Ruhleben Collection, file 3.

17 The film itself does not seem to have survived, but short clips from it were used by the film company UFA for their film 'Aus alten Zeitungen' (n.d.), which can be found in the Bundesarchiv-Filmarchiv in Berlin (BSL/19077). The clip 'In Ruhleben bei den Internierten' lasts for 70 seconds only, and as well as the 'tallest man in Ruhleben', includes views of the racetrack and of women and children apparently arriving at the guardhouse to visit their husbands. Since these visits were not permitted until April 1916, this begs the question as to whether further films of the camp were made.

18 IRC, no. 7, 12 September 1915, p. 26.

19 The photographer came on Sunday mornings and charged 18 pfennigs for each picture, some of which went to the Berlin *Kommandantur* in commission – see Cohen, *The Ruhleben Prison Camp*, pp. 229–30. Prisoners were forbidden to have cameras of their own, for obvious reasons, but they were occasionally smuggled in and illegal pictures were taken, including one from inside the prison cells in barrack 11 – see Stockall, unpublished memoirs, p. 54.

20 Ketchum, *Ruhleben*, p. 72. Chapter 10 of Ketchum's book is titled 'The Explosion of Activity' – see *ibid.*, pp. 192–209.

21 On the use of POWs in German propaganda more generally see Uta Hinz, 'Die deutschen "Barbaren" sind doch die besseren Menschen. Kriegsgefangenschaft und gefangene "Feinde" in der Darstellung der deutschen Publistik, 1914–

1918', in Overmans (ed.), *In der Hand des Feindes*, pp. 339–61.

22 Käthe Schirmacher, 'Ruhleben', *Die Woche*, no. 37, 11 September 1915, p. 1313.

23 'Im Gefangenenlager Ruhleben', *Berliner Illustrierte Zeitung*, no. 47, 21 November 1915, p. 652.

24 The journalist and writer Inge Deutschkron observed a similar phenomenon among German refugees from Nazism in various parts of the world during and after the 1930s: 'Words from the new language are taken up and integrated into one's own language. For instance: "Ich gehe shopping." "Das Haus ist nearby"' – see Deutschkron, *Emigranto. Vom Überleben in fremden Sprachen* (Berlin, 2001), p. 33.

25 L. E. Filmore, 'The Seven Ages of a Kriegsgefangener', IRC, no. 1, 6 June 1915, p. 7.

26 Ketchum, *Ruhleben*, p. 98.

27 Horrall, *Popular Culture in London*, p. 191.

28 Cohen, *The Ruhleben Prison Camp*, p. 194.

29 *Ruhleben Camp News*, no. 3, 15 February 1915, p. 4. Copy in HLL-EC, box 9, file 3.

30 Ketchum, *Ruhleben*, pp. 67–8.

31 'Die Ruhleben Lorelei' (author unknown). Copy in HLL-EC, box 3, file 2. With special thanks to Matthew Jefferies for help with translation.

32 Ketchum, *Ruhleben*, pp. 283–4.

33 *Ibid.*, p. 259. See also the various programmes in LA Berlin, Rep. 129, Acc. 1884, B6c.

34 See the review of Cinderella in RCM, no. 1, March 1916, p. 8.

35 See e.g. K. M. Gwynn to Mr Bacon Phillips, 21 July 1915, in Imperial War Museum, London, Department of Documents (henceforth IWM), 99/3/1; and George Merritt, 'Ruhleben, 1914–1918', unpublished handwritten memoirs (1977), pp. 2–3, in Liddle Collection, RUH 34.

36 Stockall, unpublished memoirs, p. 64.

37 *The British Prisoner of War*, no. 2 (February 1918), p. 14.

38 Captain S. Gulston, diary entry for 12 November 1914, in IWM, 91/30/1.

39 Diary entry for 28 March 1915, in *ibid.*

40 Bury, *My Visit to Ruhleben*, pp. 49–50.

41 See e.g. the report in RCM, no. 4, August 1916, p. 3.

42 Cohen, *The Ruhleben Prison Camp*, p. 139.

43 *Daily Sketch*, 6 August 1915. Copy in HLL-EC, box 21.

44 Prussian Ministry of War, *Les prisonniers de guerre en Allemagne, accompagné d'une préface du Prof. Dr. Backhaus* (Siegen, 1915), pp. 20 and 84.

45 Programme of events for the final day, 24 May [1915], in HLL-EC, box 3, file 5.

46 Ketchum, *Ruhleben*, p. 177.

47 Jim English, 'Empire Day in Britain, 1904–1958', *The Historical Journal*, 49/1 (2006), p. 249.

48 IRC, no. 5, August 1915, p. 16.
49 *The Ruhleben Bye-Election* (Berlin, 1915).
50 *Ibid.*, pp. 13–17.
51 *Ibid.*, p. 18.
52 *Ibid.*, p. 30.
53 Cohen, *The Ruhleben Prison Camp*, p. 146.
54 Minutes of camp committee meeting, 28 March 1916, in HLL-EC, box 5, file 14. Cf. Ketchum, *Ruhleben*, p. 289.
55 IRC, no. 8, September 1915, p. 1.
56 IRC, no. 5, 15 August 1915, p. 1.
57 W. O'Sullivan Molony, *Prisoners and Captives* (London, 1933), p. 22.
58 See the material on religious services in HLL-EC, box 3, file 4.
59 Stockall, unpublished memoirs, p. 70.
60 Gerard, *My Four Years*, p. 125.
61 Thomas Cottrell-Dormer to his mother, 17 March 1915, in Liddle Collection, RUH 10.
62 Cottrell-Dormer to his mother, 24 September 1917, in *ibid.*
63 Merritt, 'Ruhleben, 1914–1918' (as n. 35), pp. 2–3.
64 Prussian Ministry of War to AA, 13 November 1917, in BA Berlin, R 901/84319. See also the Dutch diplomat Dr Römer's report on Havelberg camp, dated 16 August 1917, in *ibid.*
65 Stockall, unpublished memoirs, p. 74.
66 Vischer, *Barbed Wire Disease*, pp. 45 ff.
67 Edward V. Stibbe, *Reminiscences of a Civilian Prisoner in Germany, 1914–1918* (Castle Cary, 1969), p. 13. Ian McEwan, in his novel *Atonement*, also makes references to the famed domesticity of seamen even when forced to live on dry land (in this case in a hospital ward in London in the summer of 1940). See McEwan, *Atonement* (London, 2001), p. 287.
68 Cf. Tony Lane, *The Merchant Seamen's War* (Manchester, 1990), p. 211.
69 Francis Gribble, 'The Conditions at Ruhleben. A Memorandum for the Red Cross Society' n.d. [October 1915], p. 2. Copy in NA, FO 383/69.
70 See e.g. the material in NA, FO 383/68 and 383/69.
71 Cohen, *The Ruhleben Prison Camp*, p. 208.
72 *Ruhleben Exhibition 1919. Souvenir Album.* Published by the Central Prisoners of War Committee of the British Red Cross and the Order of St John of Jerusalem (London, 1919), p. 26.
73 Leon was a local celebrity in Jamaica and had food parcels sent to him directly by the island's governor, Sir William Manning. See *Daily Gleaner*, 6 March 1916, 19 June 1916, 17 and 18 January 1917 and 31 January 1919. I am grateful to Joy Lumsden for drawing my attention to this.
74 Stockall, unpublished memoirs, pp. 63–4. Leon is also mentioned in camp magazines – see e.g. IRC, no. 10, Xmas 1915, p. 40, and RCM, no. 6, June 1917, p. 1. Apart from being in the cast of *The Bells*, he was also its producer, according to the RCM.

75 The story told by the Irish prisoner O'Sullivan Molony about a violent battle between Arabs and Blacks in barrack 13, leading to serious injuries (including knife wounds) and one fatality, is not corroborated by any other source. See O'Sullivan Molony, *Prisoners and Captives*, pp. 111–17; and Ketchum, *Ruhleben*, p. 118.

76 Bury, *My Visit to Ruhleben*, p. 34.

77 Harold Redmayne, interview with Peter Liddle, October 1977, in Liddle Collection, RUH 44.

78 See Israel Cohen's comments in an interview with Lord Robert Cecil, 10 June 1916, in NA, FO 383/141. Cohen makes no mention of homosexuality in his published account of the camp.

79 See Magnus Hirschfeld (ed.), *Sittengeschichte des Weltkrieges*, 2 vols. (Leipzig and Vienna, 1930), vol. 2, pp. 95–6.

80 Norman Robson, interview with Peter Liddle, April 1977, in Liddle Collection, RUH 46.

81 John Balfour, interview with Peter Liddle, March 1976, in *ibid.*, RUH 02.

82 George Merritt, interview with Peter Liddle, July 1977, in *ibid.*, RUH 34.

83 See e.g. MacKenzie, *The Colditz Myth*, p. 213; Pöppinghege, *Im Lager unbesiegt*, p. 166.

84 George Merritt, interview with Peter Liddle, July 1977 (as n. 82 above).

85 On Havelberg see the archival material in BA Berlin, R 901/84319, including various critical reports published in Swiss newspapers. Also see Chapter 5 below.

86 On this theme see also Alon Rachamimov, 'The Disruptive Comforts of Drag: (Trans)Gender Performances among Prisoners of War in Russia, 1914–1920', *American Historical Review*, 111/2 (2006), pp. 362–82.

87 *Ibid*, p. 364. Cf. Pöppinghege, *Im Lager unbesiegt*, pp. 165–6, who in this respect describes the camps as 'entmannte Männergesellschaft[en]'.

88 RCM, no. 4, August 1916, p. 43.

89 Anderson, *Imagined Communities*, passim.

90 Jahr, 'Zivilisten als Kriegsgefangene', pp. 320–1; Tripp, 'Kommunikation und Vergemeinschaftung', p. 82.

91 Cf. Stuart Hall, 'National Cultures as "Imagined Communities"', in Stuart Hall, David Held and Tony McGrew (eds.), *Modernity and its Futures* (Cambridge, 1992), pp. 291–9.

92 'A Tale', in *Ruhleben Camp News*, no. 2, 27 January 1915. Copy in HLL-EC, box 9, file 2.

93 Verhey, *The Spirit of 1914*, p. 133.

94 Angus Calder, *The Myth of the Blitz* (London, 1991).

95 I have been influenced here by Richard Ivan Jobs and Patrick McDevitt's argument that we need to take greater account of 'lived experience' and the role of 'choice and agency' when considering the cultural processes by which communities are formed. See Jobs and McDevitt, 'Introduction: Where the Hell Are the People?', *Journal of Social History* (Winter 2005), pp. 309–14.

96 IRC, no. 1, 6 June 1915, pp. 12–13.

97 RCM, no. 1, March 1916, p. 22.

98 See e.g. RCM, no. 2, April 1916, p. 22.

99 Cf. Tripp, 'Kommunikation und Vergemeinschaftung', pp. 75–6; Jahr, 'Zivilisten als Kriegsgefangene', p. 304.

4

Relief, punishments and reprisals

In the first months of internment, according to John Masterman, 'everything [was] on a temporary basis for everyone expected that the exchange negotiations would be brought to a satisfactory conclusion. It was not a question of whether we should be exchanged, but only of when and on what conditions.'[1] Under such circumstances the issue of an organised relief programme for the Ruhleben prisoners, whether in cash or in kind, did not loom large in anybody's calculations. However, in the spring of 1915 the perception began to change. One factor was the complete breakdown of all negotiations over prisoner exchanges, so that the internees and their families had to adjust themselves to the prospect of a much longer stay in captivity and a much longer period of absence from home. A second factor, as we saw in Chapter 2, was the visit paid by American ambassador Gerard to Ruhleben on 3 March 1915, and his subsequent criticism of conditions prevailing there. A third factor was the rapid growth in the number of German (and Austrian) civilians held in internment camps in Britain from May 1915 onwards. Ironically one of the immediate effects of these developments was to make both governments more willing to reach an agreement on a system of camp inspections and on the delivery of relief parcels from home, including approved lists of contraband items. Additional pressure, where it was needed, also came from the International Committee of the Red Cross in Geneva and various other humanitarian groups.[2]

In general, this meant that from March 1915 the prisoners at Ruhleben were relatively well supplied with provisions of food, clothes, books, board games, sports equipment and other distractions which were collected by voluntary agencies at home and distributed via British Red Cross depots in Switzerland, Denmark and the Netherlands. The number of parcels received indeed rose from fewer than 4,000 in the month of December 1914 to in excess of 25,000 per month by the end of 1915, as the figures in Table 2 show:

Table 2 *Relief parcels received per month in Ruhleben,
November 1914–October 1915*

Month	No. of parcels received
November 1914	None
December 1914	Less than 4,000
January 1915	8,532
February 1915	10,370
March 1915	16,510
April 1915	19,368
May 1915	20,753
June 1915	26,969
July 1915	24,950
August 1915	20,470
September 1915	25,746
October 1915	27,557

Source: Harvard Law Library, Cambridge, MA, Ettinghausen
Collection, box 5, file 16

Nonetheless, the question of relief does not end here. Rather, it sheds light on a number of other developments which occurred during the war. The first is the issue of relations between the prisoners and the home front, and in particular their expectations regarding the response of the state to their material needs. Were the Ruhlebenites satisfied with their government's relief effort and grateful for the support they received? If not, what were the reasons for their grievances, and how did this fit in with their awareness of the much harsher conditions prevailing in other camps?

A second issue, which was already raised in Chapter 3, is the impact that relief had on the relations of the prisoners to each other, as revealed in their verbal and written reports on arriving back home. To what extent did the parcels coming from Britain lead to a two-tier system of material support for the Ruhleben prisoners, one for the rich and one for the less well off? And how far were prisoner expectations determined by issues of class (the 'haves' and the 'have nots'/the 'deserving' and 'undeserving' poor) or by issues of race and nationality ('real Britishers' as opposed to 'pro-Germans' and those from 'non-British' backgrounds).

A final theme is the importance of relief in shaping the relations between the prisoners and their German captors. The German government was of course not directly responsible for deciding on the quality and quantity of relief sent to the Ruhleben internees from home. Nonetheless, it could determine when, where and to whom it was delivered. For instance, individual prisoners who breached military regulations could be punished by having their relief parcels temporarily withdrawn or by being sent to other camps or prisons where access to relief parcels was much more restricted. Alternatively, a prisoner's loyalty towards his home state could be challenged through a combination of propaganda and promises of material rewards if he changed sides and agreed to fight or work for Germany. Finally, the German authorities could threaten retaliatory measures against the whole camp, such as blocking access to relief parcels, in reaction to the on-going British blockade. By the middle of 1916 there was indeed considerable political pressure inside Germany for the government to do just that. The reasons why, in the end, it shied away from direct retaliation against the Ruhleben internees, in contrast to its treatment of other prisoners, will also be discussed in greater detail below.

The British government's relief effort

When the war broke out in August 1914 the British government at first gave little thought to the welfare needs of British subjects stranded in Germany or German-occupied territory. Admittedly a sum of £5,000 was transferred from the British legation in The Hague to the American embassy in Berlin at the end of August, but this was intended for desperate cases only and was very much an afterthought.[3] As the weeks passed by the bulk of the relief effort was therefore left to a series of ad hoc initiatives undertaken by the German branch of the King Edward VII fund (also known as the Cassell fund) which had only limited monies at its disposal. Politically influential pressure groups such as the London-based Friends Emergency Committee and the Berlin-based *Auskunfts- und Hilfsstelle für Deutsche im Ausland und Ausländer in Deutschland* also emerged in the early weeks of the war. The latter was founded in October 1914 by a thirty-two-year-old Swiss woman, Elisabeth Rotten, with the assistance of Pastor Friedrich Siegmund-Schultze, a frequent visitor to Ruhleben in 1914–15.[4] Yet with the introduction of internment in November 1914 these charities were simply overwhelmed by the sheer number of new cases being brought to their attention. As the

American ambassador Gerard reported to his counterpart in London, Walter Hines Page, on 16 November:

> There are in Germany many spinsters of British nationality who have been here for years and have no home to which they could return in England. There are also many wives and widows of British subjects, of German or non-British origin, who have spent but a small part, if any, of their lives in England, and who refuse positively to leave, although told – in accordance with the wishes of the British Government – that relief cannot be granted to them indefinitely, and although they are at present without any other means of support. To these another class has been added consisting of the wives and children of men who have just [been] interned ... I have urged all such persons to leave as soon as possible, but many are unwilling to separate themselves from their husbands and many say they cannot travel on account of age or state of health or because of young children existing or anticipated. There are also old men and women who have no homes in England, and are dependant upon annuities and pensions. These cases present themselves in an infinite variety, and no two are exactly alike.[5]

In spite of this and similar reports, the attitude of the authorities in London appeared to harden rather than soften over time. The primary concern in relation to any relief programme was to avoid incurring heavy demands on the public purse, or at least this was the Treasury's position, which was backed by the Foreign Office. On top of this, there was a rather negative attitude towards the Ruhleben prisoners and their families in Whitehall circles. What were they doing in Germany anyway? Weren't most of them Germans or at least suspect as half-Germans? Reports from British diplomats in the Netherlands, who were responsible for aiding British nationals seeking repatriation from Germany, tended to confirm this impression. Thus Ernest Maxse, the British consul-general in Rotterdam, wrote to Sir Edward Grey on 4 November 1914:

> I have had occasion to remark that many British subjects, who have resided for some time in Germany, have lost all patriotic instinct. I have reported on this subject in previous dispatches dealing with the reception of British refugees in this country. I have even had a British-born woman of the educated classes in my room at this office, who told me that she sincerely hoped that Germany would win and the

British would be beaten ... I am happy to say that their number has not been great, but they have been exceedingly virulent.[6]

And in a further letter on 19 November he was even more explicit in his views:

[I]t would appear that British subjects still in Germany have been so affected by their surroundings as in many cases to become as German in their feelings as the Germans themselves. An instance came to my knowledge the other day in which an English woman on her return from Germany said that she prayed each night that Germany might win. I could quote several other instances of a similar sort.[7]

Even when the government finally gave in to the request of ambassador Gerard and agreed to establish an emergency relief fund, stringent controls were placed on who was entitled to draw from it. The money came as a loan and had to be signed for along with an agreement to pay it back at the end of the war. Furthermore, every effort was made to avoid providing financial support to persons of non-British origin, and instead a letter was drawn up at the end of 1914 instructing Gerard that payments were to be made only

(1) to persons who are compelled to remain in Germany owing to action of the German government
(2) Persons whose state of health prevents them from leaving
(3) Women whose husbands (or nearest male relative) are interned but who are able to live near them.[8]

In a letter of 8 January 1915 the regulations were further tightened so that only British-born women were entitled to draw on the relief fund, not German-born women.[9] Occasionally exceptions were made in individual cases, but in general British subjects living at liberty in Germany were expected to return home and were told that financial support from the British state would cease if they chose to remain in enemy territory. British subjects in Ruhleben, meanwhile, were entitled to draw five marks a week from the fund, again on the condition that they paid it back at the end of the war. Only those who were without other means – over half the camp in 1915 – were entitled to make a claim through their barrack captain, who in turn received the money via a sub-committee of the finance committee.[10] Pro-Germans – those who came forward as *deutschgesinnt* – were not entitled to payments at all, although there were some grey areas here. For instance, a *deutschfreundlich* prisoner who refused German offers of naturalisation might still have a claim on the relief fund, especially if he had relatives serving in the British armed forces, and appeals were often made on these grounds to the American ambassador.[11]

Alongside relief money came relief in kind. However, as far as parcels were concerned, families and private charities made all the running in the first two years of the war, and there were few checks and balances at government level. Thus Jewish prisoners got parcels from the Jewish Board of Guardians in London, and fishermen from a specialist committee in Grimsby. The people of Lancashire and Cheshire had their own locally based appeal which sent occasional gifts to Ruhleben, as did the readers of the *Cardiff Evening Express*, and so on. Meanwhile the Canadians received their parcels from the Canadian Red Cross, and the merchant sailors were supplied by the Mercantile Marine Service Association in Liverpool. All of these organisations had their own rules and regulations, and there was little, if any, contact between them.[12]

In 1916, however, the British government began to change its whole attitude towards prisoner relief, on both the domestic and international levels. In part this was motivated by Red Cross and other reports suggesting that voluntary effort alone was not sufficient to meet demand, but it also reflected a broader shift in relations between the state and private charity, with laissez-faire policies gradually giving way to greater emphasis on centralised control and public accountability. Interests of efficiency and 'fairness' went hand in hand here with redefining the nature of the rights and obligations of the 'loyal' British citizen as opposed to the refugee and humanitarian subject. As Rebecca Gill has written in relation to Belgian refugees in wartime Britain, the citizen was increasingly defined as somebody with a 'right to welfare' and an obligation to serve his/her country, whereas the humanitarian subject was somebody who carried the 'stigma of destitution' by dint of being a 'recipient of humanitarian aid'. The former had some degree of power to 'negotiate their rights' in return for their wartime service, while the latter were increasingly 'excluded from citizenship entitlements' and thus left at the mercy of the arbitrary decisions of private relief organisations.[13]

How were the Ruhleben prisoners to be classified under these new criteria? Clearly there was one view that suggested that they had not fulfilled their obligations to Britain by allowing themselves to be captured in enemy territory. As we have seen, there were doubts about the loyalty of some of the prisoners, and a handful were refused British passports even after being released from Ruhleben.[14] On the other hand, there was an equally strongly held view that the Ruhleben prisoners were performing a kind of military service since their continued detention in Germany allowed the British government to hold on to the 26,000 or so Germans it had imprisoned. By refusing to enter into an exchange agreement with the Germans, in other words, the British state may have incurred a new set of national obligations towards the Ruhleben prisoners and their families, transforming them once again into citizens with rights and entitlements.

Both of these views can indeed be found in the government records and in the records of interviews with released prisoners in the first half of 1916. Four points in particular emerge here. Firstly, relief monies paid to prisoners were allegedly being abused by being spent on drink and gambling.[15] Secondly, some voluntary charities in Britain were supposedly misusing their funds by sending parcels to pro-German prisoners.[16] Thirdly, loyal British citizens – in this case, Jewish prisoners at Ruhleben – were sometimes being denied access to relief in kind (i.e. goods from excess parcels) on the false grounds that they were pro-German.[17] And finally some prisoners – up to 250 – were receiving no parcels at all.[18] All four issues could be dealt with, it was argued, only through a more organised and centralised system of relief. Or, as released prisoner Israel Cohen put it in a memorandum for the Foreign Office at the end of June 1916:

> The present chaotic system of sending free parcels ought to be stopped as soon as possible, and replaced by a regular system of coordination and centralisation. At present many men receive more than they need; others receive not enough or even nothing. The evil could be done away with if a Central Forwarding Depot could be created in London, to which all local organisations, relief societies and private donors should send their gifts intended for Ruhleben; and the managers of the Central Depot should see to it that each prisoner received at least one parcel per week. It would be a further simplification if the local societies and private donors send gifts only of money to the Central Depot, which would then act as the sole purchasing centre for Ruhleben and organise their despatch upon a systematic basis.[19]

Dr Alonzo Taylor of the American embassy had also recommended a more centralised system in his report on conditions at Ruhleben in May 1916 so that 'all the interned men would receive an equal share' and to ensure 'there world be no waste' through duplication.[20] However, Sir Edward Grey, in a letter to Gerard on 20 May 1916, expressed his regret that 'the circumstances will not permit the adoption in practice of the recommendations made by

Dr Taylor', i.e. the voluntary principle still held.[21] This meant, according to Taylor, that 'disregarding the supplies sent from Great Britain by the families and friends of the individual prisoners, the supplies sent from Great Britain are furnished by trade-unions, lodges, Red Cross societies, relief organisations, social service societies, and by charitable individuals who have banded themselves into groups for this purpose'. Duplication and waste were the inevitable result, especially as 'several of these bodies send their supplies to any prisoner who will send in his name'.[22]

Towards the end of 1916, however, the government gave way and agreed to a partial abandonment of the voluntary principle. The result was the formation of the Central Prisoners of War Committee of the British Red Cross Society and the Order of St John of Jerusalem, which was commissioned by the War Office to act as the sole clearing house for all charitable relief parcels, thus providing a kind of 'screen' for increased state intervention.[23] From the outset, one of the remits of this body was to treat civilian POWs on a par with military POWs. Private and state funds were thus raised 'to provide for civilian prisoners, to supply the general needs of the camps and prison hospitals, such as games, medical comforts etc. and to … meet the demands from the regimental care committees'. It was also resolved 'to supply materials and personnel to enable such prisoners to receive useful training in view of employment after the war'.[24]

If civilian internees were to be given the same status as military prisoners in respect of relief, one group connected with Ruhleben was still not afforded full equality, namely the wives and children of the internees. Those opting to remain in Germany were generally shunned by the official wartime German charities even if they were German by birth and British only by marriage. As 'enemy aliens' they also found it almost impossible to secure employment. Some might literally have faced starvation had it not been for the support provided by the German branch of the King Edward VII fund and by Elisabeth Rotten's Berlin-based relief committee, as the American diplomat Ellis Loring Dresel later reported.[25] Others got by through smuggling gifts out of Ruhleben after permission was granted to the wives and children of internees to visit the camp for two hours each month in April 1916. As Ellen Prendergast, whose father was in Ruhleben, later recalled, it was common practice for visitors (including her German-born mother) to sew big pockets into their petticoats which could hold tins of food and other things. Even so, 'it was very hard to walk out of the camp with the eyes of the guards on you, things were very heavy under their dresses'.[26] Occasionally it was possible for Elisabeth Rotten's committee to find jobs for British women prepared to act as translators or language teachers, but in general – as the food-smuggling stories show – material conditions were a lot worse for enemy nationals living outside the internment camps than for those incarcerated in them.[27]

In Britain, on the other hand, the wives and other dependants of Ruhleben internees could claim welfare payments from a special fund administered by their local poor law guardians.[28] Others were more fortunate in that their husband's employer supplied an income in lieu of lost wages. But in no sense were they entitled to the separation allowances paid to the wives of servicemen and military POWs, a fact which underlined their inferior status as humanitarian subjects commanding pity rather than respect. The same applied to destitute men released from Ruhleben and repatriated to Britain before the end of the war. If they had no other means, and were too ill to work as a result of their experiences, they too had to face the poor law guardians and, in the worst case scenario, the workhouse or lunatic asylum.[29] By contrast combatant prisoners of war and members of the mercantile marine who became physically or mentally impaired while in captivity were dealt with by the Ministry of Pensions on the same basis as members of the armed forces who suffered permanent injuries while on active service.[30] This admittedly was an issue which incited a great deal of anger after the end of the war, but it barely raised an eyebrow during the war itself. However, one group of Ruhleben prisoners did write a draft letter to the Foreign Office at the end of 1917 expressing their concern:

> We ... respectfully beg His Majesty's Government for an assurance that disabled men and their families, as well as families and dependants of the deceased and of those who, because of their internment, cannot adequately provide for them, shall not be ... left to their fate and that immediate steps be taken to avert the breaking up of their homes, to provide their children with adequate education and to prevent such families from becoming a burden to charitable organisations or rate payers or to relatives who may be unable to make adequate provision for them.[31]

Whether this letter was ever sent is unclear; certainly it was not acted upon.

Relief: the prisoners' perspective

Nearly all accounts of Ruhleben written by former internees agree that things would have been a lot worse without relief parcels from home. However, this did not mean that grievances did not surface now and again, and more often than not these were directed against the government and the Treasury rather than against voluntary bodies. One complaint, for instance, related to the activities of the government-appointed finance committee in Ruhleben and its decision to lower the amount of relief paid to needy prisoners from 5 to 4 marks a week in March 1916. The official reason given for this was the shortage of canteen stocks, which meant that too much surplus money was circulating in the camp, but this explanation was not accepted by the majority of prisoners. A petition sent to the Foreign Office claimed that 'the finance committee itself had no clear grounds for the reduction and only attempted to prepare the same when challenged by the [prisoners'] delegates'. It also demanded that a prisoner in receipt of relief should be co-opted onto the finance committee's relief sub-committee, a demand that was turned down.[32]

Another grievance was over the government's insistence that relief money should be paid back at the end of the war. This was considered unfair because combatant prisoners of war continued to receive full service pay, as did members of the mercantile marine incarcerated at Ruhleben.[33] Both sets of prisoners thus had substantial sums of money waiting for them when they got home; but 'ordinary' civilian prisoners whose careers and livelihoods had been disrupted whilst in internment did not – with the exception of the very rich or those lucky enough to receive allowances from their employers. As one group of repatriated internees put it in a letter to the Central Prisoners of War Committee in January 1919:

> During our four years' internment in Ruhleben the small savings we had accumulated have been used up, and in addition our people at home have had to lay down a not inconsiderable sum of money to send us parcels of food and clothing … On our return we have to start work again very seriously handicapped. Four years' absence from our profession or employment is a serious detriment to all, especially to those of us who were newly embarked in a career. We have no status in the government's scheme for assisting men whose career has been similarly broken.[34]

Thirdly, many of the prisoners expressed anger at the way they were portrayed by Bishop Herbert Bury, the British government's official envoy who was given permission to visit the camp in November 1916. Bury's visit itself went down well enough, but it was his subsequent descriptions of the camp in the press and in book form that caused offence, mainly because he under-played the psychological and material deprivation experienced by the prisoners and did not openly support their demand for immediate government action to secure their release. In one passage he wrote that 'smoky Spandau ... reminds one of some town in our own Black Country' and described the racecourse as 'very spacious'.[35] In another he acknowledged that he may have taken 'too rosy a view ... but I am, let me repeat it again, putting down here the things that I saw, and it will be far better for those who are related to the men to think of them as they are now than to brood over what they have heard ... in the past'.[36] Later he sent a letter defending his stance to camp captain Joseph Powell:

> I am also told that some of the men are complaining in their letters home that after expressing so much sympathy with you all, I have apparently done nothing ... I wish the camp to know once more that I have done everything I could on their behalf, and have pleaded the cause both of partial and complete repatriation in the highest quarters and in every way I could, but I am sure they will all understand that a loyal subject has to yield to the express directions of the authorities in this country.[37]

Whether this did much to mollify opinion among the prisoners is doubtful. Later that month a 'Ruhlimerick' appeared in the camp magazine which expressed in humorous terms something of the alienation and disappointment they felt:

> I could really be very sarcastic,
> If I spoke of an ecclesiastic
> Whose tales when in here
> Were undoubtedly queer,
> But when he got home were fantastic.[38]

Finally, there was also a constant grievance among the 'British' prisoners that 'undeserving' elements were getting their hands on relief parcels, particularly those who were 'pro-German'. One senior Foreign Office official agreed to write to Lady Cavendish-Bentinck in July 1916 after receiving such a complaint with regard to the parcels her organisation sent.[39] Other grievances centred around being sent too much of one thing and not enough of the other, and about periodic delays in delivery. In theory the new centralised system which came into force in December 1916 should have avoided some of these inefficiencies, but this was not how the prisoners saw it. The *Ruhleben Camp Magazine* thus listed a series of ongoing problems in its June 1917 edition and described the system as being 'in chaos'. As particular causes for concern it mentioned, among other things, the inadequate clothing allowance; the constant change in regulations; the tendency of the committee to send parcels to prisoners who had declared themselves 'pro-German' or who had been released; and the anomalous position of some of the sailors who continued to receive parcels from the Mercantile Marine Service Association as well as from the new centralised body. Finally, the magazine asserted the right of the prisoners not to receive 'charity' from the government or private bodies, but to cater for themselves through parcels sent by their families:

> While agreeing that a scheme for the regulation of parcels which are not paid for by the recipients or their relatives is necessary, we protest against the undue interference with the supply of parcels to those prisoners who are self-supporting. For more than two years many of us have provided for our own wants at our own cost. We are not and do not wish to be under any obligation to charity, whether public or private, nor have we ever as individuals been a cause of embarrassment to our government.[40]

In the end, then, relief to and from Ruhleben tended to divide the prisoners more than it united them, while providing an uncomfortable reminder that they owed more to the people at home than they were able to give in return. This was also an issue that dogged their attempts to come to terms with the experience of internment after the war had ended, as we will see in Chapter 6.

Punishments and rewards

Apart from drawing up lists of contraband and opening up every item that entered the camp, the German military authorities had no control over the content of relief parcels or the number delivered. But they could exercise power in other ways. Thus the standard punishment for minor infractions of camp rules, such as drunkenness or smoking in the lofts, was three days' confinement in the camp cells in barrack 11 on a diet of black bread and water and without access to relief parcels.[41] More serious offences, such as smuggling contraband or making 'remarks offensive to the authorities', usually meant a spell in the *Stadtvogtei*, the main criminal prison in Berlin, with the average sentence ranging from five days to four months.[42]

Significantly, there were no cases of Ruhleben prisoners being tied to poles for hours on end, as happened in other POW camps and as was permitted under German military law.[43] However, those caught escaping could count on indefinite imprisonment under conditions of solitary confinement, or later in the war deportation to Havelberg camp, some 40 miles north west of Berlin. In both instances conditions were much worse than in Ruhleben and access to relief parcels was restricted or even denied altogether. As one prisoner wrote in a letter smuggled into Ruhleben from the *Stadtvogtei* in October 1916:

> There are a number of fellows here, even among the Britishers to say nothing of the Belgians, French and crowds of Poles who are absolutely dependant on the prison food to keep body and soul together; we do what we can in our own small way to help, but of course our supplies are inadequate, and when I think of the crowds of old biscuits, even biscuit crumbs, to say nothing of the cocoa and milk and one thing and another, that are going begging at Ruhleben, and which would just delight some of the poor fellows here, it seems to me that something could be done.[44]

On several occasions during 1915 and 1916 the British government protested against the 'excessive severity' of the punishments meted out to would-be escapers, emphasising that British military regulations allowed for a maximum of four months in jail only, after which the prisoner would be returned to a normal POW camp.[45] But in fact, there was nothing in international law that limited punishments for attempted escapes and insubordination, and German policy seemed to waver between extremely harsh treatment of 'other rank' prisoners who escaped to quite lenient treatment of officer prisoners in the same situation, provided they were not 'repeat offenders'.[46] Civilian internees seemed to fall somewhere between the two and it was only with considerable difficulty that the American ambassador succeeded in getting British escapees returned to Ruhleben. Wallace Ellison, for instance, spent nearly two years in the *Stadtvogtei* without any contact with the outside world before he was finally sent back to 'normal' prison camp conditions.[47]

As well as punishments, certain privileges were granted to select groups of prisoners, although usually this was not so much to reward good behaviour as for purposes of propaganda. In April 1915, for instance, seventeen Hamburg bankers of British nationality were temporarily released from Ruhleben, an act apparently motivated by the desire to ensure that German nationals in London continued to be able to work on the stock exchange.[48] However, this decision caused a certain amount of controversy in Hamburg, and was reversed within a matter of weeks following reports that both non-naturalised and naturalised German bankers had been interned across the channel in the wake of the Lusitania riots.[49] Even more contentious was the release of several British trainers and jockeys from the royal racecourse at Hoppegarten, which allegedly took place because no Germans had been found to replace them. As far as is known, they were not returned to Ruhleben.[50]

Meanwhile, some effort was also put into persuading pro-German internees to secure their freedom by accepting naturalisation and volunteering for military service. As part of this process the English-language German newspaper *The Continental Times* was put on sale in the camp, as were Berlin papers like the *Berliner Lokal-Anzeiger* and the *Vossische Zeitung*. The records reveal, however, that only around 200 of the 700 or so *deutschgesinnt* prisoners had signalled their willingness to enlist in the German army by April 1916, the majority apparently preferring to remain in Ruhleben.[51] The criteria were also surprisingly strict. Thus, according to instructions drawn up by General von Kessel, 'a declaration of intent to enlist in the army is not sufficient grounds for release. The prisoner concerned must first get hold of a certificate of acceptance from a particular regiment ... A mere application for naturalisation is not enough.'[52]

The continued presence of so many Germans in Ruhleben indeed became a source of substantial and on-going embarrassment to the German government. As early as November 1914 the women's leader Gertrud Bäumer, in her capacity as president of the *Nationaler Frauendienst*, had made representations to the Reich Office of Interior on behalf of the German-born wives of Ruhleben internees, suggesting that they be allowed to claim relief from state funds.[53] In March 1915, at a meeting of the Reichstag Main Committee, the deputies Ernst Müller-Meiningen (Progressive), Constantin Fehrenbach (Centre Party) and Franz Behrens (Christian Social) asked why it was 'that persons of German origin, who have acquired English nationality for business reasons only, are still being held at Ruhleben'.[54] Similar complaints were made by the SPD deputies Wolfgang Heine and Oskar Cohn in January and June 1916 on the floor of the Reichstag, the former referring to the government's internment policy as counter-productive and 'completely pointless' [*vollkommen sinnlos*] and the latter suggesting that many of the Ruhleben prisoners were being held – at considerable expense to the government – only because their applications for naturalisation had been turned down under the harsh and restrictive Reich citizenship law of 1913.

The real victims, Cohn continued, were the internees' families who were 'being exposed ... to the most terrible misery and hunger'.[55]

These protests indeed led to some action on the part of the military authorities who decided to make it easier for *deutschgesinnt* prisoners to secure their release without first having to complete all the formalities necessary for naturalisation. Thus an order issued by von Kessel on 1 January 1916 allowed the following categories of prisoner to be freed on parole, provided there was no doubting their loyalty to Germany:

(1) Those who have voluntarily reported for military service but have been found to be medically unfit.
(2) Those whose applications for naturalisation have been rejected.
(3) Those who have not submitted an application for naturalisation, but are over forty-five years of age.[56]

This was followed by a further order in July 1916 allowing for the release of some categories of pro-German prisoners even if they refused to apply for naturalisation. Now they could be granted parole 'if this is necessary to ensure that their pro-German families are fed, or if, through their work, they make a useful contribution [to the German war economy]'.[57] Even so, roughly 500 pro-German prisoners remained in Ruhleben at the end of 1916 and only 206 had taken advantage of these new release schemes, according to a Ministry of War statement in the Reichstag on 2 November.[58]

The final case related to attempts by the German government and Sir Roger Casement to recruit Irish prisoners for a military brigade to be used against Britain and its allies. Casement's own story has been told elsewhere and does not require detailed rehearsal here. In brief only fifty-six Irish POWs were won over to the republican cause and of them only one, Daniel Bailey, was sent to Ireland in April 1916 with Casement and Robert Monteith to take part in the failed Easter uprising. All three men were arrested soon after they came ashore.[59] What is significant, however, is that Casement is now known to have visited Ruhleben in early 1915, and to have intervened on behalf of three Irish internees, John Bradshaw from County Antrim, William Coyne from County Mayo and Thomas Hoy from County Tyrone. They were subsequently released from the camp and allowed to return home on the understanding that they were 'friends of Germany ... and will be useful in Ireland'.[60] Other prisoners in Ruhleben whom Casement spoke to, including the Scots-born journalist Robert Smyllie, later famous as the editor of the *Irish Times*, turned him down.[61] So too did William O'Sullivan Molony, an Irish Catholic from County Clare, who wrote, 'had he [Casement] never enjoyed the advantages of his previous status, one might have loved him more, but in the circumstances, seeing him, as we did, with an immaculate adjutant of the Death's Head Hussars at his heels, it was all one could do, even as an Irishman, to conceal one's distrust of such means of action as he advocated'.[62]

In the end only a limited number of prisoners were afforded automatic release without having expectations placed on them, namely those who were certified as permanently unfit for military service by a German doctor. Under an agreement brokered by Vatican mediators on behalf of Pope Benedict XV they became eligible for repatriation from August 1915; some 394 Ruhlebenites and 776 German civilians had benefited from this scheme by the end of June 1916.[63] More intriguing were the behind-the-scenes deals in 1915–16 which involved several captured German consular officials or retired army officers being exchanged for 'prominent' Ruhleben prisoners on an individual, 'man-for-man' basis. The numbers involved were small, eleven on each side, but the fact that such deals could take place at all is a telling indication that power and privilege still counted for something in the world of international diplomacy.[64] Significantly, the beneficiaries on the British side included Timothy Eden, the twenty-three-year-old elder brother of the future Prime Minister Anthony Eden, who was exchanged in July 1916 although he was neither in government service nor medically incapacitated. Instead, his name had been put on the list by the Foreign Office minister Lord Robert Cecil, as a special favour to his mother, Lady Eden, who had suffered a series of bereavements in the first half of the war.[65] Efforts to free three further 'prominents', John Balfour, Stanley Lambert and Joseph Weston foundered, apparently due to opposition from the Prussian Ministry of War.[66]

Those turned down for early release on health or other grounds undoubtedly felt the odd twinge of jealously, but surprisingly there was no evidence of overt resentment until after the war.[67] Even so, when Lord Newton became controller of the government's new prisoner of war department in October 1916 he was determined to prevent ministers of the crown from arranging individual deals for prominent prisoners, and persuaded the war cabinet to order an immediate halt to this practice except in cases where release was 'urged … on the ground of public service'. At least as far as Ruhleben was concerned, Eden's was to be the last exchange of the old-fashioned, aristocratic kind.[68]

Reprisals

While punishments and rewards could be handed out to individuals or small groups of prisoners, a different phenomenon altogether was that of reprisals. These were not penalties inflicted for acts of misconduct by prisoners, but rather retaliatory measures carried out in response to real or supposed misdeeds committed by enemy governments. As the French scholar Marc Michel explains: 'In terms of international law, reprisals are not "punishments", but "acts committed under duress [*actes de contraintes*]... legitimised in the sense that they are employed by a state in order to put a stop to illicit acts committed against it by another state or by one of its nationals".'[69] According to the German general staff's own pre-war publications on the subject, *Kriegsnotwendigkeit* or 'military necessity' could also be invoked as justification in the face of any humanitarian or legalistic objections.[70] In the worst cases, reprisals came in the form of use of prisoners as human shields or forced labour in combat zones; less serious instances involved incarceration in punishment or labour camps far from home, or withholding treasured items like tobacco, coffee or relief parcels. Officers granted 'honour walks' (i.e. set times during the week when they could go for walks outside their camp on word of honour not to escape) might also have this privilege suddenly withdrawn at a moment's notice.[71] Even in these milder cases the psychological impact on prisoners could be 'devastating', as Stéphane Audoin-Rouzeau and Annette Becker note.[72]

During the First World War reprisals were often imposed by Germany on French and Russian prisoners, less frequently on British ones, and very rarely on the Ruhlebenites. In one sense, of course, internment itself was a form of reprisal – which failed to prevent the mass round up of German and Austrian civilians in Britain in May 1915. But after this reports from British camps tended to be more favourable,[73] and there were certainly no parallels with the vicious cycle of reprisal and counter-reprisal that took place between France and Germany after 1915.[74] Furthermore, the minutes of inter-departmental meetings between representatives of the Reich Office of Interior, the Foreign Office, the Prussian Ministry of War, the supreme commander in the marches and other departments in 1915 reveal how concerned all parties were, for pragmatic reasons, to act strictly in accordance with the principle of reciprocity, a phenomenon we already encountered in Chapter 1. It was this consideration, for instance, which led to the initial decision to exempt the *Kolonialengländer* from internment, and to release the Hamburg bankers on a temporary basis in April 1915.[75]

However, things began to change again in 1916 when domestic pressure grew for some form of retaliation against Britain in response to the increasingly effective naval blockade of Germany. In March 1916, for instance, the Jena branch of the Pan-German League presented a petition to the Bundesrat demanding that all enemy aliens, regardless of age and gender, be interned in 'concentration and prison camps' [*Konzentrations- und Gefangenenlagern*] where they should be forced to exist on German civilian rations only.[76] The controversy over the American embassy reports on the diet at Ruhleben mentioned in Chapter 2, together with an article published in the National Liberal *Kölnische Zeitung* in June 1916 advocating the withdrawal of the right of British POWs to receive food parcels from Red Cross sources, further added to the poisonous atmosphere.[77] For a while it seemed that the right wing might be in the ascendancy, particularly after figures like Wolfgang Kapp and 'Junius Alter' (i.e. Franz Sontag, editor of the *Alldeutsche Blätter*) emerged to criticise the Chancellor's supposedly timid policy towards the prosecution of the war against Britain in a series of anonymous pamphlets.[78] In one particularly shocking case a private petitioner even suggested that the Foreign Office might threaten prisoners of war with death through starvation as a means of compelling the enemy to surrender.[79] But in the end the government resisted such pressure and decided against a policy of reprisals in relation to the Ruhleben prisoners. Why was this the case? In effect, it is possible to identify four key factors.

Firstly, there were obvious concerns that the British government would retaliate by refusing to allow parcels to be sent to German prisoners in Britain. Indeed, in terms of sheer numbers Britain held all the trump cards: 26,000 Germans versus 4,000 British civilian prisoners in Germany. (By contrast, as Bernard Delpal points out, Germany held far more French civilians in occupied territory and on the home front than France did German civilians.)[80] Any worsening of the conditions for the 26,000 German civilian POWs in Britain could have a serious impact on morale in Germany, especially in Hamburg, where many of them came from. The Hamburg senate was already in receipt of a number of petitions from concerned families who were anxious to get their loved ones back home as soon as possible.[81] In September 1916 one of their spokesman, Max T. Hayn, also petitioned the Foreign Office in Berlin:

> My son, who has been held as a civilian prisoner at Wakefield
> Camp in England for over two years, and who is in as good a
> physical condition as the circumstances allow, nonetheless writes
> with increasing urgency that life in the camp is making the prisoners
> extraordinarily depressed and that they are gradually going mad, in

spite of the many distractions, such as sports or theatrical and musical events, or [academic] lectures, on offer.[82]

Secondly, the Ruhleben prisoners had a number of prominent supporters in Germany, including not only the SPD/USPD Reichstag deputies Wolfgang Heine and Oskar Cohn, but also influential left-liberals who were concerned that civilian internment was damaging Germany's image abroad and/or harming prospects of reconciliation with Britain after the war. Thus Theodor Wolff, the editor of the *Berliner Tageblatt*, called in private for the release of the Ruhleben prisoners as early as July 1915,[83] while several other leading figures from the world of business and politics provided funds for the King Edward VII fund and Elisabeth Rotten's Berlin committee, most notably Bernhard Dernburg, Walther Rathenau, Hugo Simon, Oskar Tietz and Max Warburg. Any attempt to inflict reprisals on the Ruhleben prisoners would almost certainly have been opposed by this influential group, thus further threatening the Chancellor's already very fragile *Burgfrieden* strategy.[84]

Thirdly, in a more limited way, the German government was also influenced by the views of the Vatican, which had already taken a great interest in the fate of civilian prisoners of war and continued to do so.[85] Thus, as we have seen, in August 1915 the Holy See had already arranged a deal between Britain and Germany on the exchange of civilian internees who were permanently unfit for military service. In July 1916 Benedict XV urged Bethmann Hollweg, via the archbishop of Cologne, Felix von Hartmann, to negotiate a more comprehensive settlement with the UK allowing for the release of all civilian prisoners.[86] This was followed by a significant intervention in the Budget Committee of the Reichstag from the Catholic Centre Party, which tabled a new motion on 10 October 1916:

> The Reich Chancellor [is] requested to bring about, through the good offices of the Holy See, an arrangement between the powers at war to take immediate effect, by which 1) The position of prisoners of war shall be considerably improved 2) Reprisals of all kinds shall be abolished 3) All civil prisoners without distinction of age shall be sent back to their own country, on the explicit promise of the respective states that those persons liberated shall not be enrolled in the armed forces.[87]

The Social Democrats agreed to support the motion provided that the words 'or of another neutral power' were inserted after 'Holy See' and provided that it was made clear that those released from civilian internment would be returned to their own country only 'if they so desire'. The motion and the two amendments were accepted and approved by a majority vote on 13 October 1916, thus predating the Reichstag peace resolution of July 1917 by nine months and opening a new era in relations between parliament and government.[88]

Finally, the records indicate that senior figures in the German military, although unlikely to look sympathetically on the views of the Vatican, the ICRC or the Reichstag, were also opposed to the use of reprisals against the Ruhleben prisoners. The director of the *Unterkunftsdepartement* in the Prussian Ministry of War, Colonel (later General) Emil Friedrich, was particularly anxious to play by the rules, for both pragmatic and humanitarian reasons, as British and American officials acknowledged.[89] He was also aware, as were his superiors in the Ministry of War, that Ruhleben's proximity to Berlin made it a special case. Unlike the detention and forced labour camps for French and Belgian civilians in occupied territory, for instance, conditions at Ruhleben could not be hidden from public view.[90] In addition to these situational factors there were also cultural ones. In particular the Ruhleben prisoners did not suffer from the 'franc-tireur' complex that coloured German attitudes towards French and Belgian civilians in the opening stages of the war.[91] Nor, after 1914, were they accused of collective acts of resistance or sabotage on the home front.[92] In German propaganda it was the British government, but not British civilians as individuals, who were held responsible for alleged breaches of the customs of war, particularly as regards their treatment of German nationals.[93] The preferred solution was therefore to end internment and dissolve the camp at Ruhleben, if only a suitable bargain, acceptable to public opinion in Germany, could be made with Britain. The British war office and admiralty refused every offer of an 'all-for-all' exchange, however, instead insisting on a 'man-for-man' exchange which to the Prussian Ministry of War was entirely out of the question.[94]

In August 1916 Friedrich nonetheless signalled to the German Foreign Office that his superiors were willing to make further concessions to bring about the dissolution of Ruhleben. Two offers were now to be made to Britain, either a universal exchange of internees, whereby both sides agreed not to recruit released prisoners into their respective armed forces, or a straightforward exchange of all internees over forty-five years of age.[95] In the ongoing negotiations, conducted via American mediators, Friedrich continued to press for the former option,[96] but after weeks of uncertainty and vacillation the German authorities were finally forced to accept the lesser deal covering the 'over-forty-fives' only. Even then, the British government was able to insist on a clause that allowed both parties to the agreement to hold back up to twenty persons otherwise eligible for release 'for military reasons'.[97] After further delays, the scheme finally came into effect on 2 January 1917, but was almost immediately suspended by the British owing to the German announcement of unrestricted submarine warfare.[98] This made it impossible for the German authorities to consider releasing the remaining Ruhleben prisoners on a unilateral basis, even when, as we shall see in Chapter 5, feeding them and guarding them became an increasingly difficult task in the final eighteen months of the war.

Notes

1 Masterman, *On the Chariot Wheel*, p. 102.
2 Stibbe, 'The Internment of Civilians', passim.
3 Sir Alan Johnstone to the FO, 26 August 1914, in NA, FO 369/712.
4 On this organisation see also Matthew Stibbe, 'Elisabeth Rotten and the "Auskunfts- und Hilfsstelle für Deutsche im Ausland und Ausländer in Deutschland", 1914–1919', in Alison S. Fell and Ingrid Sharp (eds.), *The Women's Movement in Wartime. International Perspectives, 1914–19* (Basingstoke, 2007), pp. 194–210.
5 Gerard to Page, 16 November 1914, in NA, FO 369/712.
6 Maxse to Grey, 4 November 1914, in NA, FO 369/714.
7 Maxse to Grey, 19 November 1914, in *ibid.*
8 Law to Page, 24 December 1914, in NA, FO 369/712.
9 FO to Page, 8 January 1915, in BA Berlin, R 1501/112365, Bl. 54–6. The reason given for this was that British-born wives of German internees in Britain were now entitled to relief monies from the British state.
10 Ketchum, *Ruhleben*, p. 101.
11 On the subtle distinction between *deutschfreundlich* and *deutschgesinnt* see the regulations outlined in HLL-EC, box 5, file 10: '"Deutschgesinnt" is one who has made up his mind to accept German nationality in its entirety, to have his children brought up as Germans and to allow them to serve in the German army, in short one who renounces all allegiance to the British empire for self and family. "Deutschfreundlich" on the other hand is one who in spite of the war retains his friendship and respect for Germany without in any way disavowing his allegiance to the British empire.'
12 See the list of donor organisations in HLL-EC, box 5, file 18.
13 Rebecca Gill, 'Calculating Compassion in War: The "New Humanitarian" Ethos in Britain, 1870–1918', unpublished PhD thesis, University of Manchester, 2005, pp. 181–95.
14 Jahr, 'Zivilisten als Kriegsgefangene', pp. 317–18.
15 See e.g. notes on interview conducted by Lord Robert Cecil with released prisoners Beaumont and Hawkins, 7 April 1916, in NA, FO 383/140.

16 Notes on interview conducted by Lord Robert Cecil with released prisoner Moresby White, 13 July 1916, in NA, FO 383/141.

17 Israel Cohen, Memorandum on conditions in Ruhleben camp, 29 June 1916, in NA, FO 383/141.

18 Powell to Gerard, 15 July 1916, in NA, FO 383/141.

19 Cohen, Memorandum on conditions in Ruhleben camp (as n. 17 above).

20 Alonzo E. Taylor, *Report on the conditions of diet and nutrition in the internment camp at Ruhleben* (= misc. no. 18) (London, 1916), p. 7.

21 *Ibid.*, p. 12.

22 *Ibid.*, p. 7.

23 On the government's use of ostensibly voluntary bodies to act as 'screens' for state intervention see Gill, 'Calculating Compassion in War', pp. 180 and 187.

24 See the leaflet on the Central Prisoners of War Committee, dated October 1916, in HLL-EC, box 6, file 15.

25 Dresel to Sir Horace Rumbold, 11 November 1916, in Houghton Library, Cambridge, MA, Dresel papers, b MS Am 1549 (346).

26 Ellen Prendergast, née Firth, unpublished typewritten memoirs, n.d., p. 4. I am grateful to Mary Firth for permission to quote from this source.

27 Auskunfts- und Hilfsstelle für Deutsche im Ausland und Ausländer in Deutschland, report dated April 1916. Copy in Archive du Comité International de la Croix-Rouge, Geneva (henceforth ACICR), C G1 419/XI.

28 As reported by Elisabeth Rotten in a letter forwarded to the Reich Office of Interior on 4 April 1918, in BA Berlin, R 1501/112371, Bl. 133–5.

29 See e.g. South Shoreham Union to the FO, 16 September 1918, in NA, FO 383/422. The author of this letter writes: 'On the 19th ultimo five civilian lunatics returned from Germany were landed at Boston in Lincolnshire, and transferred to the Royal Victoria Hospital, Netley, in this Union. From hence they were transferred to the Hants County Lunatic Asylum, Fareham, chargeable to my board ... Under the circumstances I am directed to ask that steps be taken to prevent men landed in the North or other parts of the country being brought to this Union and allowed to become a financial burden.' A note in the same file indicates that of 368 Ruhleben prisoners repatriated in January 1918 eight were certified insane on arrival at Boston, Lincolnshire, and immediately transferred to the local asylum.

30 G. R. Warner (prisoner of war department) to the Treasury, 14 January 1919, in NA, T 1/12295.

31 Draft letter to the Secretary of State for Foreign Affairs, London, December 1917, drawn up by Ruhleben prisoners Clements, Ford, Higgins, Hopf, Logie, Moland and Woolner for presentation to the barrack captains. Copy in HLL-EC, box 5, file 14.

32 See the archival material in *ibid.*, box 6, file 9.

33 Cf. Treasury to the prisoner of war department, 1 April 1919, in NA, FO 383/520.

34 Letter signed by twelve ex-prisoners to the chairman and members of the prisoner of war committee, Westminster, n.d. [January 1919], in NA, T 1/12295.

35 Bury, *My Visit to Ruhleben*, p. 29.

36 *Ibid.*, p. 30.

37 Bury to Powell, 15 June 1917, in HLL-EC, box 3, file 4.

38 RCM, no. 6, June 1917, p. 24.

39 Handwritten note by [Sir] H[orace] Rumbold, 14 July 1916, in NA, FO 383/141.

40 RCM, no. 6, June 1917, pp. 34–5.

41 Cohen, *The Ruhleben Prison Camp*, p. 56.

42 *Ibid.*, p. 58.

43 Cf. Jones, 'The Enemy Disarmed', p. 106.

44 H.W. Dixon to C.W. Donnelly, 10 October 1916. Extract in HLL-EC, box 6, file 9.

45 See e.g. FO to Page, 16 July 1915, in NA, FO 383/68, and FO to Page, 22 December 1915, in *ibid.*, FO 383/76.

46 Cf. Hinz, *Gefangen im Großen Krieg*, pp. 178–85.

47 See Wallace Ellison, *Escapes and Adventures* (Edinburgh, 1928), for his lengthy description of life in the *Stadtvogtei*.

48 See the minutes of the inter-departmental meeting on enemy aliens held at the Reich Office of Interior, 29 March 1915, in BA Berlin, R 1501/112365, Bl. 204–5.

49 See Reich Naval Office to the Reich Office of Interior, 8 May 1915, in BA Berlin, R 1501/112367, Bl. 18; and minutes of the inter-departmental meeting on enemy aliens held at the Reich Office of Interior on 19 May 1915 in *ibid.*, Bl. 36.

50 See e.g. the undated article 'Freilassung in Ruhleben internierter englischer Trainer', in BA Berlin, R 1501/112363, Bl. 280.

51 Figures given by the deputy Prussian Minister of War, General von Wandel, in the Reichstag on 7 April 1916 – see *Verhandlungen des Reichstags*, vol. 307, p. 918.

52 Supreme commander in the marches to the Reich Chancellor (Reich Office of Interior), 14 November 1914. Copy in StA Hamburg, Senatskriegsakten 111–2, Lz1.

53 Gertrud Bäumer to the Reich Office of Interior, 27 November 1914, in BA Berlin, R 1501/112364, Bl. 157. The request was turned down and instead German-born wives were directed to the King Edward VII fund. Cf. the minutes of an inter-departmental meeting on enemy aliens in the Reich Office of Interior, 26 January 1915, in R 1501/112365, Bl. 31–4.

54 *Der Hauptausschuß des Reichstags*, vol. 1, pp. 13–14 (sitting on 11 March 1915). The quotation comes from the comments of Fehrenbach, which were endorsed by Behrens and Müller-Meiningen.

55 *Verhandlungen des Reichstags*, vol. 306, p. 750 (session for 18 January 1916) and

vol. 307, pp. 1562–5 (session for 6 June 1916). On the German citizenship law of 1913 see Nathans, *The Politics of Citizenship in Germany*, esp. pp. 169–98.

56 Supreme commander in the marches to the Reich Chancellor (Reich Office of Interior), 1 January 1916, in BA Berlin, R 1501/112368, Bl. 314.

57 Supreme commander in the marches to the Reich Chancellor (Reich Office of Interior), 3 July 1916, in BA Berlin, R 1501/112369, Bl. 155.

58 See *Verhandlungen des Reichstags*, vol. 308, p. 1998.

59 Reinhard R. Doerries, *Prelude to the Easter Rising. Sir Roger Casement in Imperial Germany* (London, 2000), pp. 15 and passim.

60 Sir Roger Casement to Count Georg von Wedel, 3 March 1915, reproduced in *ibid.*, p. 85. Cf. minute by Lord Robert Cecil, 30 October 1915, in NA, FO 383/69, who notes that the three men were 'ostensibly released as being medically unfit, [although] it is significant that at the time of their release there was no agreement for the exchange of invalids' and further that they were questioned at the Home Office on arrival in the UK. What happened to them subsequently is not clear.

61 Masterman, *On the Chariot Wheel*, p. 105.

62 O'Sullivan Molony, *Prisoners and Captives*, p. 31.

63 As reported in *The Times*, 4 July 1916. On the Vatican agreement of August 1915 see Panayi, *The Enemy in Our Midst*, pp. 85–6. Also the archival materials in BA Berlin, R 901/83952 and NA, FO 383/104.

64 See the relevant documents in NA, FO 383/23 and FO 383/170.

65 *Ibid.* Interestingly, Cecil had already tried to get Eden out in 1915 in exchange for a captured German officer in the Turkish army, but the plan fell through. See the documents in NA, FO 383/59. Lady Eden had already suffered two bereavements in the war: her husband, Sir William Eden, died in February 1915 after a short illness, and her eldest son, Lieutenant John Eden, was killed at Ypres in October 1914. Another son, midshipman Nicholas Eden, perished at Jutland shortly before Sir Timothy's release from Ruhleben.

66 Cf. the further evidence in NA, FO 383/170 and 383/315.

67 In a letter to the president of the board of trade, William Graham, and the Labour MP Philip Noel-Baker, on 17 February 1930, the former internee Herbert Cooper complained, among other things, that 'by the special exchange and repatriation of civilians of high social and financial standing the British government displayed a class partisanship much to be regretted'. He also referred specifically to the example of Timothy Eden. For a copy of this letter see Liddle Collection, RUH 11.

68 Newton, *Retrospection*, p. 220. Even after this negotiations continued for the exchange of individuals but, at Newton's insistence, the new cases were restricted to those who had been in government service or essential war work of some kind. See e.g. the material in NA, FO 383/312 and 383/315.

69 Michel, 'Intoxication ou "brutalisation"?', p. 177.

70 See Hinz, *Gefangen im Großen Krieg*, pp. 64–5, who makes reference to the publication *Kriegsbrauch im Landkriege*, edited by the Kriegsgeschichtliche

71 *Ibid.*, p. 89.

72 Audoin-Rouzeau and Becker, *1914–1918*, p. 86.

73 See e.g. *Rapports de MM. Ed. Naville and V. van Berchem, Dr. C. de Marval et A. Eugster sur leurs visites aux camps de prisonniers en Angleterre, France et Allemagne* (Geneva and Paris, 1915). Copy in ACICR, C G1/432/II/1.

74 Michel, 'Intoxication ou "brutalisation"?', passim, provides a detailed account of French POWs sent to special punishment camps in Germany and the occupied zones of Russia after 1915 in retaliation for the supposed mistreatment of German prisoners (including women and children) captured by French troops in the Cameroons and Togoland or deported from metropolitan France to North Africa. See also the evidence of escalating cycles of violent reprisals against POWs on the western front in spring 1917 in Jones, 'The Enemy Disarmed', Chapter 3.

75 Cf. the minutes of the inter-departmental meeting held at the Reich Office of Interior, 19 January 1915, in BA Berlin, R 1501/112365, Bl. 21–2.

76 Eingabe der Ortsgruppe Jena des Alldeutschen Verbandes an den Bundesrat, in BA Berlin, R 1501/112366.

77 *Kölnische Zeitung*, 27 June 1916.

78 On right-wing attacks on the Chancellor in the first half of 1916 see Stibbe, *German Anglophobia*, pp. 110–19.

79 Hinz, *Gefangen im Großen Krieg*, p. 217.

80 Bernard Delpal, 'Zwischen Vergeltung und Humanisierung der Lebensverhältnisse. Kriegsgefangene in Frankreich, 1914–1920', in Oltmer (ed.), *Kriegsgefangene im Europa des Ersten Weltkriegs*, p. 151.

81 See the materials in StA Hamburg, Senatskriegsakten 111–2, Lz1.

82 Hayn to AA, 9 September 1916, in BA Berlin, R 901/83953.

83 Theodor Wolff, *Tagebücher, 1914–1919. Der Erste Weltkrieg und die Entstehung der Weimarer Republik in Tagebüchern, Leitartikeln und Briefen des Chefredakteurs am "Berliner Tageblatt" und Mitbegründer der "Deutschen Demokratischen Partei"*, ed. Bernd Sösemann, 2 vols. (Boppard am Rhein, 1984), vol. I, p. 259 (diary entry for 18 July 1915).

84 See the archival materials on a fund raising event held at the house of Prince Lichnowsky on 20 June 1916, in EZA Berlin, Bestand 51 C III a 5. Also Stibbe, 'Elisabeth Rotten', pp. 202 and passim.

85 On the Vatican's involvement see also Matthias Erzberger, *Erlebnisse im Weltkrieg* (Stuttgart and Berlin, 1920), p. 44.

86 Felix von Hartmann to Bethmann Hollweg, 23 July 1916, in BA Berlin, R901/83953.

87 Cited in *Ruhleben Daily News*, 11 October 1916. Copy in HLL-EC, box 9, file 7.

88 'Mündlicher Bericht des Ausschusses für den Reichshaushalt über Fragen der Gefangenenbehandlung', 13 October 1916, in *Verhandlungen des Reichstags*, vol. 319, p. 864.

89 See e.g. Newton to Dresel, 27 July 1918, in Houghton Library, Cambridge, MA, Dresel papers, b MS Am 1549 (299); and Newton, *Retrospection*, p. 263.

90 As director of the *Unterkunftsdepartement* Friedrich had no control over camps in occupied territory. The latter came under the direct authority of the high command and were not subject to any form of ministerial or international scrutiny. See Hinz, *Gefangen im Großen Krieg*, pp. 72 and 79–80.

91 For further details see Horne and Kramer, 'War Between Soldiers and Enemy Civilians', esp. pp. 163–8.

92 On the 'sabotage hysteria' of 1917, which affected French POWs in particular, see Hinz, *Gefangen im Großen Krieg*, pp. 144–9.

93 See e.g. 'Im Internierungslager Ruhleben', *Berliner Illustrierte Zeitung*, no. 35, 27 August 1916, p. 4.

94 See the minutes of the inter-departmental discussion chaired by Friedrich on 28 June 1916, in BA Berlin, R 901/83953.

95 Friedrich to AA, 25 August 1916, in *ibid.*

96 See e.g. Friedrich to AA, 30 September 1916, in StA Hamburg, Senatskriegsakten 111–2, Lz1.

97 Cf. the minutes of the inter-departmental meeting held in the Reich Office of Interior, 15 December 1916, in BA Berlin, R 901/83954. Also *Further correspondence respecting the proposed release of civilians interned in the British and German empires* (= misc. no. 35) (London, 1916).

98 See Newton's statement in the House of Lords on 14 June 1917, in *Parliamentary Debates, House of Lords*, fifth series, vol. XXV (London, 1917), pp. 446–8. Also Garner, 'Treatment of Enemy Aliens', p. 37.

5

The end of internment

In 1917 and 1918 diplomatic negotiations over the fate of civilian internees were caught up under the broader question of how to help POWs of all categories who had spent eighteen months or more in captivity. A bilateral exchange agreement reached between Germany and France at Berne in May 1917 was followed by a similar agreement between Germany and Britain at The Hague in July 1917, although in both instances progress towards implementation was painfully slow.[1] Now older prisoners or those suffering from a much broader range of health problems could in theory apply for repatriation or internment in a neutral country, either Switzerland or the Netherlands. In the case of British prisoners, this applied automatically to anybody over forty-five years of age, so that the earlier agreement of 2 January 1917 was now revived within a new framework.[2] 'Barbed wire disease' was also given formal recognition as a medical condition and those diagnosed as sufferers could be considered for repatriation on the same basis as those who fell victim to physical illnesses. Reprisals and punishments were not outlawed, in spite of the efforts of the Vatican and the ICRC, but they were at least limited in scope and duration. Moreover, with reference to reprisals, it was agreed that each side would give the other 'at least four weeks notice of intention' so that negotiations might begin to find alternative forms of redress.[3] Finally, officers and NCOs who had been in captivity for more than eighteen months could apply for neutral internment whatever their age or state of health, but this right was not extended to civilian prisoners or to rank-and-file military prisoners until a further agreement signed at The Hague on 14 July 1918.[4]

In Germany itself, meanwhile, pressure from the military was also growing to reduce the numbers of internees being held in the main camps (*Stammlager*) and/or to offset the costs of guarding and feeding them by integrating them into the German war economy. Beginning in April 1915 the *Unterkunftsdepartement* of the Prussian Ministry of War had made regular calls for the recruitment of French, Belgian and Russian civilian POWs into paid employment in agriculture and industry,[5] and in March 1916 this was taken one stage further when new guidelines were issued stating that those internees who refused offers of work should 'not be encouraged to make comfortable lives for themselves in the camps'.[6] In December 1916 the high command itself took up this theme, ordering, as part of the auxiliary labour law, an investigation into the number of non-combatant prisoners of enemy nationality who remained economically inactive, and demanding the mobilisation of those 'whose labour can be put to good use' into special *Arbeitskommandos* or work detachments.[7] Meanwhile, thousands more enemy nationals were deported to the Reich from occupied territory, so much so that the number of civilian prisoners in Germany continued to grow at the rate of about 350–400 per week in the last two years of the war, according to ICRC estimates.[8]

The Ruhleben prisoners, as we have seen, were able to avoid exposure to such abuses, not because they were civilians, but because their nationality afforded them greater protection than their French, Belgian and Russian counterparts. Indeed, as with captured British officers, little or no pressure was placed on them to join work details, and few did.[9] In the last two years of the war their fate was closely monitored by a new pressure group at home, the Ruhleben Prisoners' Release Committee, and by supporters within Germany itself, particularly Elisabeth Rotten's organisation. They also received regular visits from representatives of the Dutch legation in Berlin and the Danish Red Cross based in Copenhagen. During this time they were almost certainly better fed and clothed than ordinary German civilians on the home front, and were in a position to observe the deteriorating conditions on the other side of the barbed wire almost with an air of detachment. All the same, the final phase of captivity was undoubtedly the most frustrating and difficult to bear, particularly for those waiting to be placed on exchange lists under the 1917 and 1918 Hague agreements. This can be seen in particular in the increased rate of mental illness and in the sudden rise in escape attempts in late 1917 and 1918. Before we go on to consider these issues in more detail, however, it will first be necessary to discuss the growing prominence of Ruhleben as a political issue in Britain during the first half of 1917.

The Ruhleben Prisoners' Release Committee

On 24 October and 15 November 1916 the backbench Liberal peer Lord Devonport made two speeches in the House of Lords in which he advocated acceptance of the German offer of a general repatriation of civilian prisoners regardless of age on the grounds that the Ruhlebenites were now close to breaking point and would not survive another winter of internment. In the second speech he also referred directly to an undertaking made by Dr Johannes Kriege of the German Foreign Office, who had said publicly in the Reichstag on 2 November: 'If the negotiations for the release of civilian prisoners succeed, we bind ourselves not to incorporate the men returned into the army.' Surely, Devonport asked, it was now time to respond in a more positive manner:

> I fail to see what valid reason the government can adduce for not completing the agreement with Germany on the lines suggested, and I only say that if they remain insensible to the sufferings of those men who are left behind they will find, perhaps too late, that they have made a tragic blunder.[10]

Devonport's remarks caused a sensation, not least because they were an explicit challenge to the government's position that exchanging 4,000 Britishers for 26,000 German civilians would be disadvantageous to the allied war effort. They were followed up by a flood of letters to *The Times*, including one from the former Ruhleben prisoner Sir Timothy Eden on 22 November, who welcomed news of the imminent repatriation of the 'over-forty-fives' but expressed concern that the 'under- forty-fives' might have to wait for another two years until they were exchanged: 'Is it to be wondered that the prisoners ... murmur against the slow and comfortable deliberations of the authorities at home and complain that they are being neglected by their countrymen? There is only one way of obtaining the release of the British civilians: We must give Germany all her civilians in exchange.'[11]

On 26 November Devonport wrote to Eden in order to raise the possibility of a 'mass meeting' to put pressure on the authorities over the internment question.[12] Other declared supporters included prominent Tory women philanthropists such as Lady Cavendish-Bentinck and the Duchess of Bedford, as well as Lord Northcliffe, owner of *The Times* and the *Daily Mail*.[13] Ironically Devonport was forced to distance himself from this venture after his appointment as Food Controller in Lloyd George's first administration on 5 December, but continued to lend his support from behind the scenes (and took up the mantle again after his resignation from the government in June 1917).[14] In the meantime rallies were held at the Kingsway Hall in London on 26 February 1917[15] and at several other venues up and down the country between March and May 1917, including Aberdeen,

Banbury, Birmingham, Bristol, Cardiff, Croydon, Edinburgh, Glasgow, Ilford, Liverpool, Manchester, Oxford and Southend-on-Sea.[16] The purpose of these events was to publicise the launching of a Ruhleben Prisoners' Release Committee, chaired by Sir Thomas D. Pile and including among its members the former Rulebenites Timothy Eden and Israel Cohen. Their case was that the British government had been too slow to take up the German offer of an 'all-for-all' exchange of civilian prisoners, as publicly announced in the Reichstag on 2 November 1916, and that

> the question of the health and safety of 4,000 Englishmen [is] a subject of national importance, and ... [should] therefore be thoroughly discussed in both Houses of Parliament at the earliest opportunity.[17]

The committee is interesting for a variety of reasons. Firstly, it showed the ability of the Ruhleben prisoners to mobilise a wide range of political support, most particularly from among the rich and powerful. Even the Archbishop of Canterbury spoke out on their behalf in the House of Lords on 22 February, describing Newton's statement for the government as 'disappointing' and insisting that the 'wisest course' would be to accept the German offer 'notwithstanding the disparity of numbers'.[18] Viscount Bryce (Liberal) and Lord Beresford (Conservative) also argued in favour of a general exchange, the former noting that he could 'understand that the War Office and the admiralty should have the last word ... with regard to the exchange of military prisoners, but [not] ... why they should be allowed a decisive voice in the case of civilian prisoners'.[19] For the first time, the government was coming under serious scrutiny in relation to its policy on British internees in Germany.

Secondly, in spite of the upper-class character of the Ruhleben Prisoners' Release Committee, its propaganda made clear that internment was a national rather than sectional issue, and that people from all walks of life had been affected by it. One of the pamphlets produced by the committee thus contained extracts from what we must assume are authentic letters sent to it by the wives or parents of Ruhleben internees:

> Yorkshire, 23 January 1917:
> My son has been interned since August 4 1914. He was one of the crew of the SS ——, of ——. They were at ——, in Germany, when the war broke out. I am his mother and am quite alone; 83 years of age come June. I would like to have him home if only the Government would intercede.

London, 21 January 1917:

Ever since he has been [at Ruhleben] I have sent [my husband] two parcels of food each week, also bread from Berne ... it does not seem fair that we should have to keep them and ourselves as well. My husband's firm allows me so much every week. Otherwise I should have to sell my home. I go out to work while the women here who are married to interned Germans are allowed 11/6 per week, and so much for each child.

Essex, 24 January 1917

We were living in Berlin when my husband was taken. I stayed there over a year to send him food, and paid our rent, and then had to leave so as to send food from home to him, and also money. I might say we have lost all. I have had to keep him for over two years.[20]

Admittedly another publication issued by the committee, consisting of a series of letters from an unnamed prisoner to his mother, was much more aristocratic in flavour, the prisoner obviously coming from the same privileged background as Eden. In the foreword he was indeed described as an 'Oxford undergraduate' whose 'zest' and 'earnest Christianity' were a sign of hope for 'the many wives and parents who are yearning for their husbands and their sons in bondage at Ruhleben':

The writer... lives and moves and has his being in the *Classes* of the Camp School and the *Circles* of the Arts and Science Union; he studies; he dwells with pride and affection on the work of his fellow-students and fellow-lecturers; he conducts religious services; he rejoices in his opportunities of meeting, under circumstances which lead to familiarity and friendship, with men of occupations far removed from his own (e.g., we may suppose, the sailors of the mast, of whom there are many in Ruhleben).[21]

His name, in fact, was Thomas Cottrell-Dormer, the old Etonian whom we already encountered in Chapter 3.[22]

Finally the committee is interesting because its campaign deliberately sought to exploit the depth of anti-German feeling in Britain as a means of putting further pressure on the government. This can also be seen in an article in the *Daily Mail* on 16 February 1917, which supported the case for an 'all-for-all exchange' on the grounds that this would rid Britain of thousands of 'unwanted' German immigrants:

[T]here are sound reasons for accepting the German proposals, unfair though they are. By sending these German civilians back to Germany we should rid this country and the Empire of people whose presence is dangerous enough today, but will be even more dangerous when peace is made. We should prevent the interned Germans from spying on us, and stealing British trade. We should inject into the veins of Germany the baccillus of freedom. For these Huns, who have lived among us under free institutions, could hardly be expected to return with enthusiasm to German militarism, German feudalism, and all the irksome accompaniments of life in the Fatherland. They might even in time persuade their countrymen to establish something like constitutional government. They should be condemned to live in their own country until they have rescued it from the Prussian drill sergeant.[23]

The fact that a fiercely right-wing newspaper like the *Daily Mail* should make such demands after more than two and a half years of war also provides a strange sequel to the protests about British concentration camps in South Africa at the turn of the century. Here the argument was turned on its head: Britain, as a modern democratic nation at war, was bound to put the interests of its own citizens first. Yet Belgian and even German refugees in Britain were supposedly getting more financial help from the British state than the Ruhleben families. Humanitarianism had turned out to be hollow, while violence against enemy civilians (in this case, expulsion or forced repatriation) was legitimised on the grounds of national security and well-being. The (misleading) comparison with the concentration camps in the Boer war had an even greater poignancy, because Emily Hobhouse – the foremost British critic of conditions in the South African camps in the early 1900s – had visited Ruhleben in June 1916 and declared it to be 'first rate, better than any camp in England' [*ganz vorzüglich eingerichtet, besser als irgend ein Lager in England*].[24] Her visit, which was undertaken without the prior knowledge or approval of the government, unsurprisingly provoked a great deal of anger in the British press and among MPs, and was used once again to draw attention to Ruhleben as a symbol of German brutality and disrespect for international law (rather than – as she had intended – as a symbol of the wrong-headedness of internment and war in general).[25] Indeed, alongside Bishop Bury, Hobhouse was *persona non grata* among the Ruhleben prisoners and their families, albeit for different reasons.[26]

In the end, of course, the Ruhleben Prisoners' Release Committee failed in its immediate objective, namely to persuade the War Office and admiralty to shift their ground on the question of prisoner exchanges. Instead on 28 March 1917 the cabinet resolved in secret that 'a general exchange of interned civilians was impracticable and not in the interests of the state'.[27] Nor is there any evidence that public opinion as a whole sided with the Ruhleben prisoners and their supporters. Nonetheless, the Devonport–Eden campaign did succeed, at least in part, in raising public and political awareness of the Ruhleben issue, and forced the government (represented by Lord Newton) onto the defensive during several further parliamentary exchanges in 1917 and 1918.[28] Indirectly it may have influenced British policy during the negotiations at The Hague in June–July 1917 which, as we have seen, led to a renewal of the agreement to repatriate prisoners over forty-five and a new deal to allow a fixed number of invalid prisoners on both sides to be interned in neutral Dutch territory. Finally, it also had the consequence of prodding the government-controlled Central Prisoners of War Committee of the Red Cross into greater action in support of the material needs of the Ruhleben prisoners, especially from the second half of 1917 onwards. It is to this organisation, and its equivalents in Germany, that we shall now turn.

Support for internees within Germany

While the British government faced growing domestic pressure over its attitude towards the Ruhleben prisoners in 1917, the crisis faced by the German authorities was even greater. Here the main problem, put quite simply, was food. How could the Prussian Ministry of War continue to justify supplying the Ruhleben camp with meals and fuel, on top of their relief parcels from home, when German civilians were going cold and hungry?[29] This question became even more acute because the Ruhleben prisoners, unlike many other civilian POWs in Germany, were not compelled to work and for the most part refused offers of voluntary employment outside the camp. The Reichstag peace resolution of 19 July 1917, to which the new Chancellor Georg Michaelis was in theory committed, further underlined the government's precarious domestic position and the collapse of the original *Burgfrieden* strategy. Yet when it came to resolving the internment question, the numbers still stacked up in Britain's favour: by August 1917 there were only 3,320 prisoners at Ruhleben compared to roughly 36,000 German civilian POWs throughout the British empire.[30] Reprisals in these circumstances would be too dangerous a game to play.

Against this background of repeated failures to agree on an 'all-for-all exchange', both governments needed some sort of 'screen' to cover the increasing financial cost of internment to the state.[31] In Britain's case, the

Central Prisoners of War Committee functioned in that role. Over time, this body became increasingly professional and streamlined in its approach and, in spite of the many complaints from the Ruhleben prisoners, managed to keep them supplied with relief parcels right up until the November armistice (amazingly the German guards did not pilfer these gifts from Britain, although Heather Jones has found evidence of increasing theft from parcels sent to other camps from Britain and France in late 1917 and 1918).[32] Women volunteers did the packing of parcels, and the money came both from the state and voluntary contributions. The Central Prisoners of War Committee also published its own monthly newspaper from January 1918, *The British Prisoner of War*, which was aimed at prisoners' families in the UK and included features on Ruhleben in almost every edition.[33] Finally, it was instrumental in helping to organise a public exhibition of arts and crafts produced by the prisoners in the camp, an event which eventually took place at Westminster Hall in January 1919 although the original plan was to hold it in July 1918 with the money raised being used to support the prisoners and their dependants.[34]

The German government, meanwhile, had used the German branch of the King Edward VII fund as its 'screen'. Indeed, Dr Theodor Lewald, a ministerial director in the Reich Office of Interior, was one of the three members of the executive committee of this charity, and helped to organise an interest-free loan of 100,000 marks granted by the Hamburg banker Max Warburg in February 1915, which by and large kept the fund afloat until the end of 1917.[35] By this time, however, not only were the fund's resources running out, but suddenly it had a lot more claims to meet. The main reason for this was that some of the German wives of the Ruhleben internees were from middle-class backgrounds and had managed to subsist on private savings for the first three years of the war. However, eventually they too faced financial ruin and the prospect of destitution.[36]

One other possibility was for the German government to turn to Elisabeth Rotten's voluntary organisation, the *Auskunfts- und Hilfsstelle für Deutsche im Ausland und Ausländer in Deutschland*. However, this was easier said than done. Rotten had many enemies inside the government and especially inside the military, not least because of her membership of the anti-war *Bund Neues Vaterland* (BNV), which she had represented at the international women's peace conference at The Hague in 1915. Her Swiss nationality also meant that she lived under constant surveillance, especially after the BNV was closed down in February 1916 and its leader Lilli Jannasch taken into military custody.[37] Nonetheless, she was also useful in many ways, as her organisation provided a safety net for the German-born wives of British internees, thus removing pressure on the King Edward fund and deflecting criticism from the government itself. In April 1916 she was able to persuade the military authorities to permit monthly visits from internees' wives and children, provided that the latter were resident in Germany.[38] She was also in contact with Max Warburg, who was chief fund-raiser for the King Edward fund and a highly influential figure in business circles.[39] It is therefore significant that in March 1917 the military removed the year-long ban on her making appeals for voluntary contributions.[40] This had an immediate effect, as Rotten was now able to collect donations from leading German industrialists, women's groups and private charities, and channel them into relief work among destitute aliens.[41] Even so, her organisation's finances remained precarious, as did the situation of many of the internees' families.

Meanwhile, from March 1917 Rotten's links to the Ruhleben prisoners themselves became more direct. This began when a request was made by Dr Eric Higgins, the head of the Arts and Sciences Union at Ruhleben and director of its research laboratories (housed in the loft of barrack 6), for various instruments, including a spectroscope, to be sent from London. The request was passed on by Bishop Bury, and eventually, through the Friends Emergency Committee, a similar instrument was sent 'by proxy' to the interned German scientists at Knockaloe camp on the Isle of Man. As a result, Higgins was offered a 'Rubens'-type spectroscope from the firm Hans Heele in Berlin, and was granted temporary leave to discuss the arrangements with Rotten in her offices. Rotten immediately exploited the opportunity to seek information about the broader educational needs of the Ruhleben inmates, and offered to help Higgins through the regular supply of books and (where possible) equipment for his laboratories.[42] This new humanitarian action would be based on the principle of 'reprisals of good', as advocated by Edward Winton, the Bishop of Winchester, in a letter to *The Times* on 29 September 1916. In other words, anything Rotten procured for Ruhleben would be matched for German prisoners in Britain, and vice versa.[43]

On this basis, Rotten was able to arrange the delivery of over £1,000 worth of scientific apparatus, offered voluntarily by German firms, as well as botanical and zoological specimens, a quantity of chemicals (bizarrely, given the German paranoia about sabotage), and a huge number of scientific books donated privately by university professors or supplied on loan from leading German libraries, including the Royal Prussian State Library (*Königliche Staatsbibliothek*) in Berlin.[44] The number of books averaged fifty per week, and among the donors was Albert Einstein whom Rotten knew through her work with the BNV.[45] Further offers of help poured in after Rotten arranged a newspaper article in the *Berliner Tageblatt* in November 1917 drawing attention to the educational opportunities now offered to German internees at Wakefield camp through the loan of books and equipment from the University of Leeds.[46] By this stage a number of German university professors had declared their willingness to tutor Ruhleben internees, and Rotten gained permission from the Prussian Ministry of Education for them to visit the University of Berlin as day students. However, this arrangement was vetoed by the British authorities acting through the Netherlands legation in Berlin.[47] Instead, as an alternative, it was arranged for students at the Ruhleben camp school to sit for university exams in the camp itself, and, where relevant, for degrees to be awarded by the University of London. Special negotiations had to be completed with the German military authorities to ensure the censoring and secrecy of both the exam papers and the exam scripts as they entered and left the camp.[48] Students taking technical and commercial subjects were also issued with certificates by the London Chamber of Commerce and the Royal Society of Arts, Manufactures and Commerce, a situation which, as *The Times* commented, was without precedent in the history of British education.[49]

Finally, Rotten was a key contact in the organisation of the Ruhleben Exhibition. The background to this was the formation of a handicrafts department in the camp under Higgins' direction, with special workshops for textiles, clothes dyeing, bookbinding, leatherwork and silverwork, and so on (Figure 15). The raw materials were obtained from suppliers in Denmark and Switzerland while Rotten managed to gain permission from the German military authorities for their import as 'Liebesgaben' and the export of the finished products to the British Red Cross for sale or as potential exhibits. However, opposition from the British authorities prevented the import of these goods to Britain until after the war had finished.[50]

The fact that Rotten was able to collect such varied donations is partly a testimony to her own hard work, but also to the fact that some German companies and individuals were now looking ahead to a less than complete German victory in the war, and were considering ways of reviving relations with Britain in the post-war years. For instance, the electrical giants Siemens–Schuckert and the AEG proved very co-operative in this respect, partly because they had employees in Ruhleben, but partly too because of their natural interest in rebuilding overseas markets after the war.[51] Genuine idealism also cannot be ruled out as a motive, and nor can the desire to help German prisoners in Britain through the 'reprisals of good' principle. Finally, intellectual curiosity was a factor in explaining the interest of some German academics in Ruhleben. The sexologist Magnus Hirschfeld, for

15   The Ruhleben handicrafts department, c. 1918

example, was introduced to Higgins through Rotten and used this contact (among others) to gather material for his research institute's study on human sexuality in different wartime settings.[52]

Even so, Rotten still had many enemies in Germany, not least in the Berlin *Kommandantur* where she was viewed as a security risk because of her Swiss nationality and pacifist leanings. This became even clearer on 27 July 1918 when Higgins was arrested at Ruhleben and taken to the *Stadtvogtei*, where he was held for several weeks in solitary confinement and accused of 'acting in the interests of the British secret service'. Rotten, he was told by his interrogators, 'had been arrested, tried and convicted upon this charge after having made a full confession'. He would be allowed to return to Ruhleben if he pleaded guilty and provided details of Rotten's involvement. However, he turned this offer down, and was eventually released without charge in early November 1918.[53]

Rotten was saved not only by Higgins' refusal to make a false confession, but also by events taking place at the highest level of politics. At a meeting of the new war cabinet headed by Max von Baden on 24 October 1918 Walter Simons, a *Vortragender Rat* (senior civil servant) in the German Foreign Office, warned that

> The committee for aiding enemy aliens (led by Frl. Dr Rotten) has
> been treated very badly by the local *Kommandantur* and has been the
> victim of a number of unworthy tricks. The committee merely acts
> according to the Christian duty of love towards one's neighbours and
> should not be exposed to unfair treatment. A few days ago it was
> subject to a fresh ban on its activities. This will make a very poor
> impression abroad.[54]

Matthias Erzberger, state secretary without portfolio and later head of the
German armistice commission, agreed with Simons and demanded that the
ban be rescinded instantly.[55] By now Rotten's work was extremely important
in attempts to present the Reich's treatment of enemy POWs in a good
light, and the new rulers in Berlin were anxious to display their links to
this organisation rather than distancing themselves from it. Interestingly,
in December 1918 Rotten also shared a platform with Walther Schücking,
appointed by Erzberger to investigate complaints of German mistreatment
of prisoners, at a pacifist rally in Berlin at which she (and Schücking) called
for Germany to be treated as an equal partner in the forthcoming peace
negotiations.[56] In the big scheme of things this made little difference: British
newspapers continued to insist that Germany would be punished, not least
for its alleged abuse of civilian and military prisoners.[57] Nonetheless, there
is one postscript to this story which is less well known. In early 1919, as
Germany entered its fifth winter under blockade, the Friends Emergency
Committee (FEC) and the American Quakers organised a series of convoys
carrying food supplies and sterilising equipment for German mothers with
young babies. The allied military authorities at first refused to allow the
humanitarian aid convoys through but later backed down on the express
undertaking that the goods were intended for distribution through Rotten's
committee alone, and would not fall into anybody else's hands. By this
means between 500,000 and 1 million under-nourished children were fed
in Germany in the years 1919–20, a testament to what 'reprisals of good'
could do.[58]

Conditions in the camp in the final year of the war

Rotten's efforts (backed by the FEC and the British Red Cross society
in London) undoubtedly were of some importance in helping to make
conditions in Ruhleben reasonably comfortable in the final year of the war.
Indeed, even the camp captain, Joseph Powell, who followed instructions
from the Netherlands legation in Berlin to the letter and thus refused to have

anything to do with Rotten while the war was still on, eventually relented. The camp, he agreed, owed a great debt to this courageous women, whom he greeted when she was finally allowed to visit the camp on 13 November 1918. Without her support, many more prisoners would have succumbed to melancholy, or, worse still, would have gone mad, he said.[59]

Over and above this, however, it is difficult to come to any definite conclusion on the nature of conditions at Ruhleben in the final year of the war. The weekly reports of the Netherlands legation are mostly quite bland and gave little cause for serious concern.[60] The notes made by British officials on their interviews with released prisoners likewise contain surprisingly little detail about material hardships, and dwell much more on the increasingly poor relations between members of the Arts and Science Union and the captains' committee under Powell. Most of those interviewed were indeed very critical of Powell, although he was eventually returned as camp captain by a large majority in elections held in the camp in October 1918.[61] Finally, German newspaper articles continued to present Ruhleben in a positive light, and for that reason tell us more about the propaganda war between Britain and Germany than they do about the real condition of the prisoners. As late as October 1918, for instance, the *Berliner Illustrierte Zeitung* carried a feature-length article, replete with pictures of happy prisoners, in order to show 'that all the complaints that appear … in English newspapers about the poor treatment of English internees have no basis in fact'. Perhaps somewhat disingenuously (given the terrible food situation in Berlin) the article went on to tell an anecdote about a German businessman, Herr Wittkowski, who had allegedly begged the commandant of Ruhleben to take in his two sons 'since they will be well fed there and above all else will enjoy "a first rate education"'.[62]

Another article, written by a Swedish journalist and appearing in the *Stockholms Dagblad* in April 1918, was translated into French for distribution to neutral countries by the German Foreign Office, again for propaganda purposes. Here we find:

Ruhleben is amply and even abundantly provisioned [*suffisamment et même abondamment ravitaillé*]. Judging by their conversations, the prisoners have no cause for complaint about their treatment. Their accommodation has been subject to gradual improvements and the problem of overcrowding has been remedied … the prisoners can take part in all kinds of sport, such as lawn tennis, football, ice skating and skiing … Theatrical and cinematic performances are equally well appreciated by the internees, who attend each showing in large numbers. There is thus plenty to keep them entertained. The visit ended with an inspection of the kitchens, where the material needs of the internees are catered for with a remarkable degree of professionalism by the camp's cooks.[63]

Propaganda aside, there is evidence to suggest that conditions in Ruhleben remained relatively good in the last months of the war. In June 1918, for instance, there was so much surplus food and tobacco in the camp that the captains' committee was making inquiries to the Netherlands legation as to whether it would be possible to send some of it on to British officers' camps in the nearby region.[64] Other accounts talk of German guards rummaging through the bins at night looking for usable items discarded by the prisoners, or attempting to barter with them.[65] Some guards even proved willing to talk about the difficulties they were experiencing in feeding their families, and their desire for an end to the war. Certainly there was a general awareness that 'ordinary' Berliners were facing serious shortages, as Christoph Jahr has shown.[66] One prisoner remembered getting a close up view of a column of munitions workers as they marched past the camp on their way from Spandau to Berlin during the January 1918 strikes: 'The wretched half-starved creatures were a pitiable spectacle. For there was real hunger in Germany, such as was unknown in England.'[67]

Even so conditions in Ruhleben were far from brilliant, and morale did gradually begin to decline in the fourth year of internment. One indication of this was a rise in the number of escapes from the late summer of 1917 onwards. Usually the culprits were returned to Ruhleben, but some forty-five 'repeat offenders' were transferred to Havelberg camp in November 1917 after serving their sentences in the *Stadtvogtei*, allegedly because this camp was 'under stricter observation'.[68] The precise number of escapees is difficult to ascertain, although it certainly exceeded 100, especially if those who absconded after being released on temporary parole are included.

The motives for escape varied. Some prisoners were serious about getting out of Germany, and drew up detailed plans of how to reach the Dutch, Danish or Swiss borders. They were undoubtedly helped by the fact that the guards were more susceptible to bribery by 1918.[69] Others just wanted to spend a few hours outside the camp and expected – or even wanted – to be caught. Uta Hinz, who has studied escape attempts by military POWs, also notes that some officers were guided by an individualistic need for 'self-legitimisation' over and above any patriotic concern to serve their country.[70] This may have influenced some of the upper-class Ruhlebenites as well. John Masterman, for instance, remembered that his reservations about escaping were overcome when a fellow internee reminded him that they were 'too comfortable' in Ruhleben and had a 'duty to try and get out': 'That was decisive for me and I agreed to join him. My escape attempt was not sparked by an overpowering wish for liberty, still less by dislike of or impatience with camp life. I knew quite well that I could last out the war in security and without discomfort.'[71]

Masterman was caught on 6 August 1918 at a railway station 50 miles from the Dutch border, and was lucky to get away with a short spell in prison followed by a triumphant return to Ruhleben. The less fortunate escapers were, as mentioned above, sent to Havelberg, where opportunities for reading, sport and recreation were much more limited and where, as the Dutch representative Jonkheer Snouck-Hurgronje wrote, conditions amounted to 'a second punishment for the same offence'.[72] In October 1918, however, after a concerted campaign by the British Red Cross and the Dutch authorities in Berlin, the British prisoners at Havelberg were brought back to Ruhleben, some of them after a break of eleven months or more.[73]

Meanwhile, another indication of falling morale was the rise in the number of so-called 'mental cases', i.e. of prisoners suffering from nervous disorders of various kinds.[74] Here cause is difficult to separate from effect, but growing frustrations at the slow pace of exchanges and periodic interruptions in the supply of parcels seem to be linked in some way. Even the camp captain, Joseph Powell, appears to have suffered a breakdown at the end of October 1917; he was sent to Dr Weiler's sanatorium to recover and did not return to Ruhleben until May 1918.[75] Worse was to follow, however, for in April 1918 the British government suddenly announced through the Dutch legation that it would no longer fund places at Dr Weiler's for those patients whose families could not afford to underwrite the costs.[76] Thenceforth the more seriously ill patients were dispatched to the state-run *Irrenanstalt* at Neu Ruppin, which was rumoured in the camp to be a 'typical madhouse, complete with straight jackets and padded cells'. Individual accounts of the last year at Ruhleben indeed often contain lurid stories of prisoners who went sent to Neu Ruppin and either never came back or returned as mere shadows of their former selves, although Ketchum believes that the claim of 100 cases requiring treatment outside the camp is probably exaggerated.[77]

An even greater threat, potentially, was the outbreak of Spanish 'flu which swept the camp in July 1918. Between 3 and 18 July, out of a camp population of 2,336 men, some 1,565 cases of infection were reported. However, this resulted in two deaths only, partly because of the quick action of the civilian camp authorities who closed off parts of the camp and prevented prisoners from visiting the theatre and the cinema between 5 and 13 July.[78] This can be compared with the 187,000 German civilians and the many thousands of POWs of all nationalities estimated to have died from influenza during the two great epidemics of summer and autumn 1918.[79] The good hygiene conditions at Ruhleben and the low turnover of prisoners may have helped to stop the spread of the infection, although it is also possible that the camp simply experienced a milder strain of the virus.[80] Already on 11 July Ketchum reported that the '"flu" was slacking off' in his barrack, and by the end of the month the epidemic had disappeared 'as abruptly as it began'.[81] This was indeed the last major outbreak in the camp before its dissolution, although throughout the summer and autumn it was reported that small groups of prisoners, weakened by ill-health, were being transferred to the Netherlands under the terms of the 1917 Hague agreement.[82]

The November Revolution

When in October 1918 the failed escaper William O'Sullivan Molony arrived back in Ruhleben after more than two years' absence spent in the *Stadtvogtei* and at Havelberg, his impression was one of serious decline:

> From a mental and spiritual point of view the camp seemed dead; life seemed to have been extinguished all around us. Where Havelberg ... was about to come to life, Ruhleben ... had lost much of its active manly character and dwindled into a state which even verged on black insanity.[83]

How far this reflected reality is difficult to say. Other evidence, for instance, points to 'business as usual' in the last weeks of the war, with the new football season already 'in full swing' and six new theatre productions on show between 15 September and 4 November.[84] Some students even sat exams for the Chartered Institute of Secretaries in the first week of November.[85] Even so, behind the scenes the newly elected camp council, headed by Powell, began making preparations for the dissolution of the camp should the German guards desert their posts (Figure 16). The measures considered included plans 'to seize all the arms and ammunition and organise a defensive force' in case the camp was attacked by hungry Spandau residents looking for Red Cross parcels or weapons or both.[86] The atmosphere was thus anything but calm, and this may account for the depressed mood encountered by Molony. One prisoner remembered:

16   The Ruhleben camp council, October 1918; the camp captain, Joseph Powell, is on the back row, second from the left

I and my messmates thought it probable that sooner or later the camp would be raided for food. So we made what was ostensibly a window-box and hung it outside the window of our horse-box, with emergency rations of canned beef, tripe etc., buried in it and a few flowers planted on top. We never needed it.[87]

In fact, the revolution, when it did come, was considerably less violent than some of the Ruhlebenites had anticipated. Rumours were already beginning to spread by late October 1918 that 'something was in the air'. Newspapers ceased to arrive in the camp but a visit on 4 November by a sailor from Kiel, who had apparently befriended one of the seamen in Ruhleben, confirmed that the revolution had begun.[88] Finally, on 8 November the guards formed a soldiers' council and deposed their officers, stripping them of their swords and epaulettes. Later that day the Prussian monarchical flag was lowered from its place on 'Trafalgar Square' in the middle of the camp and a red flag – supplied by some sympathetic prisoners who used a tablecloth and some red dye from the camp workshop – was hoisted in its place (Figure 17).[89] The new soldiers' council also issued a written declaration stating that Germans and Englishmen were 'brothers' and that Germany was still a proud nation which 'would never beg; rather would it go to ruin' (Figure 18). The

17   The red flag flies on Trafalgar Square: Ruhleben during the November
revolution

prisoners were told that their release was now 'only a matter of days' but in
the meantime they were advised to stay in the camp for their own safety. In
at least one account the red flag remained flying at Ruhleben 'to avoid risk of
being fired on', while nearly all agree that the members of the new *Soldatenrat*
were 'moderate' socialists, not 'radicals' or 'spartacists'.[90]

Disregarding the advice given to them, most of the prisoners made
trips into Berlin over the following days and found a city where life was
surprisingly 'normal', in spite of the abdication of the Kaiser and the
declaration of a republic. One prisoner, Jeffrey Messent, later wrote:

> The socialists organised the revolution well and there was little
> bloodshed. There was sporadic sniping from house tops for some
> days afterwards, but remarkably few casualties. On the day of the
> actual revolution in Berlin (November 9th) trains, trams and other
> services were crowded with jubilant workers, many riding on roofs,
> buffers etc. There was an atmosphere of rejoicing and of holiday like
> that of November 11th in England. In fact Berlin was so absorbed
> in celebrating the revolution that the Armistice was hardly noticed
> – also there were obvious reasons why this was not celebrated as it
> was in England.[91]

ENGLÄNDER!

Brüder von jenseits des Kanals

Es ist tragisch, tief, tief tragisch das es erst einer Million von Toten bedurfte von jeder Seite, um uns zu der Erkenntnis zu bringen das wir Brüder Stammesgenossen trotz allem sind. Haben sich je ausser jezt Deutsche u England zerfleicht? Nach unseren persönlichen Eindrücken, die wir gestern an massgebender Stelle empfing ist es nur eine Frage von Tagen und Ihr werdet frei sein. Wenn Ihr wieder drüben seid so wirkt aufklärend dahin, dass das deutsche Volk trotz all der Siege Kraft genug behalten hat, seine Geschicke selbst in die Hand zu nehmen und diesmal auch zu behaupten, wirkt dahin dass das Volk sich in diesen Tagen seiner grössten Nöten die gleichzeitig aber auch die stolzesten Tage seiner Geschichte sind instinktiv seine Blicke hilfsuchend nach drüben gerichtet hat. Engländer! das deutsche ist stolz, es bettelt nie, lieber geht es zu Grunde. Brüder, oder Menchen von drüben, das deutscheVolk,auf sich ganz allein aufgewiesen,wird daran ist gar nicht zu zweifeln eventuell auc ganz allein, die Wunden überwinden und wieder gross werden. Zieht aus unserem Wörten die Konsequenzen und handelt danach wenn Ihr drüben seid.

Soldatenrat, Engländerlager, RUHLEBEN.
(gez.) Zirwes, Kieser, Plümer, Wolff, Beer, Schütze.

ENGLISHMEN!

Brothers from over the Channel.

It is tragic, deeply tragical, that a million dead on both sides were necessary in order to bring home to us that after all we are brothers, & members of the same race. Have Germans & British ever until now, torn each other to pieces? From impressions gained in competent circles yesterday, it is our personal opinion that your release is only a matter of days. When you are at home again, let it be your task to make known that the German people, in spite of all its victories, still retained sufficient strength to take its destiny into its own hand & this time to keep it there. Let your aim be to make known that the German people, in this, its time of greatest need, which is also the proudest period of its history, instinctively casts its eyes across the water, looking for help Englishmen! the German nation is proud, it will never beg, rather would it go to ruin. Brothers, or men from across the sea, the German people, left entirely to itself will eventually - there can be no doubt of this,- recover from its wounds & regain its greatness. Draw the consequences from our words & act accordingly when you are back at home. Soldiers Council, Engländerlager, RUHLEBEN.
(signed) Zirwes, Kieser, Plümer, Wolff, Beer, Schütze.

18   Declaration issued by the soldiers' council at Ruhleben, November 1918

Likewise John Masterman remembered:

> [W]hatever many have been the case elsewhere, [in Berlin] the revolution was strangely orderly. Once in the Tiergarten there was a splutter of machine-gun fire and the crowd scattered, but even then, so strong was the engrained habit of discipline, that hardly a German disobeyed the notices which forbade them to step on the grass. 'Verboten' was still 'Verboten' even in November 1918.[92]

Other prisoners were less interested in the political events happening around them than in the new opportunities for making money by selling goods like soap and toothpaste on the black market or for making sexual conquests of various kinds. The actor George Merritt, for instance, boasted to Peter Liddle in July 1977 about the wild nights he had had in Berlin during the revolution, with alcohol and women allegedly both freely available.[93] Several Ruhlebenites also took pliers into the Tiergarten and prized nails from the famous 'Iron Hindenburg' statue to take home as souvenirs. One of these nails was later presented to King George V when he visited the Ruhleben Exhibition in London on 10 February 1919.[94] Another can be found in the Liddle Collection at the University of Leeds, among the papers of former internee A. R. Cusden.[95]

Against the background of defeat, the arrangements for repatriating the prisoners were made surprisingly quickly. At the highest levels article 10 of the armistice signed at Compiègne on 11 November 1918 had stipulated the immediate return of all allied and associated POWs without any guarantee of reciprocity.[96] At ground level members of a British Red Cross team sent to Berlin in mid-November negotiated directly with the city's new civilian commandant, the Social Democrat Otto Wels, and arranged for two trains to take the prisoners out of the city. Through the efforts of Elisabeth Rotten permission was also granted for the Berlin-based wives and children of the internees to be brought to Ruhleben, where they stayed from 13 November.[97] Finally, on 22 and 24 November a total of 1,500 prisoners and their families were allowed to proceed to Copenhagen via Sassnitz. From there they were given free passage on Danish ships sailing to Hull or Leith. After spending a few days at special reception centres for returning prisoners they were released to make the last leg of their journey home.[98] Some employees of the British section of the Netherlands legation and several hundred 'ordinary' prisoners chose to remain in Germany for the time being, or (in a handful of cases) were refused passports by the British authorities. Unfortunately there are no further records of what happened to them, although the majority probably resumed their lives in the new Germany without further incident and there were certainly no moves to expel them by force.[99]

Meanwhile, the camp itself did not stay empty for long. A report sent by the British section of the Netherlands legation to the German Foreign Office on 28 November complained that extensive looting had taken place immediately after the departure of the last British prisoners, with both soldiers and ordinary civilians involved. Two days later a large group of Russian prisoners, who had been evacuated from camps on the left bank of the Rhine, arrived in Berlin and were billeted at Ruhleben (and other camps) on Wels' orders. This made it impossible, the report continued, for the Dutch diplomatic authorities to carry out a proper inventory of the camp or to accept responsibility for any damage done after the departure of the British internees.[100] How long the Russians stayed is unclear, but the camp was returned to its former owners, the Ruhleben *Trabrennbahn*, only in 1921, and the first season of the post-war years did not open until 1924, following a break of almost ten years.[101]

Notes

1 Speed, *Prisoners, Diplomats and the Great War*, pp. 37–8; Newton, *Retrospection*, pp. 237–9.
2 Even so, the remaining 'over-forty-fives' in Ruhleben were not actually repatriated until January 1918, owing to continued delays in reaching agreement over the practicalities of effecting an exchange, including the question of which ports to use. See Ketchum, *Ruhleben*, p. 349. Also Prussian Ministry of War to the AA, 10 September 1917, in BA Berlin, R 901/83955.
3 The full text of the Hague agreement of 2 July 1917 can be found in ACICR, C G 1 411/IX.
4 On the 14 July 1918 agreement see ACICR, C G 1 411/XXVIII and GLA Karlsruhe, Bestand 456/F8, no. 289. This treaty was not ratified by the German government until 3 November 1918, eight days before the armistice, and was therefore of only limited importance in determining the fate of the Ruhleben prisoners. Cf. *Journal de Genève*, 5 November 1918.
5 Unterkunftsdepartement to all deputy general commands, 22 April 1915, in HStA Stuttgart, M 77/1, no. 868, Bl. 1. See also further instructions issued at regular intervals between then and March 1917 in the same volume.
6 Unterkunftsdepartement to all deputy general commands, 13 March 1916, in *ibid.*, Bl. 9.
7 This order is referred to in a letter from the Prussian Ministry of War to the Reich Office of Interior, 22 October 1917, in BA Berlin, R 1501/112370, Bl. 387.

8   *Rapport général du Comité international de la Croix-Rouge sur son activité de 1912 à 1920* (Geneva, 1921), pp. 136–7.

9   A military notice, dated 9 May 1918, in HLL-EC, box 5, file 13, suggests that only 180 men had volunteered for farm work in Ostfriesland, although up to 500 places had been made available by the German military.

10   See *Parliamentary Debates, House of Lords*, fifth series, vol. XXIII, p. 501. Also *Verhandlungen des Reichstags*, vol. 308, p. 1983.

11   Sir Timothy Eden, 'Civilian Prisoners: The Case for their Release', *The Times*, 22 November 1916. See also the many letters in support of Eden published in *The Times* on 24, 25, 27, 28 and 30 November 1916.

12   Devonport to Eden, 26 November 1916, in Liddle Collection, RUH 18.

13   See e.g. Adelaide, Duchess of Bedford, to Eden, 8 November 1916, and Northcliffe to Eden, 31 October 1916 and 12 February 1917, all in *ibid.*

14   See e.g. Devonport's repeated interventions in the debate in the House of Lords on 7 March 1918, in *Parliamentary Debates, House of Lords*, fifth series, vol. XXIX, pp. 327–55.

15   See the report in *The Times*, 27 February 1917.

16   *The Ruhleben Prisoners. The Government Attitude*, pamphlet no. 3, issued by the Ruhleben Prisoners' Release Committee, p. 30, in Liddle Collection, RUH 46.

17   *The Ruhleben Prisoners. The Case for their Release*, pamphlet no. 1, p. 44, in *ibid.*

18   *Parliamentary Debates, House of Lords*, fifth series, vol. XXIV, p. 244.

19   *Ibid.*, p. 247.

20   *The Ruhleben Prisoners. The Case for their Release*, pp. 41–2.

21   Douglas Sladen (ed.), *In Ruhleben. Letters from a Prisoner to His Mother* (London, 1917), p. 2.

22   Cf. Ruhleben Prisoners' Release Committee to Mrs Cottrell-Dormer, 11 May 1917, in Liddle Collection, RUH 10.

23   'Send them all home', *Daily Mail*, 16 February 1917. On Northcliffe's ongoing role in demanding the expulsion of Germans from Britain see also Thomas Wittek, *Auf ewig Feind? Das Deutschlandbild in den britischen Massenmedien nach dem Ersten Weltkrieg* (Munich, 2005), pp. 215–27.

24   See Minna Cauer diaries, 21 June 1916, in Internationaal Instituut voor Sociale Geschiedenis (IISG), Amsterdam. Also the article 'Eine unbequeme Zeugin', *Frankfurter Zeitung*, 9 November 1916.

25   See e.g. the letter from a 'returned Ruhlebenite' published in *The Times*, 31 October 1916. Also the questions raised by various MPs in the House of Commons on 26 and 31 October and 1 November 1916, in *Parliamentary Debates, House of Commons*, vol. LXXXVI, pp. 1270–1, 1495–8, 1697 and 1745–7.

26   For a more sympathetic account of Hobhouse's visit to Germany and occupied Belgium see John V. Crangle and Joseph O. Baylen, 'Emily Hobhouse's Peace Mission, 1916', *Journal of Contemporary History*, 14/4 (1979), pp. 731–44.

27 Panayi, *The Enemy in Our Midst*, p. 87.
28 See e.g. *The Ruhleben Prisoners. The Government Attitude*, pamphlet no. 3; *The Ruhleben Prisoners. Some Recent Parliamentary References*, pamphlet no. 4. Copies of both in Liddle Collection, RUH 46.
29 On the food question see Davis, *Home Fires Burning*, passim.
30 The figures can be found in BA Berlin, R 1501/112370, Bl. 327. See also Panayi, *The Enemy in Our Midst*, p. 87.
31 Gill, 'Calculating Compassion in War', p. 187.
32 Jones, 'The Enemy Disarmed', pp. 324–5.
33 *The British Prisoner of War*, published by the Central Prisoners of War Committee of the British Red Cross and the Order of St John, vol. 1, nos. 1–12 (January to December 1918).
34 Friends Emergency Committee, meeting of camps sub-committee, 9 May 1918, in Society of Friends Library, London (henceforth FEWVRC), Camps/1/M2.
35 Protokolle der Sitzung des Verwaltungsausschusses des König Eduards VII. Stiftung, 4 February 1915, in BA Berlin, R 1501/112365, Bl. 60–3.
36 Lewald to Reich Chancellor Hertling, 14 May 1918, in BA Berlin, R 1501/112371, Bl. 173–4.
37 Minna Cauer diaries, 18 February 1916, in IISG Amsterdam.
38 Rotten to the FEC, 24 June 1916, in EZA Berlin, Bestand 51 C III a 6/2.
39 See the voluminous correspondence between Rotten and Warburg in *ibid.*, a 6/5 and a 7/4.
40 Protokoll der Sitzung der Auskunfts- und Hilfsstelle für Deutsche im Ausland und Ausländer in Deutschland, 21 March 1917, in *ibid.*, a 4/2.
41 See e.g the lists of donors in *ibid.*, a 6/1, and Stibbe, 'Elisabeth Rotten', passim.
42 Eric Higgins 'Connection of Dr. Rotten with Ruhleben', report dated 10 March 1919, in NA, FO 383/524.
43 Edward Winton, 'Reprisals of Good. Assistance to Enemy Aliens', *The Times*, 29 September 1916. See also Dr Markel to Rotten, 27 February 1918, and Markel to Higgins, 19 March 1918, copies in BA Berlin, R 901/83957.
44 See n. 42 above. Also the archival material (including correspondence between Higgins and Rotten) in EZA Berlin, Bestand 51 C II b 4.
45 Undated postcard Einstein to Rotten, [January 1918], in *ibid.*, Bestand 51 C II b 4 c/1. Cf. Hubert Goenner, *Einstein in Berlin, 1914–1933* (Munich, 2005) pp. 79–80; Tripp, 'Kommunikation und Vergemeinschaftung', p. 58.
46 'Deutsche Hochschule in einem englischen Gefangenenlager', *Berliner Tageblatt*, 14 November 1917.
47 Rotten to Dr Eckardt (AA), 11 June 1918, in BA Berlin, R 901/83957; Higgins, 'Connection of Dr. Rotten with Ruhleben' (as n. 42 above), p. 4.
48 See e.g. the 'papers relating to examinations taken at Ruhleben, June–December 1918', in Liddle Collection, RUH 33. Also Ketchum, *Ruhleben*, pp. 234–5.

49 'Matriculation at Ruhleben', *The Times*, 1 November 1918.

50 Friends Emergency Committee, meetings of camps sub-committee, 8 March 1917, 12 April 1917, 10 May 1917, 14 June 1917 and 10 October 1918, in FEWVRC Camps/1/M2.

51 Cf. my discussion of this issue in Stibbe, 'Elisabeth Rotten', passim.

52 Higgins, 'Connection of Dr. Rotten with Ruhleben' (as n. 42 above), p. 3. Cf. Hirschfeld (ed.), *Sittengeschichte des Weltkrieges*, esp. vol. 2, pp. 81–102.

53 See Higgins' 11-page report on his 'illegal' imprisonment, dated 12 March 1919, in NA, FO 383/524.

54 Sitzung des Kriegskabinetts, 24 October 1918, in Erich Matthias and Rudolf Morsey (eds.), *Die Regierung des Prinzen Max von Baden* (Düsseldorf, 1962), p. 322.

55 *Ibid.*

56 The speeches were reprinted as a BNV pamphlet – *Durch zum Rechtsfrieden. Ein Appell an das Weltgewissen von Professor W. Schücking, Dr. Helene Stöcker und Dr. Elisabeth Rotten* (Berlin, 1919). On the Schücking commission see also Jones, 'The Enemy Disarmed', pp. 370–1.

57 See e.g. 'British Prisoners. German Excuses not Accepted', *The Times*, 28 November 1918.

58 Stibbe, 'Elisabeth Rotten', p. 204.

59 Higgins, 'Connection of Dr. Rotten with Ruhleben' (as n. 42), p. 5; Powell and Gribble, *The History of Ruhleben*, p. 244.

60 The reports can be found in NA, MT 9/1244.

61 See e.g. the interview records in NA, FO 383/424. Also Powell and Gribble, *The History of Ruhleben*, p. 233.

62 'Bei den englischen Zivilinternierten in Ruhleben', *Berliner Illustrierte Zeitung*, no. 41, 13 October 1918, pp. 324–5.

63 'Ruhleben après trois ans et demi de guerre', French translation of article published in the *Stockholms Dagblad*, 9 April 1918, in BA Berlin, R 901/84424. According to a letter from the AA to the chief of the general staff, 26 May 1918, in *ibid.*, the plan was to send copies to Argentina, Chile, Columbia, Denmark, Dominican Republic, Luxembourg, Mexico, the Netherlands, Norway, Persia, Spain, Sweden and Switzerland.

64 Minutes of barrack captains' committee, 20 June 1918, in HLL-EC, box 5, file 15.

65 Sumner F. Austin, interview with Peter Liddle, October 1977, in Liddle Collection, RUH 01.

66 Jahr, 'Zivilisten als Kriegsgefangene', p. 313.

67 Jeffrey Sutton Messent, 'The German Revolution of November 1918', unpublished typescript recollections (November 1936), p. 1, in Liddle Collection, RUH 35.

68 Jonkheer Snouck-Hurgronje to C. Ridder van Rappard, 17 December 1917, in NA, FO 383/425. Cf. Prussian Ministry of War to AA, 13 November 1917, in BA Berlin, R 901/84319.

69 Ketchum, *Ruhleben*, p. 353.

70 Hinz, *Gefangen im Großen Krieg*, p. 170.

71 Masterman, *On the Chariot Wheel*, p. 107.

72 Snouck-Hurgronje to van Rappard, 17 December 1917 (as n. 68 above).

73 O'Sullivan Molony, *Prisoners and Captives*, pp. 244–8. See also the letter from the Central Prisoners of War Committee to Sir Arthur Stanley of the British Red Cross, 29 July 1918, in NA, FO 383/425.

74 See e.g. the report by Dr R. Römer of the Netherlands legation in Berlin, 8 October 1917, in BA Berlin, R 901/84424. Also Rotten to Eckardt, 11 June 1918, in *ibid.*, R 901/83957.

75 Powell and Gribble, *The History of Ruhleben*, p. 222; Ketchum, *Ruhleben*, p. 286.

76 Minutes of barrack captains' committee, 19 April 1918, 17 May 1918 and 25 June 1918, in HLL-EC, box 5, file 15.

77 Ketchum, *Ruhleben*, pp. 167–8.

78 Minutes of barrack captains' committee, 18 July 1918, in HLL-EC, box 5, file 15.

79 Jones, 'The Enemy Disarmed', p. 334.

80 *Ibid.*, pp. 330–1.

81 Ketchum, *Ruhleben*, p. 165.

82 See *ibid.*, p. 349. Also the reports of the Netherlands legation, 20 and 27 August 1918, in NA, MT 9/1244, and further evidence of periodic releases continuing until early November 1918 in BA Berlin, R 901/83978–9.

83 O'Sullivan Molony, *Prisoners and Captives*, p. 251.

84 Ketchum, *Ruhleben*, pp. 346–8; Masterman, *On the Chariot Wheel*, p. 112.

85 See the announcement in *The Times*, 6 November 1918.

86 Powell and Gribble, *The History of Ruhleben*, p. 239.

87 Messent, 'The German Revolution of November 1918', p. 1.

88 Powell and Gribble, *The History of Ruhleben*, p. 236.

89 Harold Redmayne, 'Ruhleben, 1914–1918', unpublished recollections, no date, pp. 15–16, in Liddle Collection, RUH 44.

90 Messent, 'The German Revolution of November 1918', p. 3; Powell and Gribble, *The History of Ruhleben*, p. 238. The one dissenting voice is that of O'Sullivan Molony, *Prisoners and Captives*, pp. 265–7, who wrote that the camp was taken over by spartacist sailors whom the British sailors objected to, leading to a series of fist fights: 'We were not going to support the disgraceful presence of these men.' However, there is no independent corroboration of this story.

91 Messent, 'The German Revolution of November 1918', p. 2.

92 Masterman, *On the Chariot Wheel*, pp. 112–13.

93 George Merritt, interview with Peter Liddle, July 1977, in Liddle Collection, RUH 34.

94 See 'Ruhleben Exhibition: Visit of the King and Queen', *The Times*, 11 February 1919.

95 See Liddle Collection, RUH 13.

96 Hinz, *Gefangen im Großen Krieg*, p. 330.

97 Powell and Gribble, *The History of Ruhleben*, p. 244.

98 See the report in *The Times*, 28 November 1918.

99 There are one or two documents in the Staatsarchiv Hamburg, Senatskriegsakten 111–2, Lz1, pertaining to the renewal of residency permits to former Ruhleben inmates by the local police authorities between November 1918 and January 1919. However, this relates to individual cases only, and there are no clear figures for the numbers involved. Mary Firth of Washington State has also kept her grandfather Albert Firth's release papers from Ruhleben, dated 14 November 1918, which allowed him passage to and residency in Bremen conditional on registering with the local police authorities – Mary Firth to the author, 21 December 2006, enclosing photocopy of the same.

100 Netherlands legation, British section, to the AA, 28 November 1918, in BA Berlin, R 901/84424. Cf. Ministry of War to the AA, 22 September 1919, in *ibid.*, which confirms the accuracy of these claims.

101 Bruno Hettwer (ed.), *Deutsches Traber-Derby. Ruhleben, 1924/5* (Berlin, 1924).

6

Ruhleben in British memory

The story of the Ruhleben prisoners did not end with the dissolution of the camp in November 1918. While most of those released disappeared into obscurity, a significant minority sought to publicise their experiences, either through writing memoirs, accepting invitations to act as after-dinner speakers, or involving themselves in the Ruhleben Exhibition project. They also found a willing audience. Thus several of the more prominent Ruhlebenites received OBEs and MBEs for their contribution to the war effort and the welfare of British prisoners, and others were celebrated as heroes in their own communities.[1] Members of the royal family and thousands of ordinary Londoners visited the Ruhleben Exhibition when it finally opened at Westminster Hall in January 1919; here they were greeted by a range of musical and theatrical performances as well as arts and crafts produced by prisoners in the camp. The British Red Cross Society also used this event to advertise its own particular role in war relief and charity.[2]

However, in spite of all this publicity, the story of internment never received due recognition in the official commemorations of the war, and was very rapidly superseded by a focus on grieving families and the men who did not return. Just twelve months after the guns had fallen silent, governments, communities and veterans' organisations were all too busy mourning the dead or creating 'multi-vocal' languages of sacrifice and redemption to think about the problems facing prisoners or ex-soldiers after they returned home.[3] By the end of 1919 very little was heard or said about Ruhleben in the newspapers or the publishing industry, and in 1928, on the tenth anniversary of the end of the war, hardly a line was printed in support of civilian war victims and their battle for financial compensation.

It would therefore seem fitting to devote the final chapter of this book to considering why such a high-profile community as Ruhleben gradually drifted out of official British memory of the war. Was it simply that there were too few ex–internees, especially in comparison to ex-soldiers, to make their experiences count? Or were other factors at work? First, though, it will be necessary to consider the place of Ruhleben in individual memory and in what Jay Winter and Emmanuel Sivan have termed 'collective remembrance', meaning shared acts of 'public recollection' at the communal and associational level.[4]

Individual memory

'Individuals', as Joanna Bourke writes, '"remember", "repress", "forget" and are "traumatized", not societies'.[5] Memory-based studies must therefore begin with the individual and move from there to the collective, although the boundaries between the two are often blurred.[6] Changes in group values or social priorities do impact on individual memory, just as some individuals' memories can help to change group or social priorities. Sadly for historians, the Ruhlebenites did more repressing than remembering. Returning home in 1918, most could not explain how they felt, even to their own relatives. They saw themselves as victims rather than agents in their personal war, and a sense of powerlessness and low self-esteem remained with them after release, preventing them from 'bearing witness' in the same way as soldier-heroes returning from the battlefield. Silence was their only recourse. Some were probably suffering from 'barbed wire disease', the symptoms of mental illness found in prisoners of war across the globe, and described by the Swiss physician Adolf Lukas Vischer in his book of the same name.[7] Others had flashbacks, moments of blind panic, and a general inability to mix socially with 'normal people', especially women. One former internee told Peter Liddle in an interview in 1977 that the experience of Ruhleben had made him and his fellow prisoners 'abnormal':

> Well, we didn't know it in the camp. I mean we were there amongst our own, but when I came out you know I can still remember if I went to the office. If I had something to eat say in the Lyons shop. I couldn't sit at a table there with anybody opposite me. That sort of thing. I mean it took an awful long time, you were amongst people who were different. I mean our language was simply awful. Swearing and so on ... I still use bad language when I am on my own. I hope that I won't be overheard. I mean it's just a relief you know.[8]

Occasionally, more sanitised aspects of the internment experience were narrated to family members and thus became part of family history. Ellen

Prendergast, the daughter of internee Albert Firth, recalled that her father 'would talk just a very little about it' while firmly rejecting any feelings of hatred for Germany: '"It was time of war"', he would say, '"people are not themselves at a time like that".'[9] Families indeed do seem to be good at remembering and decoding stories from their relatives' pasts, although the historical value of such memories varies from case to case. To take another example, in April 2004 Louise Argent from Bristol contacted me. She was looking for information about Ruhleben, as her great grandfather, a merchant sailor on the *Sappho*, had been in the camp. The little that she knew about this had been passed down to her by relatives. During the Second World War, she told me, when the bombing of Bristol began, her great grandfather was reported to have been 'visibly very petrified'. Family members attributed this to his experiences in Ruhleben, without going into details.[10] Unfortunately, this reflects the limits of what we can know, as historians, about an individual's memory as retold by a later generation. We have to fill in the gaps and make assumptions which are at best informed guesswork and at worst mere conjecture.

In my own case, I was aware from a young age that my grandfather, Edward Stibbe, had been in Ruhleben, that the camp was a former racecourse, and that when my grandparents married in 1920 the best man, Douglas Munro, had been in Ruhleben too. It is possible that, when in the company of former friends and associates from Ruhleben, my grandfather engaged in acts of collective remembrance of the kind that Jay Winter categorises under the heading 'fictive kinship'.[11] Friendships were indeed forged for life in Ruhleben, particularly among those who had shared the same living quarters for four years. The horse-boxes were in effect substitute families, some of them quite functional, others less so. I have absolutely no idea how my grandfather remembered Ruhleben in private, however, and he seems rarely to have talked about it with other family members, even with his children. In this case, too, there is relatively little to go on; the memories die with the individual and his 'fictive kin'.

There are, however, one or two instances known to me where individuals recorded their memories of Ruhleben for private purposes, not intending them to be published, at least in their own lifetimes, but nonetheless hoping to leave their families with a permanent record about an important event in their personal history. In 2003 I was given various papers and artifacts belonging to Frank Stockall, an internee from Loughborough in Leicestershire, including a memoir of Ruhleben he had written in 1961, just before his death. It is one of the most vivid accounts of life in Ruhleben I have read, and is narrated as if the events had occurred just weeks before.

The intervening forty years had also conditioned what Stockall had to say, however, and there is a profound sense that he is trying to come to terms with an experience which, in retrospect, shaped the rest of his life. In an especially poignant passage towards the end, Stockall writes:

> On the good side I did, I think, gain in four short years an insight into human behaviour under many different circumstances. I learnt ... a real appreciation of the role of womanhood as a civilising factor in our own lives. I was able to study languages, economics, drama and music – which I probably should not have had time or opportunity to do. On the other hand I left the camp weak in health [and] the ill effects lasted until well into 1935. I was left in an extremely nervous condition [and] hated meeting 'new' people, a condition which still persists ... Finally, the general condition of my health and altered temperament forced me into an occupation (until 1937) for which I was most unsuited.[12]

The question remains, nonetheless, whether a personal narrative such as this is really a contribution to the history of Ruhleben or merely the story of one man's war. To paraphrase Samuel Hynes, 'one man's Ruhleben is not everyman's'.[13] Stockall's memoir is extremely detailed, but even he admits, in an earlier passage: 'There is much that I have deliberately omitted. All prison camps in 1914 to 1918 were not run as ours was. Many lives were lost in the salt mines, many died later as the result of their hardship ... We lived in constant fear of being transferred to these camps.'[14] Already here we can see signs of the kind of self-censorship which prevented people like Stockall from doing more to publicise their own stories. But even in its unpublished form, how can we be sure that Stockall's voice speaks for the many in Ruhleben, in other words that it is more than just a personal reflection? The limitations of personal memory are more apparent when we remember just how little of it is shared.

Collective remembrance

Where individual memory meets family memory, we begin to approach the first level of 'collective remembrance'. Fragments of the past are gathered together for family consumption, or for the consumption of future generations. Inevitably fact becomes confused with legend, and exact details remain muddled or obscure. More often than not, the memories are of the individual and not of the historical event itself. For instance, when my father decided to publish his own father's unpublished memoir of Ruhleben in 1969, he did so not to remember Ruhleben, but to remember his father, who had died a few years before.[15]

Attempts to bring Ruhleben to a wider, more public audience, are a different matter, however, and require a search for different kinds of sources. Thus, the one act of public commemoration which did receive significant national attention was the above-mentioned Ruhleben Exhibition, held at Westminster Hall in early 1919 and attended by a range of dignitaries, including King George V and Queen Mary.[16] In the first months after the war a great deal of coverage was also given in the Northcliffe press to the possibility of obtaining compensation from the German government for the suffering of British civilian prisoners, for their loss of business and earnings, and for the money their families had spent on food parcels.[17] Returning internees were indeed encouraged to register any individual claims with the Foreign Claims Office housed within the Foreign Office.[18] Hopes were raised by the final version of the Treaty of Versailles, which required Germany, under article 232, to pay compensation

> to civilian victims of acts of cruelty, violence or maltreatment (including injuries to life or health as a consequence of imprisonment, deportation, internment or evacuation, of exposure at sea or of being forced to labour), wherever arising, and to the surviving dependants of such victims.[19]

However, not long after this a decision was taken in the corridors of Whitehall that the Treasury would take sole charge of all monies received from Germany by way of reparations, and would distribute them as it saw fit, on the basis of the Crown's prerogative to decide what was in the national interest. This position was announced in the House of Commons on 4 May 1920 by the Chancellor of the Exchequer, Sir Austen Chamberlain:

> His Majesty's Government have given careful consideration to the position of individuals in respect to whose losses reparation will be claimed by His Majesty's Government. It must be understood that the claims to be made are claims by the British Government in respect of a wrong done to the State, and not claims by individuals in respect of private wrongs, and that the Government do not act as agents of any individual to put forward his personal claim. Any payments that may be received from Germany are therefore the property of the nation, and no individual will have any claim in law for any sum

which the British Government may receive from Germany in respect of reparation.[20]

A sum of £5 million would be set aside as an 'act of grace', Chamberlain continued, but claims would be considered 'on the basis of the strength of the case for compensation' and not on the basis of actual damage done to businesses, livelihoods and health.[21]

After this very little publicity was given either to the individual claims of ex–internees, or to the treatment of civilian victims of the war more generally. Politics – and public sentiment in general – dictated that the military and naval victims of the war should receive the largest slice of the cake, and civilian prisoners were subsequently pushed to the bottom of the pile, much to their own dismay and the dismay of their families and supporters. The same applied to public recognition of war service and sacrifice as well. Rightly or wrongly, governments and communities framed their commemorations of the war around the families who had lost loved ones and the veterans who had seen their comrades fall; the annual 2-minute silence staged up and down the country on Armistice Day during the inter-war years, and the sale of poppies to raise funds for the British Legion, reflected similar concerns and priorities.[22]

Nonetheless, on a small-scale level there were efforts to retell and commemorate the story of Ruhleben for a public audience. Some of this at least was motivated by an exasperation with politicians and bureaucrats who talked empty talk about reparations and compensation for the civilian victims of war and then failed to deliver. But concern to preserve the memory of Ruhleben for its own sake and pride in the cultural and intellectual achievements of the Ruhleben community were also important factors, and became more so as time went on.

For instance, like many other veterans, the former Ruhlebenites established an exclusive club of their own, the Ruhleben Association. At first this was affiliated with the Civilian War Claimants' Association, a pressure group founded in 1925 to challenge the government's decision 'to withhold and not account for moneys paid by Germany to compensate civilians who suffered wrongs inflicted upon themselves or their property during the war'.[23] The chairman of the executive committee of the Civilian War Claimants' Association, Mr G. M. Judd, spoke on several occasions to the annual gatherings of the Ruhleben Association, and kept it informed of the progress of its legal action against the government.[24] This action finally failed in November 1931, when the Law Lords threw out an appeal made by barristers acting for Judd on the grounds that there was 'no precedent' for believing that the Treasury could act as 'agents or trustees in the matter of individual claims against foreign governments'.[25]

However, compensation was not a dominant theme for the Ruhleben Association, and its membership was largely made up of the more financially secure among the ex-prisoners, particularly those who had been linked to the Arts and Science Union led by John Masterman. The aim was to commemorate the collective experience of internment through regular rehearsal of particular moments, the most important of which was the practice of singing the Ruhleben song at the annual dinner in London. In the 1960s proposals were made to suspend these reunions on account of dwindling numbers, but in fact they continued through to 1974, the sixtieth anniversary of internment, when there were still sixty members of the Ruhleben Association known to be alive.[26] Christoph Jahr is undoubtedly correct when he writes that the members of this group represented 'a narrow upper-class elite' which 'cultivated their specific memory of the camp' without showing much concern to preserve the memories of other internees, whether black, white, British, German or Jewish.[27] Nonetheless, the group itself is also an indication of the importance of collective ritual in expanding a particular memory's 'shelf-life', especially when that memory threatened to be all but obliterated by the impact of the Second World War. It is thus no coincidence that the same familiar faces turned up year after year at the annual dinners, anxious to remember with like-minded people an experience which had shaped their attitude towards life and towards others.[28]

Apart from the Ruhleben Association, several individual internees wrote memoirs, some of them taken up by commercial publishers and others printed privately for circulation among friends and family. Most of those that were published appeared during the war or in the months immediately following the armistice; after 1919 there was a remarkable tailing off of Ruhleben memoirs.[29] Francis Gribble's *Seen in Passing* is one possible exception; this book appeared in 1929, and included a few short chapters on the Ruhleben experience at the end of a long narrative about life as a journalist and travel writer in pre-war Europe. However, Gribble had been released in September 1915 in the first exchange party and had not seen the worst years of internment. Certainly he did not regard his captivity as a central or enduring feature of his personal war, as it was for other internees. His views on the Germans were also much more restrained, as one would expect for a book published in 1929 rather than 1919. Few people in fact are criticised in this book, and internment is presented simply as an unfortunate and unavoidable consequence of war – it was 'just something that ... happened, pretty much as an earthquake might happen'.[30]

Finally, from the 1920s onwards various individuals associated with Ruhleben made efforts to preserve material artifacts and documents relating to the internment experience. The largest of these collections was – and still is – based at the Harvard Law Library in Cambridge, Massachusetts, and was the work of one man, Dr Maurice Ettinghausen, an antiquarian bookseller from London and one time captain of barrack 6, who sold it to the Law Library in 1932. It includes a whole host of military orders and announcements, theatre and concert tickets, lecture notes, programmes for sporting events and so on, as well as the minutes of the barrack captains' committee and near complete runs of all the camp newspapers and magazines.[31] The Toronto-based social psychologist John Davidson Ketchum also collected material, including contemporary diaries and letters, as well as interviews with fellow ex-prisoners, for a book he began writing in the 1930s and had almost completed at the time of his death in 1962. His aim, as he wrote, was to trace the 'moments and changes through which four thousand detached individuals became a close-knit society, and [to explain] the functioning of that society during its four years of life'.[32] At the same time, though, he was also interested in documenting 'the extraordinary nature of Ruhleben's population' and 'the challenging conditions of their internment' to a world that now seemed to take 'the mass internment of aliens in wartime … for granted'.[33]

Following the posthumous publication of Ketchum's work in 1965, the British historian Peter Liddle gathered new evidence, including transcripts of interviews with several ex-prisoners, a number of diaries and other personal recollections, and hundreds of photographs and letters. All of this is now housed in the Liddle Collection at the Brotherton Library, University of Leeds.[34] A smaller collection, relating mainly to the experiences of seamen and fishermen from the Humber ports, can be found in the Central Library in Grimsby; this includes material brought together for a special memorial exhibition to mark the sixtieth anniversary of the return of the Ruhleben men in November 1978. The pamphlet that accompanied this event indeed indicates that at least thirty local families, as well as a number of libraries, archives and maritime organisations, supplied material of various kinds. The name Ruhleben still clearly had a resonance within this particular part of the country, and it remains an important part of the Humber region's history during the Great War.[35]

However, in spite of all these efforts to preserve memories of internment and associated artifacts and visual images, the story of Ruhleben never became part of official 'British memory' of the Great War and barely receives a mention in any of the standard histories. Why was this the case?

Official commemoration

In his book *The Soldiers' Tale*, the literary historian Samuel Hynes points to the cultural hegemony achieved by accounts of the western front in writing on the Great War from the 1920s onwards. All other fronts, he argues, became mere 'sideshows' in the collective body of memoir literature on the war.[36] However, Ruhleben was not always regarded a 'sideshow'. During the war there were regular debates about internment in the House of Commons and the House of Lords, as we have seen, and the press also carried frequent reports on life in Germany's most famous prison camp. Sebastian Tripp, for instance, in a search of the London *Times*, found no fewer than 300 entries under the heading 'Ruhleben' between 1914 and 1920.[37] Likewise Chris Paton, who hosts a website on Ruhleben, claims to have discovered 240 articles on Ruhleben published by the *Scotsman* between 1914 and 1919.[38] This is on top of the government's own miscellaneous white papers on the subject, which were published at regular intervals and provoked much comment in parliament and press, and the material produced by the Ruhleben Prisoners' Release Committee in the years 1917–18.[39] However, after 1920 Ruhleben did indeed largely disappear from public discussion of the war.

Firstly, there is the cultural explanation, put forward by Hynes, Rachamimov and others, which stresses how the experience of wartime captivity did not fit into changing public perceptions of the war as the 1920s turned into the 1930s. Put simply, the Ruhleben story, like other POW narratives, was seen as an inadequate way of representing the destructive violence, youthful camaraderie and sheer madness of the war. It was hard to square, for instance, with the dominant myth of an 'heroic masculinity' which, as Graham Dawson has shown, continued to have a powerful presence in British imperial culture after 1918, particularly in popular adventure stories and war films.[40] Yet it was equally incompatible with the 'lost generation' idea, as put forward in the late 1920s by disillusioned ex-soldiers and war veterans like Edmund Blunden, Robert Graves and Siegfried Sassoon. Even the visual imagery of the camp – a trotting course inhabited by men in civilian outfits playing cricket and tennis or pottering about 'Bond Street' and 'Trafalgar Square' – reminded one of peacetime 'normality' and the moral certainties of the Edwardian era rather than the brutal dehumanising aspects of modern warfare. Publishers were far more interested in the latter, of course, especially from the late 1920s onwards. If they were interested in captivity at all, then only in escape stories, such as Geoffrey Pyke's *To Ruhleben and Back*.[41] Internment itself was seen as a boring subject, especially at a time when, in the words of George Robb, the books that really sold well were those that 'contradicted patriotic propaganda and exposed the public to the gruesome details of trench warfare and the mortal consequences of military blunders'.[42]

This point can also be illustrated by looking at the varied fortunes of Wallace Ellison's account of life in Ruhleben and in the punishment cells of the *Stadtvogtei* in Berlin, where he spent over two years after one of his many escape attempts went horribly wrong. First published in 1918, just before the war ended, *Escaped! Adventures in German Captivity* was an immediate success and a runaway hit with the critics. Admittedly this was partly because it had been preceded by Ellison making speaking engagements all over the country, especially in the area around his home town of Southport in Lancashire where he was feted as a local hero after finally getting out of Germany on his fifth attempt.[43] However, this original version had been heavily cut to remove details likely to harm people who had helped him on his way through Germany to the Dutch border in late 1917. In 1928, therefore, his publishers, Blackwood & Sons of Edinburgh, decided to bring out a new, uncensored edition in which Ellison would tell the full story for the first time. On this occasion, though, the book was a flop and was poorly received by the critics. The *Manchester Guardian* led the way, with its literary editor declaring in a highly significant passage:

> This is a record of the escapes of a non-combatant from German camps and prisons, and they very likely were – they must have been – more exciting to participate in than they are to read about. It is not easy to be moved now by the account of the second attempt to get out of Ruhleben, in which the author climbs over the high barbed fence only to find a sentry near him – and so climbs back in again. A little later he tries once more with the same result and climbs back in for a second time! In fact, these prisoners seem to have done pretty much as they liked and were fed by supplies from home on a scale far above German civil or military standards.[44]

The *Times Literary Supplement*, was a little more generous but still noted that while 'other books [on the war] are primarily about action, his is about inaction'.[45] Clearly ten years after the war there was little sympathy in literary circles with the suffering of someone who had spent over two years in solitary confinement, and a new-found willingness to gloss over accounts of German wartime brutality, whatever guise they came in.[46]

The second explanation for the lack of public interest in the Ruhleben experience after 1920 is related less to publishing and literary tastes and more directly to attitudes in Whitehall, however. It is no secret that civilian POWs found few symapthisers within the corridors of power. The official view was summed up by one Treasury official in early 1919:

> The old theory was that a British citizen went outside the territory and jurisdiction of the Government at his own risk. The only reason for treating persons caught in Germany at the outbreak of war as exceptions to this rule is their number, and it will be remembered that some of these persons were holiday-makers who suffered from lack of foresight and that a good many were pro-Germans through many years of residence in that country ... It would be ridiculous to apply anything that may be done for soldiers captured and ill-treated as a precedent to the case of those people who were in Germany of their own free will.[47]

This attitude led to a refusal to pay maintenance allowances to the German-born wives of internees, as we have seen, but it also led to various other acts of petty meanness which underlined the inferior status of civilian prisoners of war. For instance, Ruhleben prisoners repatriated in the period up to the end of October 1918 were expected to pay for their own fares home, in contrast to repatriated military personnel. One former civilian POW wrote to Sir George Cave, the home secretary, on 6 November 1918:

> [O]n March 22nd this year I was released with 100 other prisoners as an invalid from Ruhleben for internment in Holland and had to pay the sum of 54 Marks for the railway fare from Berlin to The Hague. At the end of September I was examined by a Dutch medical commission and invalided to England, arriving at Boston on October 3rd. After waiting until midnight on the quay, I was put to bed in a Red Cross hospital train for St Pancras, but before being allowed to proceed, the fare, amounting to 13/4 – was demanded from me by ... the officer in charge of the Boston quay; his alternative being immediate removal from the train ... the whole incident savoured of Prussian treatment rather than English, and it is hardly what I expected on arrival in England after 3 1/2 years' internment in Germany.[48]

Lord Newton was able to get a reversal of this policy only in late October 1918, just in time for the final repatriation of the remaining prisoners a month later. Now the Treasury agreed to pay for the board, lodging and medical treatment of British prisoners arriving in the Netherlands and Denmark, and for the cost of their travel home, including third-class rail tickets.[49] However, in general Newton's long-running campaign to persuade Whitehall officials to treat civilian prisoners in an equal manner to military prisoners fell on deaf ears. There was no sympathy, for instance, for his view that

> the detention of British civilians in Germany has … prevent[ed] the employment of some 30,000 German civilians in the German army, and that therefore British civilian prisoners have rendered a very considerable service to this country and at great personal sacrifice amounting in some cases to absolute ruin.[50]

Rather, the Treasury 'thought it clear that the obligation of His Majesty's Government towards soldiers or sailors, who have been captured by the enemy in military or naval operations, was much greater' and adopted this principle in all its subsequent dealings with Newton's office.[51]

Post-war political life was also dominated by people whose sympathies lay with the view that veterans deserved prior consideration over civilian prisoners. As George Mosse, John Horne and others have shown, the link between military service, nationhood and citizenship was central to the 'democratisation' of the war experience and the renegotiation of gender roles in many countries in the 1920s and 1930s, casting a shadow of doubt over all those men of fighting age who had not been in uniform.[52] Veterans and their families of course formed a much larger part of the electorate, and political parties and newspapers were conscious of this. In Britain, many different groups felt that they had been overlooked in the peace settlement, but when efforts were made to draw public attention to the nation's 'debt of honour', this was nearly always a reference to those who had fought and died on the battlefield and to the bereaved families, rather than to the suffering of miners, steel workers or fishing communities. The *Daily Express*, for instance, commented in an article on the eve of Armistice Day in 1927:

> Cenotaphery is not enough. Prayers and hymns are not enough. Brass bands and pipes are not enough. Episcopal benedictions are not enough … Our Glorious Living do not ask of us any sacrifice comparable with theirs. They do not beg for alms. They only demand a little share of the heritage which they and their dead comrades won for us and our children.[53]

The idea that former internees were entitled to greater public recognition for their war service was a minority opinion, shared by Lord Newton and one or two independently minded MPs but otherwise ignored. Indeed, the government had little difficulty in defeating the legal challenge to its decision not to account for monies received by way of reparation from Germany, and there was no formal debate in either House of Parliament on the issue. As a pamphlet produced by the Civilian War Claimants' Association put it:

> If the unfortunate subject who has been injured should bring his Petition of Right [i.e. the ancient method of bringing to the notice of his Sovereign an invasion of the subject's rights] he has first of all to obtain from the Attorney General, who may be a member of the cabinet who is responsible for committing the wrong from which he has suffered, permission to proceed against the Crown, and, if such permission be refused, he has no remedy.[54]

There was thus little hope of winning the case for greater compensation. Politically and legally, every effort was made after 1920 to marginalise the civilian claimants, and this was also reflected in their relatively low status in official commemorations of the war.

However, having said this, it is also important to recognise that Britain was not a dictatorship and that publishing and other forms of cultural production were not under the control of the state. As in all pluralistic societies, there was at least the potential for alternatives to the dominant hegemonic interpretations of the war's meaning to emerge. Studies by Adrian Gregory, Alex King, Jay Winter and others, for instance, have shown that the creation of memorials to those killed in the war could produce competing definitions and diverse reactions among the different 'communities in mourning'.[55] Internment was not a cataclysmic event in the same sense, and it affected far fewer individuals and communities, but it was something experienced by a significant minority. Why didn't this minority do more to champion its own cause and its own memories?

The final explanation in fact lies more with the internees themselves than with outside pressures. As Jay Winter and Emmanuel Sivan point out, when it comes to the production of collective remembrance the state is 'neither ubiquitous nor omnipotent'. Rather, in their own words:

> If some voices are weaker than others, at least in the context of a pluralistic society, this is not only because they lack resources ... They may also be weak because of self-censorship due to lack of moral status in the eyes of others, or due to a low self-image.[56]

It is here that we can see the real dilemma of the Ruhlebenites. Many returned from Germany fully aware of the 'relativity' of their suffering, and somehow ashamed of their enforced inactivity during the war.[57] Like the French officer–prisoner Georges Connes, who penned an unpublished memoir of life as a POW in Germany in 1925, they wanted to tell their story and yet at the same time felt obliged to be 'discrete, even silent ... out of respect for those who were condemned to continue the battle', and out of respect for those who fought on the home front too.[58] The self-effacing tone of many Ruhleben memoirists is indeed captured most vividly by Cyrus Harry Brooks, author of the Ruhleben song, who wrote shortly after his release and repatriation in January 1918:

> It is a feminine part that we have been called on to play – more conventionally feminine than that of our mothers and sisters in England. They see their dear ones march away to war, and they are left to wait and watch at home; but their waiting and watching is not a dumb, inexpressive thing – there is work into which they can throw themselves, work as necessary as that of the fighting men, and which can still their yearnings in the consciousness that they are giving their energies truly and directly to their country. We watch from afar the danger of our brothers but we may not share it, we watch the toil of our sisters and the shame of inactivity falls upon us.[59]

This impression was confirmed for the Ruhlebenites after they returned home. During the war they were treated as heroes in Britain, but after the war 'only the fallen heroes were assigned full posthumous glory'.[60] Here the interests of the state dovetailed nicely with the interests of civil society. True, there were one or two counter-voices to be heard, and these counter-voices mobilised prominent sympathisers, including King George V and his immediate family.[61] The ICRC also continued after 1919 to campaign against civilian internment, but there is little evidence that anybody took any notice.[62] Indeed when the former German civilian POW Paul Cohen-Portheim wrote about the 'futility' of internment in his 1931 memoir *Time Stood Still* he was also reflecting on the futility of writing about it in the face of a society that had internalised war and had forgotten its most defenceless victims, the unarmed civilians.[63] However, the cost of forgetting was destined to be much higher than anybody can have imagined from the vantage point of the 1920s and early 1930s.

Internment in the Second World War

British public consciousness of twentieth-century wars, and of their impact on civilians, is dominated not by the First but by the Second World War.[64] The same applies to consciousness of the meaning of wartime internment and captivity. The success of novels like Michael Frayn's *Spies* (2002) and David Baddiel's *The Secret Purposes* (2004), both of which are set against the background of the internment of German and Austrian refugees on the Isle of Man in the summer of 1940, is a case in point.[65] This 'submerged area' of British history is now viewed, quite rightly, as a shameful episode brought about by a widespread fear of a Nazi 'fifth column' operating in Britain and by the unwholesome influence of Lord Rothermere's *Daily Mail* on British public life.[66] For a fiction-writer like David Baddiel, however, the main interest is in the internees themselves as well as official attitudes towards them. At one point in *The Secret Purposes* the following dialogue takes place between two of the main protagonists, both of them interned Jewish refugees:

'Have you ever thought, Kaufmann ...' said Isaac, leaning across him, and picking up the timetable, 'have you ever wondered about *this?*'
'What?'
'All this teaching. And learning. Lectures, classes, seminars. Look what languages we can learn – not just English, no, why stop at something so useful? Look, we can learn French, and Spanish, and Italian, and Greek, and Russian, and classical Hebrew of course. We can go to lectures on Byzantine art, and Renaissance architecture, and modern European theatre, and biochemistry, and Talmudic history, and applied mathematics, and medicine'.
'What point are you making, Fabian?' said Kaufmann, looking a little uncomfortable.
'The point I'm making, good Herman, is that any other racial group, put in this position – essentially made prisoners of war – *unjustly* made prisoners of war – would organise themselves along ... military lines – they would try to replicate, as best they could, the conditions of their own army. But what do we do, we Jews? ... We organise ourselves along *academic* lines. We're here twenty seconds, and we've established a university. The University of the Interned Jew'.[67]

From our point of view, this dialogue is interesting not only because it suggests a strong continuity in the behaviour of British and German internees between the First and Second World Wars, but also because so few people today seem to be aware of this continuity.[68] As we have seen, the Ruhleben prisoners also organised academic lectures and busied themselves with attending debating societies, plays and musical concerts. They also felt the terrible powerlessness and loneliness of their situation. The key difference, of course, was the 'double injustice' faced by German–Jewish internees in particular, having first been driven from their homeland and then finding that the country that had granted them asylum no longer trusted them or wanted them as part of its war effort. Many also lived in the knowledge that their friends and families in Nazi Germany were in much greater danger than they were themselves.

The failure of the British state – and of British society in general – to reflect on the suffering of First World War internees and other civilian victims of that conflict had a role to play here for two reasons. Firstly, it undermined the efforts of the ICRC and of neutral governments to limit warfare to combatants only. Instead, civilian internment increased massively as an instrument of warfare in the 1930s and 1940s, affecting not only genuine 'enemy aliens' but also stateless refugees and members of established immigrant communities targeted because of suspected political disloyalty (as in the case of the Italians in Britain in 1940 and the Japanese in America in 1941–2). Ironically, in 1939 policy-makers in Britain had at first appeared willing to restrict internment of enemy subjects to a handful of suspected spies. All 'innocent' German civilians would in principle be allowed to go home, it was decided, as long as reciprocity could be guaranteed by way of American mediation. However, it soon became obvious that this applied only to loyal Nazis who could be used as 'bargaining counters' in negotiations over the fate of British civilians in German hands, and not to refugees who had no desire whatsoever to return to Germany. It was the latter who became the target of an increasingly hostile press campaign in the early months of 1940, much of it motivated by an anti-immigrant agenda several times more virulent than that of 1914.[69]

Secondly, the failure of the British government to correct misinformation about refugees from Nazi Germany in the Rothermere press reinforced the impression that they were not quite as 'innocent' or 'deserving' as 'ordinary' German civilians and that they may well have been partly responsible for their own misfortune. Whereas in 1914, for instance, official British propaganda had made a lot of capital out of alleged German atrocities in Belgium, lending a form of legitimacy to Belgian refugees in the process,[70] in 1939–40 the policy was to downplay any talk of Nazi aggression against civilians. In a revealing internal memorandum issued by the Ministry of Information to its employees in April 1940 we find the words:

Horror must be used very sparingly, and must deal with the treatment
of indisputably innocent people. Not with violent political opponents.
And not with Jews.[71]

Such a stance cannot of course be compared with the policy of the Nazis,
who had already begun to murder concentration camp victims in 1933, and
did so with even greater impunity after the outbreak of the Second World
War. Nonetheless, it is indicative of the type of reasoning that led republican
France to lock up Spanish refugees and foreign communists in 1939, Britain
to arrest large numbers of anti-fascist Germans and Italians in the summer
of 1940, and the USA to intern several thousand Japanese–Americans in
1941–2. The nightmare vision which Franz Kafka had developed in his
book *The Trial* had, for the victims of civilian internment in the Second
World War, become a living reality. No longer were they held as potential
combatants or even as bargaining counters, but as criminals and suspects,
unwanted, stateless persons, undesirables, outcasts or (to borrow Arthur
Koestler's phrase) the 'scum of the earth'.[72]

The internment story has another possible ending too, however. The
closer contact between British servicemen and the home front in the Second
World War, combined with the rise of the 'people's war' mythology in
the winter of 1940–1, when the entire war effort seemed to be centred
around withstanding the Blitz, not only served to undermine the traditional
distinction between soldiers and civilians, but also helped to soften attitudes
towards internees.[73] By the middle of 1941, when the idea of the 'people's
war' had almost entirely replaced the 'myth of the war experience' as
a means of communicating ideas about patriotic sacrifice, a significant
section of public opinion also began to demand an end to the 'injustice'
of internment. This meant that, unlike the First World War, internment
in Britain was, for most of its victims, a temporary, if highly unpleasant,
experience ending in early release and opportunities to participate in the
war against fascism. As their part of the bargain, though, former internees
had to submerge their own grievances. Too much complaining would only
highlight their 'outsider status' and lack of 'British' reserve.[74]

In more recent years, the greater acceptance of Britain as a multi-cultural
society, the increased understanding of the plight of refugees, and the
growth of ethnic and minority studies within academia, have all helped to
some extent to push the issue of alien internment in the Second World War
into public consciousness. Baddiel's novel is undoubtedly a welcome part
of this process, as is the recent and very moving exhibition of internees'
paintings of life in the Huyton camp held at the Walker Art Gallery in

Liverpool in 2004.[75] However, the injustice committed towards First World War internees, whether those held in Germany or in Britain, or in other parts of Europe and the wider world, still lies largely forgotten, as does their creativity and inventiveness in the face of crushing boredom and anxiety about the future. This study, has, I hope, made a small contribution towards reversing that trend.

Notes

1 OBEs were awarded to five individuals associated with Ruhleben: John Philips Jones (in charge of the British section of the US embassy and the Netherlands legation in Berlin); Stanley Harrison Lambert (in change of the invalids' barrack); John Harold Platford (camp treasurer); Joseph Powell (camp captain); and Reverend Henry Williams (Anglican chaplain at Berlin). MBEs also went to nine further Ruhlebenites. For further details see NA, FO 383/537.

2 See the reports in *The Times*, 14 and 15 January 1919. Also *Ruhleben Exhibition 1919. Souvenir Album*, passim.

3 Gregory, *The Silence of Memory*, pp. 7 and 225–6.

4 Winter and Sivan, 'Setting the Framework', in Winter and Sivan (eds.), *War and Remembrance in the Twentieth Century*, p. 6.

5 Joanna Bourke, 'Introduction: "Remembering" War', *Journal of Contemporary History*, 39/4 (2004), p. 473.

6 On the possible synergies between individual and collective forms of memory see Cole, 'Scales of Memory, Layers of Memory', p. 131.

7 Vischer, *Barbed Wire Disease*, passim.

8 H. Richard Lorenz, interview with Peter Liddle, October 1977, in Liddle Collection, RUH 31.

9 Ellen Prendergast, unpublished typewritten memoirs, p. 2.

10 Louise Argent to the author, 17 April 2004.

11 Jay Winter, 'Forms of Kinship and Remembrance in the Aftermath of the Great War', in Winter and Sivan (eds.), *War and Remembrance in the Twentieth Century*, pp. 40–60. As Winter explains, 'the term "fictive" implies "constructed' and "created", rather than "imaginary" or "untrue"'. It refers to the 'social bonds created and maintained through stories and acts' rather than through blood ties or adoptive parenthood (*ibid.*, p. 41, n. 1).

12 Stockall, unpublished memoirs, pp. 104–5.

13 Samuel Hynes, 'Personal Narratives and Commemoration', in Winter and Sivan (eds.), *War and Remembrance in the Twentieth Century*, p. 206. For some insightful comments on the problems posed by individual POW narratives see also Pöppinghege, *Im Lager unbesiegt*, pp. 26–7.

14 Stockall, unpublished memoirs, p. 103.

15 Edward V. Stibbe, *Reminiscences of a Civilian Prisoner in Germany, 1914–1918*.

16 'Ruhleben Exhibition: Visit of the King and Queen', *The Times*, 11 February 1919.

17 Cf. Wittek, *Auf ewig Feind?*, p. 217.

18 See the Foreign Office communiqué, January 1919, in NA, FO 383/520. Also material in the papers of former internee Herbert Smith, in IWM, 01/55/1.

19 See www.lib.byu.edu/~rdh/wwi/versailles.html (Treaty of Versailles, article 232, annex 1, point 2).

20 *Parliamentary Debates, House of Commons*, fifth series, vol. 128, p. 1874.

21 *Ibid.*, p. 1875.

22 Gregory, *The Silence of Memory*, passim.

23 *The Civilian War Sufferer. Compiled from the Records of the Civilian War Claimants' Association* (London, n.d. [1933?]), p. 1.

24 See the material in HLL-EC, box 6, file 13.

25 *The Times*, 20 November 1931.

26 See Major General R. Llewellyn Brown to W. E. Swale, 28 November 1974, in Liddle Collection, RUH 52, box 2.

27 Jahr, 'Zivilisten als Kriegsgefangene', p. 320.

28 On the 'shelf-life' of memories see Winter and Sivan, 'Setting the Framework', pp. 16–17.

29 See the list of books and articles on Ruhleben listed in Ketchum, *Ruhleben*, pp. xxi–xxiii. Of the forty-nine items listed, only eight were published after 1919, and not all of them, strictly speaking, were about Ruhleben camp itself.

30 Gribble, *Seen in Passing*, p. 334.

31 See the web page 'Ruhleben Gefangenenlager. Records, 1914–1937. A Finding Aid', at http://oasis.harvard.edu/html/law00029/html.

32 Ketchum, *Ruhleben*, pp. xiv–xv.

33 *Ibid.*, pp. 3 and xviii.

34 See the web page for this collection at www.leeds.ac.uk/library/spcoll/liddle/.

35 Humberside Libraries and Amenities (ed.), *Ruhleben. An Exhibition to Mark the 60th Anniversary of the Release of Local Men From the Ruhleben Internment Camp* (Kingston upon Hull, 1978).

36 Samuel Hynes, *The Soldiers' Tale. Bearing Witness to Modern War* (London, 1998), p. 74.

37 Tripp, 'Kommunikation und Vergemeinschaftung', p. 3.

38 Chris Paton, 'The Ruhleben Story', http://ruhleben.tripod.com/id18.html.

39 See the bibliography at the end of this book, and Chapter 5 above.

40 Graham Dawson, *Soldier Heroes. British Adventure, Empire and the Imagining of Masculinities* (London, 1994), pp. 171–2.

41 This book was first published in London in 1916 and went through several editions. It has recently been republished by McSweeney's Books with a foreword by Paul Collins (New York, 2002).

42 George Robb, *British Culture and the First World War* (London, 2002), p. 220.

43 See the extensive press cuttings in Liddle Collection, RUH 20, box 1.
44 *Manchester Guardian*, 5 December 1928. Cf. the glowing review of the earlier version of the book in *Manchester Guardian*, 18 November 1918. Copies of both in *ibid.*
45 *Times Literary Supplement*, 8 November 1928. Copy in *ibid.*
46 Cf. Horne and Kramer, *German Atrocities 1914*, p. 382; Jones 'The Enemy Disarmed', pp. 391–400.
47 Written notes by Robert Chalmers (Chief Secretary to the Treasury), 21 January 1919, in NA, T1/12295.
48 Percy Hull to Sir George Cave, 6 November 1918, in NA, FO 383/422.
49 See the correspondence between Newton's office and the Treasury in *ibid.*, esp. Treasury to Warner, 8 November 1918. Also FO to Rumbold, 19 October 1918, in NA, FO 383/364.
50 Newton to Treasury, 2 September 1918, in NA, FO 383/422.
51 Treasury to Newton, 16 May 1918, in *ibid.*
52 George L. Mosse, *Fallen Soldiers. Reshaping the Memory of the World Wars* (Oxford, 1990), pp. 70–106; John Horne, 'Masculinity in Politics and War in the Age of Nation-States and World Wars, 1850–1950', in Stefan Dudink, Karen Hagemann and John Tosh (eds.), *Masculinities in Politics and War. Gendering Modern History* (Manchester, 2004), pp. 31–4.
53 *Daily Express*, 10 November 1927. Cited in Gregory, *The Silence of Memory*, p. 80.
54 *The Civilian War Sufferer*, pp. 15–16.
55 Gregory, *The Silence of Memory*, passim; Winter, *Sites of Memory*, passim; Alex King, *Memorials of the Great War in Britain* (Oxford, 1998).
56 Winter and Sivan, 'Setting the Framework', p. 30.
57 Rachamimov also talks about the 'relativity of POW suffering' – see *POWs and the Great War*, p. 224.
58 Georges Connes, *A POW's Memoir of the First World War. The Other Ordeal*, trans. Marie-Claire Connes Wrages (Oxford, 2004), p. 1.
59 Cyrus Harry Brooks, 'Inside the Wire', article in unidentifiable newspaper, 18 January 1918. Copy in Liddle Collection, RUH 52, box 1.
60 Audoin-Rouzeau and Becker, *1914–1918*, p. 233.
61 The Civil Claimants' Association acknowledged George V's personal support for internees and suggested that the government's refusal to award the proper sums to civilian war victims 'is the more odious from its association with the name of the Sovereign'. See *The Civilian War Sufferer*, pp. 19–20. On George V's personal interest in POW questions see also Newton, *Retrospection*, pp. 221 and 254.
62 Cf. Stibbe, 'The Internment of Civilians', passim.
63 Cohen-Portheim, *Time Stood Still*, p. 2.
64 Cf. Gregory, *The Silence of Memory*, pp. 212–15.
65 Michael Frayn, *Spies* (London, 2002); David Baddiel, *The Secret Purposes* (London, 2004).

66 The earliest treatment of this subject, written from a highly critical perspective, is François Lafitte's *The Internment of Aliens* (London, 1940, new edn, London, 1988). See also Peter and Leni Gillman, *'Collar the Lot!' How Britain Interned and Expelled its Wartime Refugees* (London, 1980); and various essays in Cesarani and Kushner (eds.), *The Internment of Aliens*, passim.

67 Baddiel, *The Secret Purposes*, pp. 108–9.

68 For evidence of academic lectures and *Lager-Universitäten* in other camps in Britain and Germany between 1914 and 1918 see also Panayi, *The Enemy in Our Midst*, pp. 121–4 and Hinz, *Gefangen im Großen Krieg*, p. 118.

69 Gillman and Gillman, *'Collar the Lot!'*, passim.

70 Cf. Gill, 'Calculating Compassion in War', pp. 173–81.

71 NA, INF 1/251. Cited in Baddiel, *The Secret Purposes*, p. 64.

72 Arthur Koestler, *Scum of the Earth* (London, 1941). This book provides an account of Koestler's internment in the notorious Le Vernet camp in the Ariège region of France in 1939–40.

73 On the role of liberal-progressive myth-making in reshaping public opinion on the alien question in 1940–41 see Calder, *The Myth of the Blitz*, esp. pp. 117–18. On the 'people's war' mythology more generally see also Gregory, *The Silence of Memory*, p. 214.

74 Cesarani and Kushner (eds.), *The Internment of Aliens*, p. 5.

75 See the accompanying exhibition catalogue written by Jessica Feather, *Art Behind the Barbed Wire* (Liverpool, 2004).

Conclusion

The absence of Ruhleben in many official accounts and commemorations of the war still leaves open the question of why this camp became – at least for a time – a fundamental part of Britain's wartime self-image and an important part of German propaganda too. What, in other words, can Ruhleben tell us about the significance of First World War internment, over and above its position in British memory of the war? To what extent did it contribute to cultural mobilisation for war in Britain and Germany and therefore motivate people to fight to the finish? Or, conversely, how far did its existence help to disguise the 'darker' sides of captivity as experienced by other civilian POWs in Germany?

Internment, as we have seen, was practiced by all belligerents in the war, and even by some neutral countries like Switzerland and the Netherlands. Around 32,000 enemy nationals were held in Britain and up to 60,000 in France, but in Germany the total was officially 111,879 and in reality almost certainly higher.[1] Many of these prisoners were deportees from the occupied parts of their own countries rather than 'enemy aliens' living in Germany when the war broke out. Some of them were housed in the main camps (*Stammlager*) but significant numbers, especially after 1917, found themselves in ordinary jails, in prison-style work camps and in punishment camps dotted around the Reich and in occupied territory. Such prisoners had only limited access to Red Cross visitors, relief parcels or letters from home, and were forced to subsist on very meager rations, often while working directly for the German war economy. These were the truly forgotten victims of the war; in spite of the excellent work of Annette Becker and others,[2] we still know relatively little about them, and even their precise number is unclear.

The British prisoners at Ruhleben were, in strictly legal terms, in the same position. In other words, they too had no formal status in terms of international conventions and only limited protection under domestic German military law. Yet this was by no means a typical camp. The main reason it stood out was the relatively good conditions there, at least after the first winter of the war. This can be attributed to four main factors. Firstly, Ruhleben's geographical position close to the heart of the Reich capital favoured greater observation by neutral parties. Secondly, the camp's population was also fairly stable, with little turnover of prisoners between November 1914 and November 1918. Thirdly, humanitarian organisations and private individuals worked hard to maintain not only decent material conditions, but also aid in the form of books, games and other pastimes. And finally there was the good, indeed almost exemplary treatment of German internees in Britain. Indeed, as Panikos Panayi has shown, in spite of the domestic pressures to do so, the British authorities did not engage in reprisals or other abuses on a serious level, making it difficult for the German government to justify doing likewise.[3]

In this sense, what Uta Hinz refers to as the *Gegenseitigkeitsprinzip* worked to the advantage of both sets of prisoners, and ensured that their post-war memoirs of internment were not framed around eschatological themes like exile, disease, cruelty and death, but around cultural themes, such as the development of *Lageruniversitäten* and contacts with home.[4] *Gegenseitigkeit* was of course a utilitarian principle, linked to political and pragmatic concerns, and to considerations of social class, but we should also not ignore the humanitarian impulse that sprang from 'reprisals of good' as practiced by Elisabeth Rotten and her small band of assistants in Germany and Britain. The propaganda produced by her organisation, the *Auskunfts- und Hilfsstelle für Deutsche im Ausland und Ausländer in Deutschland*, was clever and effective. It also enjoyed backing from powerful lobby groups: the Society of Friends in London, the ICRC in Geneva, the ecumenical movement on both sides of the channel, and representatives of German high finance like Max Warburg.[5]

Internment nonetheless contributed to the development of virulent war cultures in other ways. For the British authorities Ruhleben, alongside Belgium, served as a symbol of German barbarity and criminality, whereas its own camps on the Isle of Man and at Wakefield and Alexandra Palace were presented as models of humane efficiency. As Sir Edward Grey was quick to point out to the US ambassador in London, Walter Hines Page, in November 1914:

> The German Government have not the same excuse for proceeding to the wholesale arrest of British subjects in Germany, since owing to the small number of them, and the scattered condition in which they live, they cannot, under any circumstances, be regarded as constituting the same danger to Germany as the 50,000 or so Germans in Britain.[6]

The British were also fortunate in that the ICRC and other neutral bodies were willing to confirm that good conditions prevailed in their camps. The final report of the ICRC on its activities during the war, for instance, noted that British lists of civilian prisoners were always 'very complete', something which it pointedly did not say of Germany, Austria-Hungary or Russia.[7] ICRC inspectors were even more positive in their account of a visit to Britain in January 1915, concluding that 'the German government and the families of the prisoners need not worry greatly [*peuvent être sans inquiétude*] about those who are being held in the camps in England'.[8]

For the German government, on the other hand, the decision to intern British civilians in November 1914 was an unmitigated disaster. In the four years that followed the Ruhleben prisoners proved virtually worthless as bargaining counters, and yet could not be forced to work for the German economy. And they had to be fed. 1916 represented the nadir of internment policy, particularly when the Germans were forced into a climb down over Dr Taylor's report on the deteriorating dietary conditions in the camp. Relations with the USA reached an all-time low, and even the Prussian Ministry of War recognised how disastrous internment had become in terms of Germany's image abroad.[9] Johannes Kriege's speech in the Reichstag in November 1916, in which he offered an 'all-for-all' exchange while promising that returned prisoners would not be recruited into the German army, was a clever piece of propaganda and exposed the British government to increased pressure at home. So too was the attempt to link conditions at Ruhleben to conditions on the German home front more generally, on the 'humanitarian' principle that allied prisoners could not expect to get more to eat than ordinary German civilians who were suffering equally under the British blockade.[10]

Yet in the end London was able to resist these tactics. The main reason why the two governments could not agree on an 'all-for-all' exchange was practical rather than ideological: put quite simply, Britain feared that its coalition partners Russia, France and Italy would not like it if up to 26,000 Germans of fighting age were repatriated to their country of origin. Even if they were not to be used directly in the war effort, their return could still have enabled the release of other German workers for service at the front. Germany was not accountable to its allies in the same way (and besides, at most 3,000 Ruhlebenites could potentially have served in the British armed forces had they been sent home before the end of the war). Here it was domestic considerations – the fear of a nationalist backlash against the government, already under pressure over its submarine policy, combined with the negative impact on morale in Hamburg in particular

– that prevented acceptance of the British offer of a 'man-for-man' exchange. The fact that several 'moderate' Reichstag deputies – including Matthias Erzberger – continued to insist that Germany's treatment of its prisoners was far more humane than that of its enemies also made it difficult to reach any agreement which fell short of a complete release of all German civilian prisoners.[11] The will to negotiate was there, in other words, but mutual distrust remained an insurmountable obstacle.

In November 1918 the *Gegenseitigkeitsprinzip* broke down when the Ruhleben prisoners were released, while over 24,000 German and Austrian internees remained in Britain.[12] Now there was nothing left to protect them from reprisals or to prevent their use as hostages. Even so the British government – and trade unions – did not follow the French example of demanding the deployment of POWs in reconstruction work, and in fact the British press and British politicians were anxious simply to expel 'unwanted' Germans.[13] The government, in other words, did not make the mistake of attempting to use prisoners as bargaining tools in the post-war era, at least after the Treaty of Versailles had been signed. Even before then, most of the civilian internees, as well as a handful of wounded and sick military prisoners, were repatriated between January and April 1919.[14] By contrast the repatriation process from France was much slower, and lasted from June to November 1919, giving rise to much bitterness and resentment on both sides.[15]

This also explains why Ruhleben was quickly forgotten at an international level and did not become part of the ongoing propaganda war in the 1920s and 1930s. There was no equivalent of the 'black horror on the Rhine' to sully Anglo-German relations and revive cultural memories of the harsh treatment of German civilian prisoners in colonial settings, for instance.[16] True, the German demand for equality remained an issue. While the British maintained that 'no comparison is possible between the treatment of prisoners of war by the German government and that of the allied and associated powers',[17] the official Reichstag inquiry into the causes of the war and of Germany's defeat refuted war guilt allegations in no uncertain terms and insisted that Britain had also committed abuses against German civilians:

> The German people had no desire to outdo the English in respect to retaliatory actions, but had a duty to demand the same treatment for its own citizens that was granted to the English subjects living in Germany.[18]

Interestingly, the Reichstag inquiry also revived claims that British civilians had sabotaged food supplies in Germany in the early months of the war by setting fire to grain warehouses.[19] But over and above this there was little desire for revenge or opening up old wounds, and – in the 1930s in particular – a growing acceptance that civilian prisoners in both countries had indeed suffered equally.[20]

This can also be seen in 1939 when the Chamberlain and Hitler governments seemed anxious to avoid the 'mistakes' of 1914 in relation to alien internment. Only Churchill – in a repeat of his position in 1914–15 – opposed exchanges and advocated all-out war against German civilians, including the removal of German merchant seamen from neutral vessels.[21] Yet the vast majority of those Germans actually interned in Britain in 1939–40 were Jewish and anti-Nazi refugees whose fate was a matter of complete indifference to the German authorities. Similarly of the millions imprisoned by the Nazis, only a handful – not more than 1,800 – were British civilians trapped in Germany when the war broke out. A further 6,000 were interned in occupied France from December 1940, but were mostly exchanged in 1943–44.[22] By contrast in the Far East 130,000 British, Dutch, French and American civilians, including 41,895 women and 40,260 children, were held in camps of varying (and often very poor) quality in areas under Japanese military control, and were not protected by any established principle of reciprocity.[23] Meanwhile, in German-occupied Europe the sheer scale and horror of the Holocaust, and the murder of up to 2 million Soviet POWs, completely and permanently overshadowed more minor acts of violence towards British subjects, civilians included. For all of these reasons, and many others, internment – and the memory of it – was a very different ball game in the Second World War.

Notes

1   See the figures in Stibbe, 'The Internment of Civilians', pp. 7–8.
2   Becker, *Oubliés de la grande guerre*, passim.
3   Panikos Panayi, 'Normalität hinter Stacheldraht. Kriegsgefangene in Großbritannien, 1914–1919', in Oltmer (ed.), *Kriegsgefangene*, pp. 126–46. Jones, 'The Enemy Disarmed', pp. 427 and 447, also notes that while there is some real evidence of British maltreatment of German prisoners, overall its record 'stands out as the least violent'. Indeed, British abuses played only a very minor role in German post-war accusations, which were directed first and foremost against France, followed by Romania, Russia, Italy and Britain in that order. See also Pöppinghege, *Im Lager unbesiegt*, pp. 105–14.
4   Hinz, *Gefangen im Großen Krieg*, passim.

5 Stibbe, 'Elisabeth Rotten', passim.

6 Grey to Page, 9 November 1914, in NA, FO 369/714.

7 *Rapport général du Comité international*, p. 137.

8 *Rapports de MM. Ed. Naville et V. van Berchem*, p. 26.

9 Cf. minutes of a discussion on 28 June 1916 in the Prussian Ministry of War, in BA Berlin, R 901/83953.

10 See also 'England und die Zivilgefangenen', *Norddeutsche Allgemeine Zeitung*, 12 December 1917.

11 On Erzberger cf. Pöppinghege, *Im Lager unbesiegt*, p. 82.

12 Panayi, *The Enemy in Our Midst*, p. 95.

13 Wittek, *Auf ewig Feind?*, pp. 215–27.

14 See e.g. German consulate in Rotterdam to AA, 23 April 1919, in BA Berlin, R 901/83959, and AA to Bavarian envoy in Berlin, 25 April 1919, in *ibid.*, R 901/83958: 11,750 Germans were nonetheless given leave to remain in Britain.

15 See 'Entlassung der Zivilinternierter aus Frankreich', article appearing in the Viennese publication *Mitteilungen der Staatskommission für Kriegsgefangenen- und Zivilinterniertenangelegenheiten*, no. 2, 21 June 1919, p. 5. Also 'Le repatriement des prisonniers', *Revue Internationale de la Croix-Rouge*, 1/11 (November 1919), pp. 1333–4.

16 Keith L. Nelson, 'The "Black Horror on the Rhine". Race as a Factor in Post-World War I Diplomacy', *Journal of Modern History*, 42 (1970), pp. 606–27.

17 Jones, 'The Enemy Disarmed', p. 314.

18 WUA, Reihe 3, Bd. III/2, p. 727.

19 *Ibid.* Cf. Chapter 1 above.

20 See e.g. Cohen-Portheim, *Time Stood Still*, passim, and Messent, 'The German Revolution of November 1918', passim.

21 Gillman and Gillman, *'Collar the Lot!'*, pp. 62–3.

22 *Ibid.*, pp. 288–9.

23 Archer, *The Internment of Western Civilians under the Japanese*, pp. 3 and ff.

Appendix[1]

British subjects resident in selected German towns and cities, autumn 1914[2]

Landespolizeibezirk Berlin[3]	1,861
Including:	
Stadtbezirk Berlin	822
Charlottenburg	393
Wilmersdorf	238
Schöneberg	223
Neukölln	48
Lichtenberg	31
Berlin jails	20
Russenlager Ruhleben-Spandau	86
Bundesstaat Hamburg[4]	2,247
Including:	
Civilians	1,182
Merchant mariners	1,065
Polizeibezirk Frankfurt-am-Main[5]	503
Regierungsbezirk Potsdam[6]	439
Including:	
Kreis Teltow	334
Berlin-Lichterfelde	62
Spandau	43
Düsseldorf	303

Hanover	230
Kiel	227
Bremen	218
Munich	215
Dresden	210
Cologne	115
Leipzig	112
Magdeburg	101
Baden-Baden	96
Nuremberg	78
Wiesbaden	78
Breslau	71
Chemnitz	71
Merseburg	69
Heidelberg	68
Cassel	67
Minden	65
Coblenz	64
Aachen	58
Stuttgart	58
Hildesheim	49
Bad Nauheim	45
Stade	45
Frankfurt an der Oder	44
Mannheim	44
Offenbach	43
Gelsenkirchen	39
Münster	39
Dortmund	34
Stettin	34
Bautzen	33
Freiburg	33
Bonn	31
Oldenburg	30
Trier	28
Arnsberg	23

Erfurt	22
Osnabrück	21
Strasbourg	19
Danzig	18
Braunschweig	17
Karlsruhe	17
Esslingen	16
Königsberg	16
Lübeck	16
Zwickau	16
Mainz	13
Posen	13
Darmstadt	10

Source: BA Berlin, Reichsamt des Innern, R 1501/112376–77

Notes

1 These figures are based on police lists delivered to the Reich Office of Interior in late October and early November 1914, according to a request issued on 8 October 1914. They relate to all British nationals, including so-called *Kolonialengländer*. They also include the German-born wives and children of British nationals, but not the British-born wives of German nationals. Finally, with the exception of Berlin, they do not include British nationals already in police or military custody on the date the census was taken, or those who had left Germany since the outbreak of war in August 1914. This partly explains the relatively low figures for towns and cities in southern Germany, and in Bavaria and Württemberg in particular.

2 Towns and villages with fewer than ten British residents have not been listed.

3 The Landespolizeibezirk Berlin included the six original *Stadtbezirke* (Mitte, Kreuzberg, Friedrichshain, Prenzlauer Berg, Wedding and Tiergarten) along with Charlottenburg, Lichtenberg, Neukölln, Schöneberg and Wilmersdorf, but did not encompass all the areas included when the boundaries were redrawn in 1920 to create today's Greater Berlin.

4 This figure is for the Bundesstaat Hamburg only, and does not include what was then still Prussian-administered Altona.

5 Excludes surrounding areas in Hesse.

6 Included here are some areas that were incorporated into Greater Berlin in 1920.

Bibliography

Archives, Libraries and Museums

Archive du Comité International de la Croix-Rouge, Geneva (ACICR)
Archive générale de l'Agence internationale des prisonniers de guerre de Genève, 1914–18 (C G1, Groupe 400)

British Library, London
Collection of pamphlets and other material relating to Ruhleben

Brotherton Library, University of Leeds
Liddle Collection (RUH 01–RUH 60)

Bundesarchiv, Berlin-Lichterfelde (BA Berlin)
Akten des Auswärtigen Amts, Abt. III (Rechtsabteilung) (R 901)
Akten des Reichsamts des Innern (R 1501)
Reichslandbund-Pressearchiv (R 8034 II)

Bundesarchiv-Filmarchiv, Berlin
Universum film studios (UFA) production 'Aus alten Zeitungen' including 'In Ruhleben bei den Internierten', date and origin unknown (BSL/19077)

Evangelisches Zentralarchiv Berlin (EZA)
Hilfsausschuß für Gefangenenseelsorge, 1914–21 (Bestand 45)
Caritas inter Arma im Ersten Weltkrieg (Bestand 51 C)

Generallandesarchiv Karlsruhe (GLA)
Akten des stellvertretenden Generalkommandos des XIV. Armeekorps (Bestand 456)

Grimsby Central Library (GCL)
Collection of material relating to local men interned at Ruhleben

Harvard Law Library, Harvard University, Cambridge, Massachusetts (HLL-EC)
Maurice Ettinghausen Collection: Ruhleben Gefangenenlager, 1914–37

Hauptstaatsarchiv Stuttgart (HStA)
Akten des stellvertretenden Generalkommandos des XIII. Armeekorps (Bestand M 77/1)

Houghton Library, Cambridge, Massachusetts
Papers of Ellis Loring Dresel (MS Am 1549)
Papers of Joseph C. Grew (MS Am 1687)

Imperial War Museum, London (IWM)
Various papers relating to ex–internees (Department of Documents)

Internationaal Instituut voor Sociale Geschiedenis, Amsterdam (IISG)
Minna Cauer papers

Landesarchiv Berlin (LA Berlin)
Rep. 30 Berlin C Polizeipräsidium (Stimmungsberichte)
Rep. 129, Acc. 1884, B6c (Kriegsgefangenen-Theater, Lager Ruhleben, 1914/18)

The National Archives, Kew, London (NA)
Foreign Office Papers
Ministry of Transport Papers
Treasury Papers

Niedersächsisches Hauptstaatsarchiv, Hanover (NHStA)
Akten betreffend Kontrolle, Festnahme und Heimbeförderung der Ausländer feindlicher Staaten, 2 vols. (Hann. 122a, no. 7010–11)

Society of Friends Library, London (FEWVRC)
Papers, correspondence and reports of the Friends Emergency Committee for the Assistance of Germans, Austrians and Hungarians in Distress, 1914–19

Staatsarchiv Hamburg (StA Hamburg)
Senatskriegsakten, 1914–18

Newspapers and journals

Berliner Illustrierte Zeitung
Berliner Tageblatt
The British Prisoner of War
Bulletin International des sociétés de la Croix-Rouge
Daily Gleaner

Daily Mail
Daily Sketch
Deutsche Tageszeitung
Frankfurter Zeitung
Hamburger Echo
Hamburger Fremdenblatt
Hamburger Nachrichten
Journal de Genève
Kölnische Zeitung
Leipziger Neueste Nachrichten
Manchester Guardian
Morning Post
Neue Preußische (Kreuz-) Zeitung
Norddeutsche Allgemeine Zeitung
In Ruhleben Camp (IRC)
The Ruhleben Camp Magazine (RCM)
The Ruhleben Camp News
The Strand Magazine
Tag
The Times
Times Literary Supplement
Vorwärts
Der Weltspiegel
Die Woche

Contemporary books, articles, pamphlets and memoirs, 1914–45

Anon., *The Civilian War Sufferer. Compiled from the Records of the Civilian War Claimants' Association* (London, n.d. [1933?])

Bund Neues Vaterland, *Durch zum Rechtsfrieden. Ein Appell an das Weltgewissen von Professor W. Schücking, Dr. Helene Stöcker und Dr. Elisabeth Rotten* (Berlin, 1919)

Bury, Herbert, *My Visit to Ruhleben* (London, 1917)

Cohen, Israel, *The Ruhleben Prison Camp. A Record of Nineteen Months' Internment* (London, 1917)

Cohen-Portheim, Paul, *Time Stood Still. My Internment in England, 1914–1918* (London, 1931)

Ellison, Wallace, *Escaped! Adventures in German Captivity* (Edinburgh, 1918)

—— *Escapes and Adventures* (Edinburgh, 1928)

Erzberger, Matthias, *Erlebnisse im Weltkrieg* (Stuttgart and Berlin, 1920)

Garner, James W., 'Treatment of Enemy Aliens. Measures in Respect of Personal Liberty', *American Journal of International Law*, 12/1 (January 1918), pp. 27–55

Gerard, James W., *My Four Years in Germany* (London, 1917)

Gribble, Francis, *Seen in Passing. A Volume of Personal Reminiscences* (London, 1929)

Hettwer, Bruno (ed.), *Deutsches Traber-Derby. Ruhleben, 1924/5* (Berlin, 1924)

Hirschfeld, Magnus (ed.), *Sittengeschichte des Weltkrieges*, 2 vols. (Leipzig and Vienna, 1930)

Koestler, Arthur, *The Scum of the Earth* (London, 1941)

Lafitte, François, *The Internment of Aliens* (London, 1940, new edn, London, 1988)

Liszt, Franz von, *Das Völkerrecht*, 10th edn (Berlin, 1915)

Newton, Lord, *Retrospection* (London, 1941)

O'Sullivan Molony, W., *Prisoners and Captives* (London, 1933)

Peters, Carl, *Das deutsche Elend in London* (Leipzig, 1914)

Powell, Joseph, with Francis Gribble, *The History of Ruhleben. A Record of British Organisation in a Prison Camp in Germany* (London, 1919)

Pyke, Geoffrey, *To Ruhleben – and Back. A Great Adventure in Three Phases*, first published 1916, new edn with an introduction by Paul Collins (New York and San Francisco, 2002)

The Ruhleben Bye-Election (Berlin, 1915)

Ruhleben Exhibition 1919. Souvenir Album, published by the Central Prisoners of War Committee of the British Red Cross and the Order of St John of Jerusalem (London, 1919)

Schirmacher, Käthe, 'Ruhleben', *Die Woche*, no. 37, 11 September 1915

Sladen, Douglas (ed.), *In Ruhleben. Letters from a Prisoner to his Mother* (London, 1917)

Stibbe, Edward V., *Reminiscences of a Civilian Prisoner in Germany, 1914–1918*, first written as a private pamphlet in Leicester in 1919, published with a foreword by Paul Stibbe (Castle Cary, 1969)

Vischer, Adolf Lukas, *Die Stacheldraht-Krankheit* (Zurich, 1918)

⸻ *Barbed Wire Disease. A Psychological Study of the Prisoner of War* (London, 1919)

British government publications

Parliamentary Debates, House of Commons, fifth series (London, 1917–1920)

Parliamentary Debates, House of Lords, fifth series (London, 1917–1918)

Parliamentary Papers, *Note from the United States ambassador transmitting a report, dated June 8, 1915, on the conditions at present existing in the internment camp at Ruhleben* (= misc. no. 13) (London, 1915)

⸻ *Correspondence with the United States ambassador respecting the conditions in the internment camp at Ruhleben* (= misc. no. 3) (London, 1916)

⸻ *Report by Dr. A. E. Taylor on the conditions of diet and nutrition in the internment camp at Ruhleben* (= misc. no. 18) (London, 1916)

⸻ *Further correspondence respecting the conditions of diet and nutrition in the internment camp at Ruhleben* (= misc. no. 21) (London, 1916)

⸻ *Further correspondence respecting the conditions of diet and nutrition in the internment camp at Ruhleben and the proposed release of interned civilians* (= misc. no. 25) (London, 1916)

⸻ *Further correspondence with the United States ambassador respecting the treatment of British prisoners of war and interned civilians in Germany* (= misc. no. 26) (London, 1916)

⸻ *Further correspondence respecting the proposed release of civilians interned in the British and German empires* (= misc. no. 35) (London, 1916)

German government publications

Deutscher Reichstag, *Verhandlungen des Reichstags. Stenographische Berichte und Anlagen zu den Stenographischen Berichten*, vols. 306–319 (Berlin, 1916–18)

────── *Das Werk des Untersuchungsausschusses, 1919–1928, Reihe 3: Völkerrecht im Weltkrieg, Bd. III/2: Gutachten des Sachverständigen Geh. Rates Prof. Dr. Meurer. Verletzungen des Kriegsgefangenenrechts* (Berlin, 1927)

────── *Der Hauptausschuß des Deutschen Reichstags, 1915–1918*. Eingeleitet von Reinhard Schiffers, bearbeitet von Reinhard Schiffers und Manfred Koch in Verbindung mit Hans Boldt, 4 vols. (Düsseldorf, 1981–83)

Matthias, Erich and Rudolf Morsey (eds.), *Die Regierung des Prinzen Max von Baden* (Düsseldorf, 1962)

Prussian Ministry of War, *Les prisonniers de guerre en Allemagne, accompagné d'une préface du Prof. Dr. Backhaus* (Siegen, 1915)

────── *Kriegsgefangene Völker. Bd. 1: Der Kriegsgefangenen Haltung und Schicksal in Deutschland*, ed. by Wilhelm Doegen on behalf of the Reichswehrministerium (Berlin, 1919)

Red Cross publications

Documents publiés à l'occasion de la guerre de 1914–1915. Rapports de MM. Ed. Naville et V. van Berchem, Dr. C. de Marval et A. Eugster sur leurs visites aux camps de prisonniers en Angleterre, France et Allemagne (Geneva and Paris, 1915)

Rapport général du Comité International de la Croix-Rouge sur son activité de 1912 à 1920 (Geneva, 1921)

Secondary sources and memoirs published after 1945

Abbal, Odon, *Soldats oubliés. Les prisonniers de guerre français* (Bez-et-Esparon, 2001)

Anderson, Benedict, *Imagined Communities. Reflections on the Origin and Spread of Nationalism*, revised edn (London, 1991)

Archer, Bernice, *The Internment of Western Civilians under the Japanese, 1941–1945. A Patchwork of Experiences* (London, 2004)

Audoin-Rouzeau, Stéphane and Annette Becker, *1914–1918. Understanding the Great War* (London, 2002)

Becker, Annette, *Oubliés de la grande guerre. Humanitaire et culture de guerre. Populations occupées, déportés civils, prisonniers de guerre* (Paris, 1998)

Bourke, Joanna, 'Introduction: "Remembering" War', *Journal of Contemporary History*, 39/4 (2004), pp. 473–85

Brinkmann, Tobias, '"Grenzerfahrungen" zwischen Ruhleben und Ellis Island. Das System der deutschen Durchwandererkontrolle im internationalen Kontext, 1880–1914', *Leipziger Beiträge zur jüdischen Geschichte und Kultur* 2 (2004), pp. 209–29

Calder, Angus, *The Myth of the Blitz* (London, 1991)

Cesarani, David and Tony Kushner (eds.), *The Internment of Aliens in Twentieth Century Britain* (London, 1993)

Cole, Tim, 'Scales of Memory, Layers of Memory: Recent Works on Memories of the Second World War and the Holocaust', *Journal of Contemporary History*, 37/1 (2002), pp. 129–38

Connes, Georges, *A POW's Memoir of the First World War. The Other Ordeal*, trans. by Marie-Claire Connes Wrages (Oxford, 2004)

Crangle, John V. and Joseph O. Baylen, 'Emily Hobhouse's Peace Mission, 1916', *Journal of Contemporary History*, 14/4 (1979), pp. 731–44

Daly, Gavin, 'Napoleon's Lost Legions: French Prisoners of War in Britain, 1803–1814', *History* 89/3 (2004), pp. 361–80

Davis, Belinda J., *Home Fires Burning. Food, Politics and Everyday Life in World War I Berlin* (Chapel Hill and London, 2000)

Dawson, Graham, *Soldier Heroes. British Adventure, Empire and the Imagining of Masculinities* (London, 1994)

Deist, Wilhelm (ed.), *Militär und Innenpolitik im Weltkrieg, 1914–1918*, 2 vols. (Düsseldorf, 1970)

Delpal, Bernard, 'Zwischen Vergeltung und Humanisierung der Lebensverhältnisse. Kriegsgefangene in Frankreich, 1914–1920', in Oltmer (ed.), *Kriegsgefangene im Europa des Ersten Weltkriegs*, pp. 147–64

Deutschkron, Inge, *Emigranto. Vom Überleben in fremden Sprachen* (Berlin, 2001)

Doerries, Reinhard R., *Prelude to the Easter Rising. Sir Roger Casement in Imperial Germany* (London, 2000)

Dülffer, Jost, *Regeln gegen den Krieg. Die Haager Friedenskonferenzen von 1899 und 1907 in der internationalen Politik* (Frankfurt/M, 1981)

Durand, André, *From Sarajevo to Hiroshima. History of the International Committee of the Red Cross* (Geneva, 1984)

English, Jim, 'Empire Day in Britain, 1904–1958', *The Historical Journal*, 49/1 (2006), pp. 247–76

Farcy, Jean-Claude, *Les camps de concentration français de la première guerre mondiale, 1914–1920* (Paris, 1995)

Ferguson, Niall, *The Pity of War* (London, 1998)

Geertz, Clifford, 'Thick Description: Toward an Interpretive Theory of Culture', in *The Interpretation of Cultures. Selected Essays by Clifford Geertz* (New York, 1973), pp. 3–30

Geinitz, Christian, *Kriegsfurcht und Kampfbereitschaft. Das Augusterlebnis in Freiburg. Eine Studie zum Kriegsbeginn 1914* (Essen, 1998)

Gillman, Peter and Leni Gillman, *'Collar the Lot!' How Britain Interned and Expelled its Wartime Refugees* (London, 1980)

Goenner, Hubert, *Einstein in Berlin, 1914–1933* (Munich, 2005)

Gregory, Adrian, *The Silence of Memory. Armistice Day, 1919–1946* (Oxford, 1994)

Gullace, Nicoletta F., 'Friends, Aliens and Enemies. Fictive Communities and the Lusitania Riots of 1915', *Journal of Social History* (Winter 2005), pp. 345–67

Hall, Stuart, 'National Cultures as "Imagined Communities"', in Stuart Hall, David Held and Tony McGrew (eds.), *Modernity and its Futures* (Cambridge, 1992), pp. 291–9

Herbert, Ulrich, *Geschichte der Ausländerbeschäftigung in Deutschland, 1880 bis 1980. Saisonarbeiter, Zwangsarbeiter, Gastarbeiter* (Bonn, 1986)

Hinz, Uta, 'Die deutschen "Barbaren" sind doch die besseren Menschen. Kriegsgefangenschaft und gefangene "Feinde" in der Darstellung der deutschen Publistik, 1914–1918', in Overmans (ed.), *In der Hand des Feindes*, pp. 339–61
―― 'Internierung', in Hirschfeld *et al.* (eds.), *Enzyklopädie Erster Weltkrieg*, pp. 582–4
―― 'Humanität im Krieg? Internationales Rotes Kreuz und Kriegsgefangenenhilfe im Ersten Weltkrieg', in Oltmer (ed.), *Kriegsgefangene im Europa des Ersten Weltkriegs*, pp. 216–36
―― *Gefangen im Großen Krieg. Kriegsgefangenschaft in Deutschland, 1914–1921* (Essen, 2006)
Hirschfeld, Gerhard, Gerd Krumeich and Irina Renz (eds.), *Enzyklopädie Erster Weltkrieg* (Paderborn, 2003)
Hobsbawm, Eric, *Nations and Nationalism since 1780. Programme, Myth, Reality*, 2nd edn (Cambridge, 1992)
Hobsbawm, Eric and Terence Ranger (eds.), *The Invention of Tradition*, 2nd edn (Cambridge, 1992)
Holmes, Colin, *John Bull's Island. Immigration and British Society, 1871–1971* (London, 1988)
Horne, John, 'Masculinity in Politics and War in the Age of Nation-States and World Wars, 1850–1950', in Stefan Dudink, Karen Hagemann and John Tosh (eds.), *Masculinities in Politics and War. Gendering Modern History* (Manchester, 2004), pp. 22–40
Horne, John and Alan Kramer, 'War Between Soldiers and Enemy Civilians, 1914–1915', in Roger Chickering and Stig Förster (eds.), *Great War, Total War. Combat and Mobilization on the Western Front, 1914–1918* (Cambridge, 2000), pp. 153–68
―― *German Atrocities 1914. A History of Denial* (New Haven and London, 2001)
Horrall, Andrew, *Popular Culture in London, c. 1890–1918. The Transformation of Entertainment* (Manchester, 2001)
Humberside Libraries and Amenities (ed.), *Ruhleben, 1914–1918. An Exhibition to Mark the 60th Anniversary of the Release of Local Men From the Ruhleben Internment Camp* (Kingston upon Hull, 1978)
Hynes, Samuel, *The Soldiers' Tale. Bearing Witness to Modern War* (London, 1998)
―― 'Personal Narratives and Commemoration', in Winter and Sivan (eds.), *War and Remembrance in the Twentieth Century*, pp. 205–20
Jahr, Christoph, 'Zivilisten als Kriegsgefangene. Die Internierung von "Feindstaaten-Ausländern" in Deutschland während des Ersten Weltkrieges am Beispiel des "Engländerlagers Ruhleben"', in Overmans (ed.), *In der Hand des Feindes*, pp. 297–321
―― 'Keine Feriengäste. "Feindstaatenausländer" im südlichen Bayern während des Ersten Weltkrieges', in Hermann J. W. Kuprian and Oswald Überegger (eds.), *Der Erste Weltkrieg im Alpenraum. Erfahrung, Deutung, Erinnerung/La Grande Guerra nell'arco alpino. Esperienza e memoria* (Innsbruck, 2006), pp. 231–45
Jobs, Richard Ivan and Patrick McDevitt, 'Introduction: Where the Hell Are the People?', *Journal of Social History* (Winter 2005), pp. 309–14
Jones, Heather, 'Encountering the "Enemy": Prisoner of War Transport and the Development of War Cultures in 1914', in Pierre Purseigle (ed.), *Warfare and*

Belligerence. Perspectives in First World War Studies (Leiden, 2005), pp. 133–62

Ketchum, John Davidson, *Ruhleben. A Prison Camp Society* (Toronto, 1965)

King, Alex, *Memorials of the Great War in Britain* (Oxford, 1998)

Kotek, Joël and Pierre Rigoulot, *Das Jahrhundert der Lager. Gefangenschaft, Zwangsarbeit, Vernichtung* (Berlin, 2001) [French original, Paris, 2000]

Kramer, Alan, 'Kriegsrecht und Kriegsverbrechen', in Hirschfeld *et al.* (eds.), *Enzyklopädie Erster Weltkrieg*, pp. 281–92

Lane, Tony, *The Merchant Seamen's War* (Manchester, 1990)

Liddle, Peter H. and S. P. MacKenzie, 'The Experience of Captivity. British and Commonwealth Prisoners in Germany', in John Bourne, Peter Liddle and Ian Whitehead (eds.), *The Great World War, 1914–45. Vol. 1. Lightning Strikes Twice* (London, 2000), pp. 310–28

Lohr, Eric, *Nationalizing the Russian Empire. The Campaign Against Enemy Aliens during World War I* (Cambridge, MA, 2003)

MacKenzie, S. P., 'The Treatment of Prisoners of War in World War II', *Journal of Modern History*, 66/3 (1994), pp. 487–520

—— *The Colditz Myth. British and Commonwealth Prisoners of War in Nazi Germany* (Oxford, 2004)

McPhail, Helen, *The Long Silence. Civilian Life under the German Occupation of Northern France, 1914–1918* (London, 1999)

Madley, Benjamin, 'From Africa to Auschwitz: How German South West Africa Incubated Ideas and Methods Adopted and Developed by the Nazis in Eastern Europe', *European History Quarterly*, 35/3 (2005), pp. 429–64

Masterman, J. C., *On the Chariot Wheel. An Autobiography* (Oxford, 1975)

Michel, Marc, 'Intoxication ou "brutalisation"? Les "represailles" de la grande guerre', *14–18 aujourd'hui today heute*, 4 (2001), pp. 175–97

Mosse, George L., *Fallen Soldiers. Reshaping the Memory of the World Wars* (Oxford, 1990)

Nathans, Eli, *The Politics of Citizenship in Germany. Ethnicity, Utility and Nationalism* (Oxford, 2004)

Nelson, Keith L., 'The "Black Horror on the Rhine". Race as a Factor in Post-World War I Diplomacy', *Journal of Modern History*, 42 (1970), pp. 606–27

Oltmer, Jochen, 'Arbeitszwang und Zwangsarbeit – Kriegsgefangene und ausländische Zivilarbeitskräfte im Ersten Weltkrieg', in Rolf Spilker and Bernd Ulrich (eds.), *Der Tod als Maschinist. Der industrialisierte Krieg, 1914–1918* (Bramsche, 1998), pp. 96–107

—— 'Zwangsmigration und Zwangsarbeit – Ausländische Arbeitskräfte und bäuerliche Ökonomie im Ersten Weltkrieg', *Tel Aviver Jahrbuch für deutsche Geschichte*, 27 (1998), pp. 135–68

—— (ed.), *Kriegsgefangene im Europa des Ersten Weltkriegs* (Paderborn, 2006)

Osterhammel, Jürgen and Niels P. Petersson, *Globalization. A Short History* (Princeton, NJ, 2005)

Overmans, Rüdiger (ed.), *In der Hand des Feindes. Kriegsgefangenschaft von der Antike bis zum Zweiten Weltkrieg* (Cologne, 1999)

Panayi, Panikos, 'Anti-German Riots in London, 1914–1918', *German History*, 7 (1989), pp. 184–203

—— *The Enemy in Our Midst. Germans in Britain During the First World War* (Oxford, 1991)

—— 'An Intolerant Act by an Intolerant Society. The Internment of Germans in Britain During the First World War', in Cesarani and Kushner (eds.), *The Internment of Aliens*, pp. 53–75

—— (ed.) *Minorities in Wartime. National and Racial Groupings in Europe, North America and Australia During the Two World Wars* (Oxford, 1993)

—— *Immigration, Ethnicity and Racism in Britain, 1815–1945* (Manchester, 1994)

—— 'Normalität hinter Stacheldraht. Kriegsgefangene in Großbritannien, 1914–1919', in Oltmer (ed.), *Kriegsgefangene*, pp. 126–46

Pöppinghege, Rainer, *Im Lager unbesiegt. Deutsche, englische und französische Kriegsgefangenen-Zeitungen im Ersten Weltkrieg* (Essen, 2006)

Procacci, Giovanna, *Soldati e prigionieri italiani nella Grande Guerra (con una raccolta di lettere inedite)* (Turin, 2000)

Rachamimov, Alon, *POWs and the Great War. Captivity on the Eastern Front* (Oxford, 2002)

—— 'The Disruptive Comforts of Drag: (Trans)Gender Performances among Prisoners of War in Russia, 1914–1920', *American Historical Review*, 111/2 (2006), pp. 362–82

Robb, George, *British Culture and the First World War* (London, 2002)

Robert, Tristan, 'Les prisonniers civils de la grande guerre. Le cas de la Picardie', *Guerres mondiales et conflits contemporains*, 190 (1998), pp. 61–78

Seddon, Peter, *Steve Bloomer. The Story of Football's First Superstar* (Derby, 1999)

Segesser, Daniel Marc, 'The International Debate on the Punishment of War Crimes during the Balkan Wars and the First World War', *Peace & Change*, 31/4 (2006), pp. 533–54

Sofsky, Wolfgang, *Die Ordnung des Terrors. Das Konzentrationslager* (Frankfurt/M, 1993)

Speed, Richard B. III, *Prisoners, Diplomats and the Great War. A Study in the Diplomacy of Captivity* (New York, 1990)

Stibbe, Matthew, *German Anglophobia and the Great War, 1914–1918* (Cambridge, 2001)

—— 'A Community at War: British Civilian Internees at the Ruhleben Camp in Germany, 1914–1918', in Jenny Macleod and Pierre Purseigle (eds.), *Uncovered Fields. Perspectives in First World War Studies* (Leiden, 2004), pp. 79–94

—— 'A Question of Retaliation? The Internment of British Civilians in Germany in November 1914', *Immigrants & Minorities*, 23/1 (2005), pp. 1–29

—— 'The Internment of Civilians by Belligerent States during the First World War and the Response of the International Committee of the Red Cross', *Journal of Contemporary History* 41/1 (2006), pp. 5–19

—— 'Elisabeth Rotten and the "Auskunfts- und Hilfsstelle für Deutsche im Ausland und Ausländer in Deutschland", 1914–1919', in Alison S. Fell and Ingrid Sharp (eds.), *The Women's Movement in Wartime. International Perspectives, 1914–19* (Basingstoke, 2007), pp. 194–210

Verhey, Jeffrey, *The Spirit of 1914. Militarism, Myth and Mobilization in Germany* (Cambridge, 2000)

White, Hayden, 'Historical Emplotment and the Problem of Truth', in Saul Friedlander (ed.), *Probing the Limits of Representation* (Cambridge, MA, 1992), pp. 34–53

Winter, Jay, *Sites of Memory, Sites of Mourning. The Great War in European Cultural History* (Cambridge, 1995)

Winter, Jay and Antoine Prost, *The Great War in History. Debates and Controversies, 1914 to the Present* (Cambridge, 2005)

Winter, Jay and Emmanuel Sivan (eds.), *War and Remembrance in the Twentieth Century* (Cambridge, 1999)

Wippich, Rolf-Harald, 'Internierung und Abschiebung von Japanern im Deutschen Reich im Jahr 1914', *Zeitschrift für Geschichtswissenschaft*, 55/1 (2007), pp. 18–40

Wittek, Thomas, *Auf ewig Feind? Das Deutschlandbild in den britischen Massenmedien nach dem Ersten Weltkrieg* (Munich, 2005)

Wolff, Theodor, *Tagebücher, 1914–1919. Der Erste Weltkrieg und die Entstehung der Weimarer Republik in Tagebüchern, Leitartikeln und Briefen des Chefredakteurs am "Berliner Tageblatt" und Mitbegründer der "Deutschen Demokratischen Partei"*, ed. by Bernd Sösemann, 2 vols. (Boppard am Rhein, 1984)

Ziemann, Benjamin, *War Experiences in Rural Germany, 1914–1923* (Oxford, 2007)

Zimmerer, Jürgen, 'The Birth of the "Ostland" out of the Spirit of Colonialism. A Postcolonial Perspective on the Nazi Policy of Conquest and Extermination', *Patterns of Prejudice*, 39/2 (2005), pp. 197–219

Novels

Baddiel, David, *The Secret Purposes* (London, 2004)

Frayn, Michael, *Spies* (London, 2002)

Jerome, Jerome K., *Three Men on the Bummel*, Penguin edn (London, 1983)

Kafka, Franz, *The Trial*, Penguin edn (London, 1994)

McEwan, Ian, *Atonement* (London, 2001)

Unpublished dissertations

Gill, Rebecca, 'Calculating Compassion in War: The "New Humanitarian" Ethos in Britain, 1870–1918', PhD dissertation, University of Manchester, 2005

Jones, Heather, 'The Enemy Disarmed. Prisoners of War and the Violence of Wartime. Britain, France and Germany, 1914–1920', PhD dissertation, Trinity College, Dublin, 2005

Tripp, Sebastian, 'Kommunikation und Vergemeinschaftung. Das "Engländerlager" Ruhleben, 1914–1918', Masters dissertation, University of Marburg, 2005

Index

Lightning Source UK Ltd.
Milton Keynes UK
UKOW06f0341120316

270071UK00028B/673/P